Sorry, I Don't Speak French.

GRAHAM FRASER

Confronting the Canadian
Crisis That Won't Go Away

⟦A DOUGLAS GIBSON BOOK⟧

100

McCLELLAND & STEWART

Library and Archives Canada Cataloguing in Publication

Fraser, Graham, 1946-
Sorry, I don't speak French : confronting the Canadian crisis
that won't go away / Graham Fraser.

Includes index.
"Douglas Gibson Books".

ISBN 13: 978-0-7710-4766-4
ISBN 10: 0-7710-4766-5

1. Language policy–Canada. 2. Canada–Languages–Political
aspects. 3. Bilingualism–Canada. I. Title.

FC97.F73 2006   306.44'971   C2005-906377-7

We acknowledge the financial support of the Government of Canada
through the Book Publishing Industry Development Program and
that of the Government of Ontario through the Ontario Media Development
Corporation's Ontario Book Initiative. We further acknowledge the
support of the Canada Council for the Arts and the Ontario Arts Council
for our publishing program.

Typeset in Minion by M&S, Toronto
Printed and bound in Canada

A Douglas Gibson Book

This book is printed on acid-free paper that is 100% recycled,
ancient-forest friendly (100% post-consumer recycled).

McClelland & Stewart Ltd.
75 Sherbourne Street
Toronto, Ontario
M5A 2P9
www.mcclelland.com

1   2   3   4   5   10   09   08   07   06

To Malcolm and Stacey
Nick and Glenda
and Lydia and Owen

Contents

Sorry, I Don't Speak French

Introduction

> *The issue is not, I believe, whether the individual historian should appear in his books, but* how *he should appear – covertly or overtly.*
>
> *MARTIN DUBERMAN*

In 1965, when I was a nineteen-year-old university student at the University of Toronto, I spent the summer working on a federal archaeological training project at Fort Lennox on Île-aux-Noix, on the Richelieu River, some fifty kilometres south of Montreal. We were about twenty students, half from Quebec and half from across Canada; it was an effort to recruit potential future archaeologists for projects like the excavation and reconstruction of Louisbourg. I joined less out of an interest in archaeology than out of a determination to learn French and something of Quebec. Just as some of my fellow students in Toronto had become fascinated by the civil rights movement in the southern United States, I had become intrigued by this society in motion, so near my own, so visible and yet so opaque.

The previous year had been a politically turbulent one: Confederation had seemed at risk, in the confrontation between Quebec and Ottawa at a federal-provincial conference over the Canada Pension Plan in the spring of 1964. In the fall, there had been violence when police attacked demonstrators protesting the Queen's visit to Quebec City. René Lévesque was a dynamic figure in Jean Lesage's cabinet; the Front de libération du Québec (FLQ) had set off bombs in mailboxes; the new Quebec student move- ment, L'Union générale des étudiants du Québec, had separated from the Canadian Union of Students.

We arrived in early May. Because local teenagers were hired to dig the trenches, French was the language of the dig. I was soon immersed in the head-spinning process of absorbing another lan- guage as it is actually spoken, rather than as it is articulated by high-school and first-year university French teachers. I found it an exhausting, often embarrassing experience, moving gradually from total incomprehension to being able to understand one person speaking slowly, if I concentrated on every expression and gesture, to managing to participate in the flow of conversation. Somewhere about the level of comprehension required for understanding con- versations at a party with loud music playing in the background came the telephone; I can remember shrinking away when the phone rang, hoping someone else was near enough to answer.

The effect was overwhelming; I had the sense of being a foreigner in my own country, one I thought I knew and under- stood. One of the Quebec students on the dig seemed to me to hate the English, sometimes almost quivering with resentment, and it was a jarring experience to encounter, for the first time, a blanket of intense but impersonal dislike. The experience of attempting to learn a new language was draining, full of groping pauses and polite, uncomprehending smiles. A totally bilingual student from the University of Ottawa told me I was very differ- ent in French from the way I was in English. "Of course I'm different in French!" I snapped. "I'm stupid, I'm inarticulate, and have no sense of humour!"

Ruefully, I realized that this is the immigrant experience, and traditionally the experience of a French-Canadian in an English-dominated society. This is what it is like to be stripped of flexibility, subtlety, humour, wit, and intelligence; inevitably, you feel imprisoned in an accent, with all the stiffness and stereotype that that implies. But perhaps more than the language difficulty, the sheer foreignness of the culture I was struggling to understand hit me with enormous force; I had an overwhelming sense of cultural distance. I had come to Quebec to learn French in part out of a sense of patriotism – and I was bombarded with a vitality that had very little to do with the country I had grown up in. That summer, Gilles Vigneault sang "Mon Pays" in a National Film Board feature by Arthur Lamothe called *La neige a fondu sur la Manicouagan*. Vigneault was not referring to Canada.

Almost forty years later, in March 2005, the Liberals held a policy convention in Ottawa, and except for a few token sentences, there was remarkably little French spoken. For the most part, delegates from Quebec who wanted to make an argument did so in English. Two weeks later, the Conservative Party held a convention in Montreal – and, despite a complaint from one delegate about French on cereal boxes, affirmed a commitment to bilingualism. A number of speakers made a valiant effort to speak French. However, most of the convention organizers were unilingual anglophones and the convention centre staff were mainly unilingual francophones; one reporter was amused at the sight of sign language breaking out whenever a table had to be moved or more chairs were required.

In the same month, Quebec films won the main Genie Awards, and one film critic was clearly taken aback that the winners – for Best Director, Best Actor, and Best Actress – spoke in French when they received their awards.

None of these things made headlines, or even caused much surprise. No flags were trampled, no anthems booed, no awards refused – just some syntax mangled here and eyebrows lifted there. Language, you see, has slipped into the background in Canadian public life; a minor discord in the public chorus of national conversation.

(At times, this seems almost an advantage. In 1988, when Brian Mulroney's government amended the Official Languages Act to bring it into accordance with the Charter of Rights and Freedoms, there was a near-revolt in the Progressive Conservative caucus. In November 2005, the next time the Act was amended – to make the federal government's commitment to promote minority language communities enforceable in the courts – it went through Parliament with barely a ripple. The Conservatives did not want to be seen opposing an extension of language rights.)

And yet this polite obliviousness often hides a deep chasm in the Canadian public consciousness, and even in the national identity. Discussion of language has become an odd kind of taboo, as if ignoring the problem represents a solution.

For years, "Sorry, I don't speak French" has been the reflexive response of English-speaking Canadians to a request, a comment, or a greeting in the other official language. Part apology, part defiance, it is a declaration of otherness. *That is not me. I don't do that. The language barrier is here, at this counter, now.*

Language, and how language barriers are overcome, have been the central elements and challenges of Canadian life. And yet, except in times of crisis, they remain on the back burner of Canadian public life. Most of the time, Canadians don't want to think, talk, or read about the language issue. It often inspires, variously, feelings of barely suppressed irritation, or politically correct guilt, or nostalgia for a time when "bilingualism" seemed like an exciting transformation of Canadian society, a word inspiring the same liberal enthusiasm in Canada as "integration" did a little earlier in the United States. Recently, discussions about language in Canada are more likely to involve litmus tests for potential political leaders, tests for public servants, teacher shortages, and court challenges. And yet, the question of how English-speaking and French-speaking Canadians communicate remains an important question – and one that is now rarely asked.

I have been thinking about this book for a long time. Learning French was one of the more important experiences in my life, just as moving to Quebec and living there for a decade was one of the most significant experiences in my professional life. Over the years, I have been fascinated by the divide between English-speaking and French-speaking Canada, and intrigued by the ramifications – political, social, and cultural – of that gap.

In 1965, a few months before my summer at Fort Lennox, the authors of the Royal Commission on Bilingualism and Biculturalism warned the country that Canada was passing through the greatest crisis in its history. With that warning, amplified in the final report and recommendations two years later, the federal government embarked on an ambitious and idealistic mission: to create a federal government that could communicate effectively with Canadians in English and in French.

There have recently been a number of compelling books about the state of Canadian democracy, the decline of Canada's foreign policy, and the need for a new Canadian role in the world – not to mention debates on health care, productivity, and the knowledge economy. But there is a more basic *sine qua non* for Canada in the twenty-first century: sustaining a national leadership that can communicate with Canadians in French and English. If Canada fails this basic test, the other challenges may be insurmountable.

Four decades after that memorable statement about what Canada was experiencing, a significant part of the crisis that the Bi and Bi Commission recognized had been resolved. The income gap between anglophones and francophones in Quebec – whose identification by the Commission had been a source of outrage and fuel for the independence movement – had vanished, and the federal government had succeeded in providing services in both official languages.

For a short period, there was a certain amount of complacency in English-speaking Canada. The Clarity Act had been passed in 2000 without the expected nationalist backlash in Quebec. The independence movement seemed to have lost steam – first with the revival of the federal Liberals in Quebec in 2000, and then with the victory of the Quebec Liberals in 2003.

But this complacency proved to be unsustainable. The sponsorship scandal exploded in 2004, contributing to the election of fifty-four Bloc Québécois MPs that spring and the resurgence of the independence movement in the polls. No pan-Canadian political party retained a solid foothold in French-speaking Quebec. The popularity of the Charest government in Quebec faded quickly. And the ripples of confusion and incomprehension over the appointment of Michaëlle Jean as governor general in 2005 confirmed that the cultural and social gaps between the language groups in Canada are still enormous.

The political culture that has developed at the centre is increasingly dysfunctional. And the emergence of a broader national leadership able to function effectively in both languages, with effective understanding of both linguistic communities, is still more of a distant dream than a current reality. To a significant degree, Canada has failed to come to terms with its French fact, and the country has gone into a state of denial about that failure.

In some ways, it is as if, on being told in 1965 that the country was going through the greatest crisis in its history, Canadians said, "Fine. We'll make public servants learn French, we'll send our brightest children to immersion French so that they can run the country in both languages – and, until they've grown up, we'll let Quebec lawyers run the country." It is now forty years on, many public servants are still unable to meet the language requirements that have been set for them, our children are not very interested in running the country, and many Canadians are tired of having Quebec lawyers doing it.

Currently, there is a national leadership deadlock, comparable in some ways to the one that existed between 1963 and 1968: a minority government headed by a prime minister who has lost key support in Quebec and cannot win sufficient support in the rest of the country for a majority, facing an opposition leader who is even more unpopular in Quebec with little prospect of a break-through. We can't go on indefinitely with the current stalemate. Quebec now acts as Canada's New Hampshire, making critical decisions on who can and cannot be prime minister. As long as that is the case – and it doesn't look as if it is going to end soon – bilingualism has to be understood as a leadership necessity. And if politics is going to be connected to the rest of Canadian life, bilingualism needs to be seen as a more general criterion for national leadership, not simply political leadership, and as a stepping stone to multilingualism.

After four decades, how do the ambitions and intentions of the originators of the policy look? Has the mission worked? If not, why not? Because it is too important a mission to fail.

Language has always been, and remains, at the heart of the Canadian experience. The fact that there is a thriving French-speaking society in Canada, and the tensions that have resulted from this fact, is as central to Canadian politics and society as race is to the United States, and class is to Great Britain. From the discussions that led to Confederation in the 1860s, through the crisis created by the hanging of Louis Riel and the conscription crises of the two world wars, the constitutional struggles that led to the patriation of the Constitution and its amendment with a Charter of Rights in 1982 and the failures of the Meech Lake and Charlottetown accords in 1990 and 1992 – not to mention the fact that Quebec has provided the backbone of every majority government in Canadian parliamentary history – the often-unspoken subtext to each of these events has been the relationship between French-speakers and English-speakers in Canada. In the 1960s, those rules changed under the pressure to deal with the explosion of nationalism in Quebec. And those who changed the rules changed the country.

Many books have been written about that surge of political nationalism in Quebec, and its political ramifications in the 1970s and 1980s. I have even written one myself. There are also shelves, if not whole libraries, of books on the constitutional response to Quebec's assertion of its own identity.

But there have been relatively few books that have looked at how the federal government has attempted to respond to the basic requirement of providing a bridge between English-speaking and French-speaking Canada, and serving both communities in their own official language.

This is what I have set out to examine here. In other words, this is not a book about Quebec, or about the Constitution; it does not look at whether Quebec is (or should be defined as) a nation, a distinct society, or one of ten equal provinces. It is not a study of the struggles of the French-language minorities outside Quebec – or of the English-language minority in Quebec. Others have tackled those subjects. It is not a history of relations between English and French in Canada – although it will touch on some aspects of that history.

No, my focus is more modest. I have looked at the pressures that led to the creation of the Royal Commission, examined its discussion primarily through the lens of the journals that André

Laurendeau and Frank Scott kept, and looked at the influence they had on Camille Laurin and Pierre Trudeau. I follow the introduction of the Official Languages Act and the work of the first Commissioner of Official Languages, Keith Spicer, look at the impact of language policy on Montreal and Ottawa, examine the changes that have occurred and not occurred in Canadian education, and briefly at the question of language in the military, voluntary associations, and the public service. Finally, I look at how language skill has become an imperative for political leadership.

I actually try to avoid use of the word *bilingual*, for I think it is misleading. It suggests a kind of equilibrium, or linguistic ambidextrousness that can be achieved only by those who grew up in families where two languages were spoken at home. What is important is the ability to communicate in another language; it is that collective ability of Canadians to communicate with each other in English or in French and to understand each other's societies that is at the core of Canada's linguistic challenge.

Making Canada's language policy work is critical to making the country work – and that central task has been treated as yesterday's news. There is a tendency to see this subject as part of Canada's past and not its future, and any discussion of language policy as an exercise in nostalgia. This has been solved, right? Well, no. I set out to look at the response of the English-speaking majority, not the French-speaking minority, and I discovered some surprises. Things are far from "solved." There are fewer and fewer institutions where French-speaking and English-speaking Canadians work together. French is less and less a requirement in Canadian schools and universities. Four decades after the government declared that the federal public service must be able to function in both languages, millions of dollars are still being spent to teach middle-aged public servants (who were in high school, for God's sake, when the policy was declared) to pass language tests.

As a journalist, in this book I look at the origins of Canada's language policy and how it was developed, explore how that policy has been applied, and, four decades later, look at how it is working. Seeing how these rules actually work now is vitally important. To put it bluntly, I believe that if Canada's language policy does not work, if it is not possible for this country to be governed effectively in both languages, then sooner or later, the already frayed ties that connect the country will disintegrate, and what we know as Canada will fall apart.

> Graham Fraser
> Ottawa
> November 2005

PART ONE

Making a Policy

Two Hundred
Years of
Language Relations

*Canada is not English – that is the first thing
to understand.*

BRUCE HUTCHISON

I am a journalist, and not a historian, as one of my former professors has reminded me before and will, I am sure, do so again if he reads this. However, the past matters in the story of language in Canada; it is hard to understand the context of the current policy without at least a sense of the historical backdrop. So let me review some of the history of the issue. Skip this chapter if your eyes glaze over at historical surveys. I've tried to make this one short. On the other hand, if you skipped the introduction, it's worth a look, since it has a bearing on the rest of the book.

There is no question that French-English relations have been one of the central themes of Canadian history. During the first century of Confederation, the unspoken rules in the relationship were clear. Indeed, on the first day of the Confederation debates, on February 3, 1865, the very first exchange in the legislature concerned language. Sir E.P. Taché had read the motion, which was based on the Quebec Conference of 1865.

"Having read the motion, the hon. gentleman commenced to speak in French, when Hon. Mr. Ross requested he should address the House in English," the Hansard entry states.

"Hon. Mr. Letellier thought, as there were two members of the government in the House, one who spoke best in French (Sir E.P. Taché), and one who did the same in English, it would be better for the Hon. Premier to speak in French, and then his colleague could do the same in English, but Hon. Sir E.P. Taché concluded that as there were English members who did not understand French at all, while the French members all understood English, it would be best for him to speak in the latter language, and proceeded to do so."

It is strangely fitting that the very first words in the debate about the terms and conditions of Confederation should be about the ground rules for the debate itself – and should focus on language. For the following century, that was the rule for bilingualism: the operating assumption was that the English did not understand French at all, while the French were expected to understand English. (Occasionally, French-speaking members took advantage of the fact that their English-speaking colleagues did not understand them – on March 8, 1865, when Joseph Perrault argued that England's goal "has always been to annihilate us as a people," Édouard Rémillard responded by saying, "Fortunately, his speech was not understood by the English members of the House, and consequently it could produce no effect upon them.") Certainly, those who were prominent enough to be elected to Parliament did understand English – and it was taken for granted that the country, its Parliament, and its capital would function in English.

For two hundred years, the rules of the relationship between English and French were clear, and taken for granted. They were rules that established when French was spoken, and who bore the burden of bilingualism.

In the debate over the Quebec Act of 1774, the British made it clear that, while they would be assuming full sovereignty over the French colonies that had been won on the battlefield, they would not be imposing their language, their religion, or their legal system. "You ought to change those laws only which relate to the French sovereignty and in their place substitute laws which should relate to the new sovereign," Sir Edward Thurlow, the Attorney-General of Great Britain told the British House of Commons. "But with respect to all other laws, all other customs and institutions what-ever, which are indifferent to the state of subjects and sovereign, humanity, justice and wisdom equally conspire to leave the people just as they were."

In other words, leave them speaking French. From the very outset, the continuation of a French-speaking society in Canada was part of the understanding.

Eighty years later, Lord Durham came to Canada to report on the Rebellion of 1837, and produced a report that was critical to the development of the country. He identified colonial powerlessness as being intimately linked to irresponsibility, and the effect on what he called "the colonial demagogue" of being "hopelessly excluded from power" – a prescient analysis in some ways, and a foreshadowing of the psychological studies of colonial powerless-ness by Albert Memmi and Frantz Fanon a century later that proved to be so influential with Quebec radicals of the 1960s. The opposi-tion leaders, he argued, had no prospect of having their ideas, policies, or claims tested by the realities of power. Opposition leaders, he wrote, were "men of strong passions, and merely declam-atory powers, who think but little of reforming the abuses which serve them as topics for exciting discontent" – a description that can be applied only too easily to some of the members of the opposition parties during the decade of Jean Chrétien's prime ministership.

But Durham is remembered better for his analysis of the French-English conflict, summed up in the comment that he found "two nations warring in the bosom of a single state," one of the more memorable phrases to emerge from a government report. Durham wrote that it was difficult to describe the degree of animosity between the two groups; that it was "difficult for us to comprehend the intensity of the hatred which the difference of language, of law, and of manners, creates between those who inhabit the same village, and are citizens of the same state."

Durham concluded that the solution was assimilation. In phrases that have been engraved on the collective memory of French Canada for more than 160 years, he concluded, "There can hardly be conceived a nationality more destitute of all that can invigorate and elevate a people, than that which is exhibited by the descendants of the French in Lower Canada, owing to their retaining of their peculiar language and manners. They are a people with no history and no literature."

And, after continuing in this vein, he wrote that he would be surprised if "the more reflecting part" of French Canada entertained any hope of preserving their nationality. "Much as they struggle against it, it is obvious that the process of assimilation to English habits is already commencing," he continued. "The English language is gaining ground, as the language of the rich and of the employers of labour naturally will." While no coercion was recommended, Durham made it clear that, in policy terms, "the first object ought to be that of making it an English Province."

Durham's recommendations led to the creation of a united Canada – Canada's only experience with a unitary state. It lasted only a quarter-century: the tensions and fault lines in the union led to Confederation in 1867. But that pre-Confederation period provided an intriguing model for French-English co-operation.

It was a co-operation that seemed unlikely at first. Durham's successor, Lord Sydenham, observed tartly, "They have only one feeling – the French hate the English and would cut their throats if they could – the English hate the French and only desire to ride rough shod over them." But the next governor, Sir Charles Bagot, concluded that the French should be drawn into government and that the colony could not be managed otherwise.

That opening drew two reformers, Robert Baldwin and Louis-Hippolyte Lafontaine, to become attorneys-general, one for Upper Canada and the other for Lower Canada. They had already established both a personal friendship and a durable political partnership; when Sydenham banned Lafontaine from the assembly, Baldwin stepped down from one of the two constituencies he represented and asked the electors of York to choose his friend. Later, when angry Tories defeated Baldwin, Lafontaine reciprocated, and Baldwin became the member for Rimouski. Baldwin took the responsibility seriously, and in 1844, asked Lafontaine advice about a French school for his son: "I must not expose him to the miserable embarrassment that I labour under myself for want of French."

It was Durham's son-in-law, Lord Elgin, who ensured that the partnership would survive; in a letter to the colonial secretary, Lord Grey, in 1848, he called for the revocation of the restriction on the official use of French. "You may perhaps americanize, but, depend upon it, by methods of this description, you will never anglicize the French inhabitants of the Province," he wrote. He resisted the pressure from angry English-speaking merchants; his decision to sign the Rebellion Losses Bill, despite being stoned by an angry mob as he made his way to the assembly, was a critical moment in the birth of Canadian democracy.

In discussions of Canadian history, it is worth remembering that, while it is a blueprint for modern Canada, the British North America Act of 1867 was also an act of separation: it separated Canada East from Canada West, and gave political powers to the

Province of Quebec, with a French-speaking majority – exactly what Durham had wanted to avoid. The successful management of relations between Quebec and the rest of Canada, and the maintenance of solid support in Quebec have been the key to majority federal government in Canada ever since Confederation.

Until very recently, history itself has been out of fashion in English-speaking Canada, and it has been easy to forget the impact that these events have always had in French-speaking Canada, a society with a long, but selective, memory. In the fall of 1989, after I had finished an interview with Lucien Bouchard, still Canada's Minister of the Environment and Brian Mulroney's Quebec lieutenant (before he dramatically quit the government in the weeks leading up to the death of the Meech Lake Accord), he pulled a copy of Donald Creighton's biography of Sir John A. Macdonald off his shelf, and, pointing to an underlined passage, remarked, "Things haven't changed much."

When I got home, I looked up the passage, and found it to be a revealing one – and not simply because Bouchard had pointed it out to me. The passage was from a letter Sir John wrote to a journalist in Montreal in 1856, in which he chided Brown Chamberlin for the attitude of what he called "British Lower Canadians" to the French-speaking majority.

"The truth is that you British Lower Canadians never can forget that you were once supreme – that Jean-Baptiste was your hewer of wood and drawer of water," Sir John wrote. "You can't and won't admit the principle that the majority must govern." The observation is one that many Quebec nationalists feel still applies.

Sir John wrote about more than just the attitudes of the English community in Montreal. In what his biographer described as a "jocular, laconic and curiously discerning fashion," he sketched out the nature of government in the country that had yet to be created.

In the same letter, he touched on the tension that for the next 130 years would be the main challenge to governing the country that he and his friend, George-Étienne Cartier, spent the next decade designing. "No man in his senses can suppose that this country can for a century to come be governed by a totally unfrenchified government," he wrote. In an often-quoted passage, he went on to describe how an anglophone should approach the problem of dealing with French Canada. "He must make friends with the French; without sacrificing the status of his race or language, we must respect their nationality. Treat them as a nation and they will act as a free people generally do – generously. Call them a faction, and they become factious."

What is also noteworthy is that Sir John foresaw the impact of demography on French Canada, and how that would affect Canadian politics. "Supposing the numerical preponderance of British in Canada becomes much greater than it is, I think the French would give more trouble than they are said now to do," he wrote. "As they become smaller and feebler, so they will be more united."

This was, don't forget, less than twenty years after Durham had prescribed political union with the ultimate goal of assimilation as the solution to the tensions. The result was merely a broadening of the battle, as the Clear Grits of Canada West raged against the dominance of Roman Catholic, French-speaking Canada East with its Napoleonic Code. For Sir John, Confederation became an exercise in conciliation; for George Brown, his Grit opponent, it became a fight to liberate Ontario from the domination of French Canada.

"All right!!!" George Brown wrote his wife triumphantly after the terms of Confederation were negotiated in 1864, sounding more like a late-twentieth-century teenager than a nineteenth-century statesman. "Confederation through at six o'clock this evening – constitution adopted – a creditable document – a complete reform of all the abuses and injustices we have complained of. Is it not wonderful? French Canadianism entirely extinguished." As historian Ramsay Cook has pointed out, the last line about French Canadianism speaks volumes.

George-Étienne Cartier, Macdonald's Quebec ally, had to unite with Brown to achieve Confederation. Against considerable odds, he succeeded. "Cartier knew that federal politics would forever centre around Quebec, the pivotal province of the new Dominion," his biographer Alastair Sweeny wrote. The issue for all these men – and for many others who continued to resent the fact – was what Cook has called "the most permanent theme in Canadian history: the relations between French- and English-speaking Canadians."

In the years following Confederation, those relations worsened as the expansion into Western Canada was led by those who were determined that the new settlements should be English and Protestant. D'Alton McCarthy, the Irish-born Conservative MP for Barrie, and a product of the anti-Catholic Orange Lodge, introduced a bill in 1890 to ban French in the legislature and courts of the North-West Territories. The French language was suppressed in the North-West Territories in 1891, the school system secularized in 1892, and the rights of francophones were eliminated when the provinces of Alberta and Saskatchewan were created in 1905. In Manitoba, French and Catholic education was suppressed. In 1912, Ontario introduced Regulation 17 outlawing the teaching of French in Ontario – a decision which, combined with the bitter debates over conscription for World War I, further embittered relations between French and English. "The Orange movement provoked the Métis persecution, attacked francophone rights and caused Ontario also to lose close to a century of balanced evolution," wrote John Ralston Saul. "Its infection of society can still be felt when unilingual movements or other reflections of prejudice break out."

In a fascinating book on French-English tensions written in 1918, *The Clash! A Study in Nationalities*, William Moore made the then-provocative argument that British traditions called for bilingualism and inclusion, contrasting them with what he shrewdly characterized (during the First World War) as the rigid Prussian approach. He criticized the anti-French reflexes in English Canada, writing, "We English-Canadians have habitually had our good eye upon French-Canadian faults and our blind eye upon our own." Similarly, he contrasted Quebec's tolerance of an English and Protestant school system with Ontario's move to eradicate French: "[Ontario] has taken fifteen of the sixteen ounces of flesh to which it is entitled under the British North America Act; Quebec has never drawn the knife."

During that period, in Quebec, the basic understanding between French and English was established: what Robert Linteau called a "non-aggression pact," and what Marc Levine described as "the rules of the game" – rules that remained in place for the next century, from the 1850s until the 1960s. In his 1990 book, Levine summarized them: Francophones would run the provincial political system, protecting French-Canadian religious, educational, and legal institutions, but the status of the English language in public life and the autonomy of anglophone institutions were untouchable. Anglophones would dominate the economy of Montreal and the province, and this would not be challenged by the powers of the Quebec state, which would support the policies favoured by the English-speaking economic elite of Montreal. Conflicts would be worked out through back-channel discussions between political leaders; anglophones would largely abstain from provincial politics, and use their economic power instead.

Maurice Lamontagne, an economist at Université Laval in the 1950s, used the language of international conflict to summarize relations between French and English. He described two distinct stages: a Cold War between Confederation and the First World War – quiet hostility marked by outbreaks over French-language schools and conscription – and a period between the wars of peaceful co-existence: peace sustained through mutual ignorance and distance.

When Quebec went through rapid industrialization in the 1930s and 1940s, French-speaking Quebeckers were locked into a position of economic inferiority. "The French Canadian, in becoming an industrial worker and a town-dweller, gets a culturally alien employer," wrote Everett C. Hughes in his classic 1943 study *French Canada in Transition*. "He works under a system whose spirit is English-American, rather than French. . . . The French-Canadian city-dweller and industrial worker, even if he speaks no English and has no English-speaking neighbours, feels the impact of alien influences."

The general assumption that Hughes discovered when he came to McGill University to do his research was that those influences would transform Quebec society. "I can tell you frankly that those of my colleagues at McGill who were the least interested in contemporary French Canada unconsciously considered it as an entity on the way to assimilation," he told a conference in 1953. "Their assumption was that French Canadians would be absorbed, sooner or later, as an ethnic group in the great English-speaking Canadian whole."

Quebec was transformed – but not that way. In the 1960s and 1970s, those rules changed, but the political realities of the country remained intact. In 1956, Michael Oliver wrote succinctly, "There can be no stable power in Canada without Quebec support." Half a century later, those words are equally valid. Every prime minister who has succeeded in winning more than one majority government has done so by juggling the pressures of maintaining support both in Quebec and in English Canada – and, in virtually every case, the fall of every government occurred when those natural tensions were not successfully managed.

Sir John A. Macdonald forged the alliance between Quebec and English Canada that led to Confederation; the alliance dissolved after the hanging of Louis Riel in 1885. Sir Wilfrid Laurier, a Liberal, managed a similar juggling act, presiding over regional language tensions in the provinces without intervening, and keeping his coalition together until the election of 1911, when a combination of nationalists in Quebec and business interests in Ontario united to defeat him on the issue of reciprocity, of free trade with the United States. But Laurier's self-styled "sunny ways" did not prevent a series of bitter conflicts over language, as Western Canada systematically moved to eradicate French-language rights.

William Lyon Mackenzie King was the most effective manager of regional and linguistic tensions in the country, riding out the Conscription Crisis of 1942. Unique among successful prime ministers, he was able to convey his party, his government, and his political support intact to his successor, Louis St. Laurent, who won two more majority governments.

Lester Pearson never succeeded in winning a majority government in the 1960s, but coped with the resurgence of nationalism in Quebec, and laid the groundwork for Pierre Trudeau's government which lasted through the October Crisis in 1970, the election of the Parti Québécois in 1976, and returned after a nine-month hiatus to fight and win the referendum in 1980, and to amend and patriate the British North America Act over the objections of the Quebec government in 1982.

Even so superficial an overview of Canadian history may suggest that Canada's international reputation for being boring is testimony to our success in managing our internal disputes, miring them in legal and constitutional wrangles, and keeping our overt hostilities largely verbal. For the hostilities have certainly been there. Historian Arthur M. Lower characterized the period immediately before Confederation in terms of "hatred as a virtue: Canada as a melting-pot of belief and prejudice." At times, that characterization still applies.

The Pressures Converge

> *Vouloir, c'est aussi vouloir les conséquences*
> *de ce qu'on veut.*
>
> MAURICE LAMONTAGNE

On September 20, 1962, Maurice Lamontagne wrote an extraordinary three-page memo to Lester Pearson that, in retrospect, laid out the Liberal agenda for the next two decades. He began by saying that, in certain ways, it was possible to believe that Canada was going through a crisis.

It is not hard to understand why he would use such a powerful word. The Liberals were still licking their wounds from their electoral defeat a few months earlier. For the previous year, tension had been increasing in Quebec; the Rassemblement pour l'indépendance nationale (RIN) had been attracting large crowds to political rallies, and Pierre Bourgault had been electrifying them with his message of Quebec independence. Quebec premier Jean Lesage had been greeted in Paris in October 1961 like a head of state; in June 1962, John Diefenbaker's government had lost its majority, and, in Quebec, had dropped from fifty seats and 45.7 per cent of the vote to fourteen seats and less than 30 per cent. But the Liberals had won only ten more seats than the twenty-five they had won in 1958, and dropped from 49 per cent of the vote in Quebec to 39 per cent. Réal Caouette had emerged, apparently out of nowhere, leading the Crédit Social to twenty-six seats with 26 per cent of the vote.

The Quebec Liberals represented a further challenge to Ottawa and the federal Liberals. As Minister of Natural Resources, René Lévesque was arguing that the private hydroelectric companies should be nationalized and, on the Labour Day weekend, won over the cabinet to his position at a cabinet retreat. On September 19, the day before Lamontagne finished his memo to Pearson, Lesage called an election on the issue, using as the Liberal slogan a phrase with a long history in Quebec nationalist rhetoric: "*Maîtres Chez Nous.*" Masters in our own home.

For Lamontagne, an economist, the events were disturbing. An adviser to Pearson, he had been forced to leave Université Laval almost a decade earlier, because Union Nationale premier Maurice Duplessis had objected to a book he had written on federalism that was critical of Duplessis and Quebec nationalism. First working as a senior public servant, he had resigned when Diefenbaker was elected and, after a short interval at the University of Ottawa, went to work for Pearson as an economic adviser and strategist on Quebec. He had run unsuccessfully in 1958 and 1962, defeated first by a Conservative and then by a Créditiste.

Although primarily an economist, Lamontagne had been thinking seriously about bilingualism and the relations between French and English for at least ten years. As Monica Heller put it, forty years later, the emergence of Quebec nationalism represented a challenge to the legitimacy of the Canadian state. Lamontagne wanted to reinforce that legitimacy.

Lamontagne was essentially optimistic, but argued in his memo that it was up to the Liberal Party to achieve three concrete objectives. First, the patriation of the Constitution "and it must include a declaration of human rights covering federal and provincial areas"; secondly, the creation of a national flag and a national anthem which will, he said, leave no doubt about the sovereignty of the country.

"Finally, all federal institutions must become bilingual and be the concrete demonstration of our bilingualism," he wrote. "These three objectives will constitute the immediate goals for the next Liberal government. If we want to maintain the integrity of Canada and assure our life together, the federal administration must become as soon as possible and as completely as possible the synthesis and the symbol of a truly bicultural Canadianism."

In four short paragraphs, in 1962, Lamontagne summed up what would turn out to be major Liberal achievements of the next two decades: the creation of a Canadian flag in 1965, the approval of "O Canada" as the national anthem in 1967, replacing "God Save the Queen," the Official Languages Act in 1969, and the patriation of the Constitution and its amendment with the Charter of Rights and Freedoms in 1982. Along with a number of others, he played a key role in the creation of the Royal Commission on Bilingualism and Biculturalism.

At that point, the Liberals were licking their wounds from their third consecutive defeat at the hands of John Diefenbaker. The shock of the 1962 election had not been merely the collapse of the Conservatives, but the election of the twenty-six Créditistes from Quebec. They were rural and, for the most part, unilingual – swept into office by Caouette's monetary theories, populist rhetoric, and his unanswerable slogan: "You've got nothing to lose." Following the fifty Quebec Tories elected in 1958, they were the second significant caucus of Quebec MPs who came, not from the local (bilingual) elite, but from the unilingual majority in rural and small-town Quebec.

In September, Lamontagne also wrote a lengthy paper recommending a strategy for the Liberals in Quebec. He argued that the Liberals should ignore the Tories in Quebec, and focus on the Créditistes, discrediting Caouette and his number two, Gilles Grégoire. ("The negative strategy consists of directly attacking Social Credit and trying to destroy it.") However, he warned, care should be taken not to mock those who had voted for them, or backbench Créditiste MPs – with the exception of Grégoire.

This was easier said than done. Grégoire was not to be underestimated. A lawyer, he was the son of a mayor of Quebec City and professor of political economy at Laval, J.-Ernest Grégoire, who became infatuated with the economic theories of Social Credit. In 1958, young Grégoire joined the Ralliement des Créditistes.

In Ottawa, Grégoire was virtually the only professional in a caucus of car salesmen, farmers, furniture store owners, undertakers, and carpenters. "My role is simple," he told political scientist Michael Stein. "In this group, I am the only one who studied law and procedures in the House . . . so I act as House leader." As House leader, he led the charge in harassing the Diefenbaker government on the issue of bilingualism.

It was a considerable charge. On the first day of the new session, Bellechasse MP Bernard Dumont asked Léon Balcer, the Minister of Transport, if it would be possible to have the announcer at the Ottawa railway station announce arrivals and departures in French as well as English. (Balcer replied that since the Conservative government had done so much for the cause of bilingualism, he would be pleased to pass on the request to the CNR.) Two days later, Antoine Bélanger, MP for Charlevoix, complained about the quality of translation in the House. The day after, Dumont raised the unilingual menu in the parliamentary restaurant. The following week, Réal Caouette asked Balcer to ensure there was service in

French on Air Canada. And the next day, Grégoire complained that Beauchesne, the Bible of parliamentary procedure, was in English only. David Ouellet, MP for Drummond-Arthabaska, complained that his MP's paycheque was in English only and, in protest, refused to cash it for several months. It continued day after day, reaching the point where an Air Canada stewardess admitted to Grégoire that the assignment on the plane had been switched at the last minute when the airline realized that Caouette and Grégoire were booked on the flight.

In the first sixty days of the session, Grégoire spoke or asked questions 134 times – in addition to a whole series of procedural questions he raised.

"I marvel at what he got going and what he set in train," Douglas Fisher said years later. "Historians will give him a lot more credit or blame for crystallizing the separatist thing. No clubby *bonne entente* for him between French and English members. He wasn't having any gentility – he raised hell about everything – from the menus in the cafeteria through to the rules of order which weren't available in French every day. He hammered at it – he converted Liberals into bilingualists."

It was in that context that on November 19, 1962, Donald Gordon, the president of Canadian National Railways, came to Ottawa to appear before the House of Commons Railway Committee. Grégoire was on the committee – and was waiting for him. As Fisher put it, "He set up a whole atmosphere and Gordon just walked into it."

Donald Gordon was, literally and figuratively, one of the giants of Canadian public administration. A Scottish-born immigrant who had left school at fifteen to become a bank clerk, he had been chairman of the Wartime Prices and Trade Board and deputy-governor of the Bank of Canada before becoming president of Canadian National Railways in 1949. He was big, tough, impetuous, hard-drinking, and hard-driving.

Grégoire was a firecracker of a man: short, shrewd, persistent, and, like Caouette, a populist demagogue of considerable power. Grégoire may have seemed like a clown, but as Peter C. Newman recalls, he was a good one. "He was a fabulous juggler, played Mozart on the piano exquisitely, and lived during the Parliamentary summers aboard a motor launch tied to the Dow's Lake boathouse with two stunning blondes," he told me. Gérard Bergeron compared Gordon and Grégoire to an elephant and a mouse: le petit Grégoire, he wrote, was "a Parliamentary knight disguised as Mickey Mouse."

Grégoire started his questioning by referring to the CNR's top executives. "I note one president, seventeen vice-presidents and ten directors and none of them is French-Canadian," he said.

Gordon responded bluntly, saying that promotion at the CNR was based on merit; the best person for the job would be selected, "and we do not care whether he is black, white, red or French." He insisted that the CNR did not practise discrimination; in fact, in ten years, as a result of the railway's university recruitment program, he was sure there would be some French-Canadian executives. Then, he uttered the memorable phrase: "As far as I am concerned, as long as I am president, promotions are not going to be made because the person is French-Canadian. He has to be something else as well."

The incongruity was obvious: a high-school dropout was suggesting that it would take ten years before Quebec university graduates would be ready for executive positions in the state-owned railway whose headquarters was in Montreal. Gordon's testimony made headlines in Quebec.

The effect was electric; there were demonstrations on November 26 in Montreal, on November 29 in Quebec, on December 1 in Trois-Rivières. On December 5, three hundred students from the University of Ottawa marched on Parliament Hill. At all the demonstrations, Gordon was burned in effigy. (The largest demonstration was in Montreal, led by the student executive at the Université de Montréal, which succeeded in getting an interview with Gordon. The student council president was Bernard Landry; the next day was the first in which his picture was on the front page of the *Globe and Mail*.)

On December 18, 1962, in the House of Commons, Grégoire called for "a complete policy statement" on bilingualism. "Mr. Speaker, I believe that it is time now to set up a Royal Commission on bilingualism and on French-Canadian participation in the civil service at all levels," he said. But his proposal was virtually ignored, overshadowed by the speech that followed.

When Grégoire sat down, Lester Pearson rose to his feet. Confederation "may not have been technically a treaty or a compact between states, but it was an understanding or a settlement between the two founding races of Canada made on the basis of an acceptable and equal partnership," he said. "To French-speaking Canadians, Confederation created a bilingual and bicultural nation."

English-Canadians, he suggested, felt that Confederation protected the rights of French-Canadians in Quebec, in Parliament, and in the courts. "But most felt – and I think it is fair to say this – that it did not go beyond those limits, at least until recently. This meant that, for all practical purposes, there would be an English-speaking Canada with a bilingual Quebec. What is called 'the French fact' was to be provincial only."

But, he said, separatism and Quebec's social revolution had provided a shock treatment. It was now clear to all that French Canadians were determined to take charge of their destiny and were also asking for full and equal opportunity to participate in the federal government – a right flowing from the equal partnership of Confederation.

Pearson then asked a series of questions which are still worth asking: "Are we ready . . . to give all young Canadians a real opportunity to become truly bilingual? If the answer is yes . . . what concrete steps should be taken . . . to bring about this opportunity, having regard to the fact that constitutional responsibility for education is, and must remain, exclusively provincial: What further responsibilities to this end have we a right to expect from radio, from television and from films in both languages? How can we encourage more frequent contacts between young Canadians?"

Then, he asked some specific questions that dealt with federal responsibility. "What are the reasons why there are relatively few French-speaking Canadians in the professional and administrative jobs of the federal civil service, including crown corporations and federal agencies? How can that situation be improved as it must be improved? Would it be desirable, for instance, to have a bilingual school of public administration operated by the federal government in Ottawa?"

He concluded by saying that the federal government and the provinces should embark on an inquiry, and if the provinces were not prepared to participate, the federal government should go it alone.

This was the speech, Pearson would later write in his memoirs, of which he was proudest. In its diffident, moderate, Pearsonian style, it is as close as one can find to an "I have a dream" speech on official bilingualism. The dream was Pearson's – and the years that followed involved fleshing out answers to the questions he asked.

The reaction in Parliament was very positive, and the next day the *Toronto Star* endorsed the idea in an editorial. The *Globe and Mail* was much more skeptical. "A wiser course, in our view, would be to let Quebec complete the task it has set itself," the paper intoned the next day, adding that the province was in good hands and reforms were underway. "If we have patience, the discovery, already made by its leaders, that English is the language of commerce and is as essential to Quebec as to the rest of us, will spread through the populace. We will find wider areas of agreement. French-speaking Canadians will retain their culture, as the Welsh and the Scots have done. We will be able in time to find the unity we seek."

In some ways, the *Globe*'s position can be seen as the starting point for English-speaking Canada in their attitude toward Quebec. They saw it as a conservative, traditional, church-dominated society that was emerging from decades of backwardness and corruption. As Quebec modernized and matured, it would learn English – and become like Scotland and Wales – societies that (then, at any rate) were seen as English-speaking societies that spoke English with a charming accent, and retained a colourful folklore. But the *Globe* editorial writer's tone, dripping with condescension, would seem almost enthusiastic compared to some of the views expressed at the public meetings that the Commission would hold.

Discussion of Pearson's proposal was soon overwhelmed by the confusion in the Diefenbaker government and the bitter debate over whether or not Canada should accept nuclear arms. When Pearson announced that Canada was obliged to do so by its signed obligations and that the Liberals would accept this responsibility, the reaction from the left wing of the party was bitter, particularly in Quebec. Editor-in-chief of *Le Devoir*, André Laurendeau, denounced Pearson, referring to Pierre Trudeau's article in *Cité libre* that called him "the defrocked priest of peace." But the crisis that Lamontagne had referred to in September intensified: the Rassemblement pour l'indépendance nationale was formed in a special convention on March 3.

The FLQ began setting off bombs in Montreal in March and April 1963, killing a night watchman, Wilfrid O'Neil, on April 21. On election night, April 8, 1963, Laurendeau was a commentator on Radio-Canada. Lamontagne won his seat in Outremont, despite the fact that Laurendeau had written an editorial saying he would vote against him. At the television studio, Lamontagne told Laurendeau, "I've got to see you again soon – you know on what subject."

For Laurendeau had been the first to talk about the need for a Royal Commission, fifteen months earlier. "Bilingual cheques is a tardy measure which in no way corresponds to the present aspirations of the French-Canadian people," he wrote on January 20, 1962.

Laurendeau proposed that there be a Royal Commission established to look into bilingualism – with three objectives: to find out what Canadians from coast to coast think about the subject; to study how Belgium and Switzerland deal with the same problems, and, thirdly, "to examine, again very closely, the role played by the two languages in the federal civil service." At stake, he said, is the French language, spoken by nearly a third of the population of Canada. "Paris, history reminds us, was worth a mass," he concluded, evoking Henry IV's conversion in order to secure the support of Catholic Paris. "Perhaps Canada is worth a Royal Commission."

Diefenbaker dismissed the idea – and responded with precisely what Laurendeau had already dismissed as out of date: bilingual federal cheques. This followed a series of incremental gestures the federal government had made over the years: bilingual postage stamps in 1927, bilingual banknotes in 1936, bilingual family allowance cheques in 1945, simultaneous translation in the House in 1959 and in the Senate in 1961. On February 7, Laurendeau called it "*trop peu, trop tard.*" Too little, too late. But over the next year, a political consensus around his idea of a Royal Commission would develop. Lamontagne had even shown Laurendeau and Gérard Pelletier, editor-in-chief of *La Presse*, a draft of Pearson's speech.

Laurendeau and Lamontagne were not the only people thinking about the need to make the public service bilingual. Montreal lawyer Eugène Therrien, a member of the Royal Commission on Government Organization headed by Grant Glassco, which published its report in 1962, wrote a stinging dissenting statement on the lack of bilingualism in the federal government. His observations were pungent: "The number of French Canadians holding key positions in the government administration is insignificant, save for a few district offices in the Province of Quebec. . . . In the federal administration, and markedly in the Armed Forces, there is little or no understanding of French Canada's claim to certain rights, especially with regard to the co-existence of the French language in Canada, nor of the way in which bilingualism bears upon efficiency in the administration. . . . French Canadians cannot feel at home all over Canada as long as the co-existence of their language goes unrecognized, not only in written texts, but in fact. They refuse to be regarded by the federal administration as second-class citizens. . . . French-Canadian public servants cannot freely use the French language as a means of communication within the federal administration."

In his own way, in ten pages included near the beginning of the Glassco Report, Therrien gave a preview of the Royal Commission: a stark description of the inequities facing French-speakers, the lack of representation of French Canadians, the failures of recruitment, the inappropriate representation of Canada abroad – and a comparison with the administrative policies in Switzerland, Belgium, and South Africa. It was a reflection of the growing unhappiness in Quebec that it emerged from a figure as conventional as Therrien: a Queen's Counsel, a member of the Montreal Board of Trade, the director-general of an insurance company, L'Économie mutuelle d'assurance, and a man selected by a Conservative government to work on a Royal Commission on government organization.

Therrien wrote his dissent in May. Less than a month later, on June 18, 1962, Diefenbaker lost his majority, falling from an unprecedented victory of 208 seats out of 265 to 116, and dropping from 55 per cent of the popular vote to 40 per cent. The Liberals had come back from the debacle of 1958, where they had got only 29 per cent of the vote, with 36 per cent. But Social Credit's gains meant that Quebec eluded them both.

In this context, both the Liberals and the Conservatives looked at what was happening in Quebec, and tried to see if they could capitalize on it. Looking at the prospects of the following election, if it came soon, Pearson made it clear to his son Geoffrey in a letter after the election that Quebec was the key to a Liberal majority. "If it were not for [Social Credit] in Quebec – our complacent party managers muffed that one – we would be forming a minority government. And that would be a real headache – in present circumstances," he wrote, imagining facing Diefenbaker and Caouette in opposition. "With a turnover of a few votes in 15 constituencies (where the Tory majority was under five hundred) and a 'reasonable' Quebec, we would be forming a majority government. That would be better – but – if we don't make any silly mistakes – it will come next time."

It was that "next time" that Lamontagne had been trying to prepare for, and, even on election night, was thinking about. The weeks that followed the April 8 election continued to be tense in Montreal. Bombs continued to explode. One night, when Laurendeau, Lévesque, labour leader Jean Marchand, and Pierre Trudeau met at Gérard Pelletier's house, as they did twice a month, a mailbox bomb went off, just down the street.

It seemed unlikely that any of them would be chosen to serve on a Royal Commission. Laurendeau, Pelletier, and Trudeau were unpopular in federal Liberal circles for their harsh criticism of the decision on nuclear weapons. And Lionel Chevrier, an aging veteran of Louis St-Laurent's cabinet who had been named to Pearson's, had told Laurendeau and Pelletier over lunch that former governor general Vincent Massey and Renaud St-Laurent, Louis's son, were being considered as possible co-chairmen. (Pelletier's response was scathing; both men pointed out to the astonished Chevrier that being the son of a former Liberal prime minister was hardly a sufficient qualification for the position, and that no one would expect much that was new or innovative from Massey, "this noble old man.")

But in June, Pearson called Laurendeau and asked if he would be part of a Royal Commission on Bilingualism and Biculturalism and have lunch with Lamontagne to discuss the details the next day. When he consulted his colleagues at *Le Devoir*, Claude Ryan – then an editorial writer and Laurendeau's successor – told him he could not in good conscience turn it down. Laurendeau had been the first to call for a commission; if he refused to participate, he could not in good conscience criticize the report.

Laurendeau was then fifty-one, but because he had become an active nationalist very young, seemed part of an older generation. He had been a student of the nationalist historian Abbé Lionel Groulx, and part of the Jeune Canada movement in the 1930s, which had endorsed separatism and flirted with fascist ideology and anti-Semitism. In February 1963, in *Le Magazine Maclean*, he recounted a conversation with a Jewish neighbour who was deeply concerned about Union Nationale leader Daniel Johnson's flattery of Caouette, who had declared shortly before that his political heroes were Mussolini and Hitler. (Her family had fled Germany in 1933, after Hitler had been elected.)

"I watched her as she was speaking. Suddenly the reality of what she was saying struck me," he wrote. "If in late 1932 or early 1933, I told myself, that German Jew hadn't decided to leave his German homeland, my neighbour wouldn't be sitting there beside me. She couldn't have urged her grandmother to get out and vote, and the whole family would have perished in the gas ovens."

He recalled, with deep embarrassment, a meeting he had helped organize in 1933 with Le Jeune Canada, a counter-demonstration to a protest against the treatment of Jews in Germany. "I wonder to this day, who or what inspired it. But we held it just the same, because a cloud of anti-Semitism had polluted the atmosphere," he said. The speeches, he confessed, were dreadful – talking about the "alleged persecution" and "so-called persecution" in Germany compared to the bad treatment "very real by contrast" which French-Canadians suffered in Quebec. "I can still see myself and hear myself braying with the best of them at that meeting, while in another part of the world a German Jew, by accepting exile, was snatching his family from death."

In 1935, Laurendeau left for Paris, and spent two years in Europe, an experience that transformed his views. He became influenced by both the doctrine of personalism of the Catholic left, and by French scholar André Siegfried, who forced him to look at Canada as a whole. "I can't deny it, the courses I took with Siegfried have influenced me," he wrote to a friend. "I wonder if there isn't a good Confederation to be established."

Laurendeau returned to Montreal in 1937 after having travelled in Italy and Belgium; he had become repelled by fascism, condemning it in Italy and Spain, and denounced Franco – which, he remarked later, "estranged me somewhat from my fellow French Canadians." Nevertheless, on his return he took over the editorship of his father's nationalist publication *L'Action nationale* and later campaigned against conscription and was elected to the Quebec legislature with the Bloc Populaire. He was one of the people Pierre Trudeau had sought out for advice in 1944, when he was trying to decide what to do after articling as a lawyer; Laurendeau told him that their society was terribly lacking in economic expertise – which helped Trudeau decide to do a joint degree in economics and political science at Harvard.

Disillusioned with partisan politics, Laurendeau resigned from the Bloc and joined *Le Devoir* in 1947 – but had also been active in the arts, writing plays. Deeply sensitive (political scientist Dale Thomson once described him as "a man of almost Florentine delicacy ... [who] wrote sensitive, carefully crafted editorials, often with a touch of wistfulness, as if regretting that the world was not as perfect as he wished it to be"), he remained a nationalist but was a bitter critic of Maurice Duplessis. Despite his interest in the renewal of nationalism among the young, he continued to reject independence as an option for Quebec, saying that he had decided in the 1930s that it was a dead end.

Over lunch with Lamontagne, Laurendeau realized that Ryan was right; he could not turn down the co-chairmanship, and then write editorials critical of the report. He asked for a week to decide – and embarked on a process of consultation. He consulted widely, and encountered mixed reactions. Lévesque drew up a list of reasons for and against with the negative list much longer, and the main reason in favour being the impact Laurendeau would have if he resigned. (At one point during the lunch, Laurendeau began a sentence by saying, "I am not a separatist . . ." and Lévesque interrupted, "Neither am I!") To Laurendeau's dismay, some of those whom he expected to be supportive were lukewarm to the idea. They were fed up with extending hands to the English. It took another two meetings with Lamontagne before he gave his agreement. Finally he said, "*Vouloir, c'est aussi vouloir les conséquences de ce qu'on veut*" – an elegant way of saying, "Be careful what you wish for."

On July 11, Laurendeau met with Pearson. One of the final things that he wanted to be sure of was that he would retain his right to keep writing on other subjects. Mischievously, Pearson said, "Now let's imagine you were studying the nuclear arms situation. You could talk about everything in *Le Devoir*, except nuclear arms." Laurendeau was impressed at the teasing reference to his editorials attacking Pearson on his decision to accept nuclear weapons.

The adventure began. In January 1962, Laurendeau had written that a Royal Commission's first objective would be to find out what Canadians thought about the subject – which would lance the abscess. "We might as well stop kidding ourselves; there is nothing to lose from knowing the truth." He was about to find out.

And what happened to the people who, wittingly or unwittingly, had such a critical influence on the creation of the
committee? Maurice Lamontagne would resign from the cabinet
in 1965, embarrassed by the revelation that he had bought furniture without a repayment plan from a furniture dealer who
subsequently went bankrupt. Named to the Senate in 1967, he
wrote a polemic during the 1980 referendum attacking the economic assumptions of separatism. He died in 1983. Gilles Grégoire
became the first *indépendantiste* in Parliament when he left the
Créditiste caucus to sit as an independent. He then left federal
politics in 1966 to lead the right-wing *indépendantiste* group
le Ralliement national – and, in 1968, became the co-founder of
the Parti Québécois, suggesting the party's name. Elected to the
Quebec National Assembly in 1976 and re-elected in 1981, he left
the PQ caucus in 1983 after being convicted for having sex with
seven underage girls, and did not run for re-election in 1985.

And Donald Gordon himself? He had become a profoundly
controversial figure – as he put it in a letter to Pearson, his appear-
ance before the parliamentary committee in November 1962 had
generated "much criticism, distortion, misunderstanding and some
public unrest." When he returned to the committee in December
1963, he was able to make an impressive progress report. He had
hired a French Canadian to be a vice president, gleefully phoning
Pearson to tell him the news. A special examination of language use
by the state-owned railways in Switzerland and Belgium was in
process, a large-scale French and English instruction program for
CNR employees had been established, a French-English dictionary
of language terminology was almost finished, an accelerated
recruitment program in French-language universities had been
started, requirements for advancement in each department had
been reassessed to make sure that there were opportunities for
advancement for French Canadians. "The objective [is] to foster an

environment in which both languages can be freely used," he told the committee.

Even Grégoire was impressed, and conceded he was surprised by the details of Gordon's report, moving a motion that it was very satisfactory. "I think you, more than many others, have understood what bilingualism is," he told Gordon.

By then the Royal Commission was underway – and would soon discover what the state of understanding was in the country.

chapter three

Two Éminences Grises

> André Laurendeau et Frank Scott furent les hommes
> de l'ouverture à l'autre.
>
> *GUY LAFOREST*

At every public session of the Royal Commission, André Laurendeau – or, if he was not there, Davidson Dunton, president of Carleton University, former head of the Wartime Information Board, and former president of the CBC – would begin by saying that there were three key questions that summed up the problem the Commission was trying to address: "Can English-speaking and French-speaking Canadians live together, and do they want to? Under what new conditions? And are they prepared to accept those conditions?"

They were quite different questions from those that Pearson had asked, which were much more institutional and functional: Was Canada ready to give young Canadians the opportunity to become bilingual? What steps should be taken to make this possible? Why were there relatively few French Canadians in the federal

civil service? How could this be improved? Would it be desirable
to have a bilingual school of public administration?

Laurendeau and Dunton were asking a much more basic,
fundamental question: Did the country want to stay together? On
May 4, 1964, Laurendeau noted in his journal that *Le Devoir*
reporter Michel Roy told him that this was the real question to
be confronted. "It would be premature to try to answer it,"
Laurendeau wrote. "Let's say only that the coexistence will be still
more difficult than I imagined. . . . For the moment, it is true that,
left to myself, I feel several times each week and even several times
a day, real internal surges towards separatism. It is a question of
elementary reactions of an emotional nature, to which I don't
ascribe any more importance than necessary. But the density, the
depth of ignorance and the prejudices are really immeasurable,
and even if sociologists could explain the reason, it remains that
these things are difficult to endure and to live through."

In terms of separatism, Laurendeau felt he had been there and
done that – three decades earlier. In 1935, he had endorsed the
position of Jeune Canada that each nation should form a state,
and thus, that French Canada should have its independent state. It
was, as Denis Monière noted in his biography, a circumstantial
engagement that would not last, a dream rather than a commitment. In a letter in 1940, he wrote that his ideas had evolved over
the preceding five years. "I figure that if it were possible, it would
be better if the French-Canadian nationality were on its own and
directed its own destinies," he wrote. ". . . And yet, I no longer
desire secession (short of some dramatic upheaval)."

His time in Paris in 1935, during which he had written a separatist pamphlet for Jeune Canada, had transformed his view, he
explained two decades later. "It was there, the following year, that
I lost my faith in separatism, and I have never regained it since."

Laurendeau may not have regained it, but he felt he understood it and could empathize with it. In 1961, in a CBC-Radio

broadcast, he said that he knew civil servants who were separatists – because they were civil servants. They were forced to work in another language and, in effect, deny who they were – or speak out and become marginalized. He said he knew journalists who were separatists – because they were journalists, and had to deal with the irrationality of translating into French stories in English that were actually based on speeches that had been made in French. He continued – as he did until he died – to insist on the distinction between being a nationalist and being a separatist, but he retained the indignation that he had felt as a young man at the state of the French language in Quebec and in Canada. As a result, he was able to keep in touch with various generations of Quebec activists and intellectuals, from his one-time mentor, Lionel Groulx, to the young neo-Marxist separatists of the magazine *Parti Pris.*

He believed in the importance of vigorous public debate. When Trudeau published his essay in a book that he edited on the Asbestos Strike, Laurendeau – who disagreed profoundly with Trudeau's attack on Quebec nationalism – applauded the essay. "Of course, it is never pleasant to see ideas challenged that one has never doubted or questioned during one's life," he told Pelletier. "But I repeated to myself on each page that it is healthy to be shaken on one's certainties and habits of thought, particularly by a mind of this quality. . . . This is the price you pay for a real intellectual climate." And similarly, during his time as a commissioner, while he noted René Lévesque's journey toward embracing sovereignty ("I found a Lévesque who was very relaxed, very disoriented and very separatist," he wrote in June 1965), Laurendeau found Lévesque's impact to be "absolutely essential" to the achievement of any kind of understanding of Quebec in the rest of Canada.

After Laurendeau's participation was confirmed, the next challenge was to establish the mandate. Lamontagne wrote it in French, and it was translated: "to inquire into and report upon the existing

state of bilingualism and biculturalism in Canada and to recom-
mend what steps should be taken to develop the Canadian
Confederation on the basis of an equal partnership between the two
founding races, taking into account the contribution made by the
other ethnic groups to the cultural enrichment of Canada and
the measures that should be taken to safeguard that contribution."

It went on to identify "all branches and agencies of the federal
government" and "the role of public and private organizations,
including the mass communications media" as part of the mandate
as well as calling for reports on how "the bilingual and basically
bicultural character of the federal administration" could be
ensured, and how "better cultural relations and a more widespread
appreciation of the basically bicultural character of our country"
could be promoted and improved.

The words themselves were tricky, in both languages. "For a
reason we had difficulty understanding, Jack Pickersgill, the
Secretary of State, asked that the word 'races' be substituted for
the word 'peoples,'" recalled Jean-Louis Gagnon in his memoirs.
"Perhaps he was thinking of 'Canada des deux races by André
Siegfried.'" According to Gagnon, Pearson later had to apologize
to a Jewish group for the use of the word *races*. But that was not
the least of it; Gagnon argued that there was no French equivalent
for the word *partnership*, and no English word for the French
word *égalité*.

On July 19, 1963, the Commission was announced: Laurendeau's
co-chair was Davidson Dunton. A calm, self-contained man, he
provided a contrast to Laurendeau, who was often stung by the
criticism that the Commission received. He had what Montreal
journalist Mark Farrell once called "the gift of silence"; he was a
careful listener. "Davie, just by nature, would not be insistent,
pressing, pushing," recalled Gordon Robertson, who was one of
his closest friends. "He was the moderate man. Davie's whole
approach was exactly right for Mike Pearson."

The other commissioners were New Brunswick priest and university administrator Clément Cormier, Quebec labour leader Jean Marchand, Ontario lawyer and Liberal organizer Royce Frith, French teacher Gertrude Laing from Calgary, J.B. Rudnyckyj of Winnipeg who was head of the Department of Slavic Studies at the University of Manitoba from 1949 until 1977, and Paul Wyczynski of Ottawa, founder of the Centre de recherche en littérature canadienne-française, which he directed from 1958 until 1973. (When Marchand resigned in 1965 to run for the Liberals, he was replaced by Paul Lacoste, who had previously been co-secretary of the commission. His presence reinforced the nationalist position on the Commission.)

The staff proved very important: Lacoste of the Université de Montréal and Neil Morrison – an old friend of Laurendeau's who had worked at the CBC – were co-secretaries, Michael Oliver of McGill was director of research, and Léon Dion of Laval was a special consultant on research. Laurendeau was closer to several of the staff members than he was to Dunton, but he became very upset at reports that there were tensions between them. "I found Mr. Dunton to be truly an ideal co-chairman, and still find him a pleasure to work with," he wrote in his journal. "Of course, a joint chairmanship is a difficult task and day-to-day operations can be complicated; this being said, I couldn't have dreamt of a better colleague."

But Laurendeau's real counterpart on the Royal Commission, his intellectual and emotional counterweight from English-speaking Canada, was Frank Scott. Like Laurendeau, he had a subtle mind, political idealism, personal charisma, and a poet's sensibility; also like Laurendeau, he had only reluctantly joined the Commission. As Guy Laforest put it in his essay on the two men, "While both were intellectuals involved in the political debates of their society, they were also artists, two figures endowed with a remarkable aesthetic sensibility." Laforest traces the parallels: both men were engaged in the arts and politically involved, both withdrew from political life somewhat at the end of the 1940s and beginning of the 1950s, and, at the end of the decade, both were *éminences grises* – intellectual leaders in their respective communities.

Laurendeau and Scott first met a quarter of a century earlier, in 1938. Laurendeau was just back from two years in Europe, where he had studied under André Siegfried. "He inspired in Laurendeau the desire to dialogue with English-Canadians as soon as he returned to the country," wrote Anne Moreau in her thesis on Scott. While similar in many ways, Moreau pointed out that their backgrounds were very different: Laurendeau was a nationalist, who studied the Catholic philosophers Jacques Maritain and Emmanuel Mounier when he was in Paris; when he was at Oxford, Scott, the son of an Anglican priest, studied the English socialists G.D.H. Cole, R.H. Tawney, and Ramsay Macdonald.

The two men formed a study group of French-speaking and English-speaking intellectuals but, as Laurendeau noted in his book on the conscription crisis, while their references were rarely the same, they did achieve friendship. But the political gap was too wide; Scott argued that a strong central government could protect French-speaking minorities outside Quebec, while Laurendeau, as Moreau points out, was suspicious of federal centralization and saw Quebec as the best protection for French-Canadian culture and identity.

The war put an end to their meetings. In a 1943 by-election in Montreal, Laurendeau was the campaign manager for the Bloc Populaire candidate, and Scott was the campaign manager for David Lewis. (Both their efforts were in vain; Fred Rose, the communist candidate, won.)

They shared an erudition, intellectual rigour, and sensuality – but while Laurendeau had an almost therapeutic sensitivity, listening to people without judging them, Scott had a cutting sense of humour. "I can still hear that great laugh that made you know he was there at a party even when he was two rooms away," wrote Michael Oliver, in 1997, twelve years after Scott's death, observing that everyone who came in contact with him knew a different Frank Scott. "For me he was myth incarnate: the co-author of the Regina Manifesto, the vanquisher of Maurice Duplessis, the man whose name the *Montreal Star* would not publish, the magician who could put social as well as personal passion into the frame of verse."

Born in Quebec City in 1899, Scott was a Rhodes Scholar who, on returning to Montreal, became caught up not only in English-speaking political and cultural life, but also engaged with French-Canadian traditions. "I could understand Stendhal reading the Code Napoleon to improve his prose style," he wrote. "One summer to occupy my spare time as a student in a Montreal law office I translated the whole of the Coûtume de Paris, the principal source of the Civil Law in Quebec prior to the adoption of her own Civil Code of 1866. The continuity of Quebec's traditions with old France, and through the civil law with ancient Rome, has always seemed to me a fascinating part of our Canadian heritage."

Scott was a socialist and a wit in conservative English Montreal when to be a socialist was an outrage and to be witty was outrageous. His laugh was unforgettable; he was a tall, handsome man, and his mouth often curled with what seemed to be the effort of keeping in the laughter. When it burst out, often loud and raucous, it would fill a room and linger like pipe smoke. His best-known commentary on bilingualism was in a poem first published in 1954, "Bonne Entente":

> The advantages of living with two cultures
> Strike one at every turn,
> Especially when one finds a notice in an office building
> "This elevator will not run on Ascension Day";
> Or reads in the *Montreal Star*:

"Tomorrow being the Feast of the Immaculate
    Conception,
There will be no garbage collection in the city";
Or sees on the restaurant menu the bilingual dish:
                    DEEP APPLE PIE
            TARTES AUX POMMES PROFONDES

At times, Scott's wit could be wry and at times bawdy and
almost bullying. In a line that some suggested applied as much to
himself as to his fellow poet, Scott quipped that the lusty Irving
Layton was "like a bull in a vagina shop."

Scott turned sixty-four two weeks after the Royal Commission was formally announced; by that time he had established
himself as a social democrat who was active in the Co-operative
Commonwealth Federation, a constitutional law scholar, a civil
libertarian, a translator, a wit, an academic, and a poet. (To add
a personal note, in 1950 my parents bought a summer place in
North Hatley, in Quebec's Eastern Townships, jointly with the
Scotts, a house I now own. My childhood and adolescent memories of him are primarily of a man who loved to laugh. Once, at
a picnic when I was a small child, he accidentally capsized a
canoe – and, convinced he had done it intentionally, I got quite
excited, calling out, "Do it again, Mr. Scott! Do it again!" – which
amused him greatly, and became part of family lore.)

In 1956, Scott had appeared before the Supreme Court challenging Duplessis's Padlock Law, and won; in 1958, he represented
Montreal restaurant owner Frank Roncarelli (whose liquor licence
had been taken away by Duplessis because he had been paying the
bail of fellow Jehovah's Witnesses) before the Supreme Court and
won. In 1961, after years of quiet disapproval and near-disavowal,
McGill made him Dean of Law – more than a decade after he was
passed over because of his political activities and affiliation.

Scott had known Laurendeau since the late 1930s. In 1939, he began meeting with a group of French-Canadian nationalists who were opposed to the war – which included Laurendeau, who was then editor of the nationalist journal *L'Action nationale*. Scott noted approvingly in his journal that he was on a first-name basis with the three French-speaking members of the Commission, but, except for Dunton, whom he had known when he was editor of the *Montreal Herald* and then president of the CBC, he knew none of his fellow commissioners from the rest of Canada.

Both Laurendeau and Scott kept journals during the period of their involvement in the Royal Commission, Laurendeau until his death in 1968, and Scott until the commission finally wrapped up its work in March 1971. The two accounts, when read with the reports of the Royal Commission, show the differing responses of a remarkable group of people brought together at a time when the country was groping for a response to the explosion that was occurring in Quebec.

The composition of the Commission itself was unusual, and highly unrepresentative of the country. Once the government had decided upon bilingualism as a criterion, the pool of potential candidates from English-speaking Canada shrank dramatically. Pearson confessed to Scott that "finding a member of the family compact in Toronto who could speak French was utterly impossible," and as a result had named Royce Frith, a young Ontario Liberal organizer originally from the Ottawa Valley town of Perth, a lawyer and private television owner who had done a graduate law degree in French at the University of Ottawa. Scott was disappointed, noting in his journal that Frith "probably could not speak for that great solid lump or heart of English Canada which is as much a fact of life as the Catholic core of Quebec is." He was similarly dubious about Gertrude Laing, the only woman on the Commission, "whom I had seen described as 'a teacher of French in Calgary.'"

Scott was soon charmed by both of them on a personal level, and remarked more than once in his journal at the warm personal relations that were established between the commissioners during the eight years and eighty-three private meetings that they spent together. ("People ask how we succeeded so well," Laing said at the Commission's last meeting. "Martinis," Scott replied. "That's just what they think," she said.)

In some ways, the congeniality was not surprising; they were a remarkably sophisticated, erudite, and articulate group, and Scott noted that their private meetings rarely went ten minutes without being interrupted by laughter. "What I notice now about our Commission in informal social intercourse is that we are able to talk about anything inside and outside Quebec. May it stay that way!" he wrote approvingly on December 19, 1963. "I notice also that we now speak almost exclusively in French outside our meetings."

But Scott became increasingly upset by two things: the degree to which, as the final report was being drafted, there was a nationalist consensus among the surviving Quebec commissioners, and, at the same time, the degree to which Frith and Laing were prepared to become part of that consensus at the expense of English-speaking Quebec.

He found the moderate, conciliatory approach, of which Pearson himself was the personification, to be deeply frustrating. Before going to see Pearson in August 1965, Scott wrote bitterly, "Being trained as a diplomat and not as a political leader he apparently is satisfied to act as the President of a United Nations composed of the Canadian provinces." Then, after the meeting, he wrote, "Mike Pearson is so charming in his manner, and so obviously a man of good will, that it is impossible to be angry with him when you are in his presence. Yet his whole nature and outlook makes him the most unsuitable Prime Minister for this present critical stage in Canada's history that could possibly have been found. He is the logical extension of the Mackenzie King policy of vacillation and prolonged inactivity. It looks as though the way Canada will end will be not with a bang but with a whimper." Scott could not think of a more damning insult than comparing Pearson to King; he had written a devastating poem after King's death, "W.L.M.K.," which concluded:

> Truly he will be remembered
> Wherever men honour ingenuity
> Ambiguity, inactivity and political longevity.
> Let us raise up a temple
> To the cult of mediocrity,
> Doing nothing by halves which can be done by quarters.

Dunton's quality of moderation, which Pearson and Robertson saw as a critical virtue, Scott saw as a cardinal sin. And later, after a meeting of the Commission in December, he complained about "two co-equal Chairmen, neither of whom has responsibility because both have it, and neither of whom is a dominant or leading personality."

In their public meetings, the commissioners encountered the range of opinions, from anger and resentment – in French Canada of the English, in English Canada of the French – to enthusiasm and support for the idea of bilingualism. They heard from people who were unable to send a telegram in French, soldiers who had been beaten up for speaking French to each other, and staff at the Château Frontenac who had been ordered to reply to guests in English even when asked questions in French. In Alberta, Laurendeau met an elderly local gentleman who asked, "I know you use French in your schools and churches and courts in Quebec, but you do speak English at home, don't you?"

They heard people in Vancouver complain that Quebec was "fifty years behind the times," and a regional school inspector who said cheerfully that there was no problem for French-speaking families living on a large base outside Quebec because within a matter of months, the children were assimilated. An editorial writer in Calgary told Laurendeau that the system of values that he had functioned with had completely disappeared, and even his own children didn't believe them any more. When Laurendeau asked what values he meant, he replied, "The Bible, Shakespeare, the Union Jack, the British Empire . . ."

Occasionally, both Laurendeau and Scott would lose patience, and break their self-imposed rule of impartial listening. In Saskatoon, after a long evening of comment about Quebec and French Canada, Laurendeau said, "Suppose that the French Canadians in Quebec are wrong. What are you going to do with them? Shoot them?" To which someone of Doukhobor origin said, "Perhaps we should disperse them across Canada." Laurendeau noted that the reaction to this was "general stupor," adding, "I didn't dare reply that you would have a few bombs in Saskatoon."

And Scott lost patience in Winnipeg, at a lunch with local businessmen where one said that he did not believe that the Franco Manitobans were at all dissatisfied with their lot. "Why should they be?" he asked. "At this point, I could not contain myself and I called out loudly 'You took away their school and language rights, didn't you? Why should they feel satisfied?'" Scott wrote. "We got nowhere after this, except exchanges of argument which changed no one's opinion. After we left the lunch, Jean Marchand remarked 'Before I joined this Commission, I was an anti-separatist.'"

What struck the commissioners most forcefully was the gap between the two language groups – the level of frustration in French-speaking Canada, and the level of ignorance and incomprehension of this in English-speaking Canada. "The concessions offered in the English-speaking community were seldom those demanded in the French-speaking communities," the commissioners wrote in the preliminary report. "Their clocks were set at a different time."

And, for all their congeniality and mutual respect, the French- and English-speaking commissioners did not come to the table with synchronized watches either. Scott had difficulty believing anybody ever uttered the phrase "Speak White!" and believed it was an urban legend, a phrase concocted from racial insults in the southern United States. Following that conversation, Laurendeau took to asking Acadians and French-Canadians in the West if they had heard the phrase, and began hearing accounts of people being told to "speak white," being told by an employer, "You must speak a white man's language," or "Go back to Quebec" if they were overheard speaking French in public.

"All in all, the fact of speaking French seems to irritate anglophones more than the fact of being French-Canadian," he noted in his journal. "It would be very interesting to be able to psychoanalyze the reaction that determines the insult: is one offended to hear a foreign language? Or particularly to hear French? Do they feel excluded: Do they have the impression that French Canadians are exchanging unfriendly remarks about them?"

Scott, on the other hand, was irritated at what he saw as Laurendeau's stereotyping of English Canada's misunderstanding of Quebec as shown by the use of the phrase "priest-ridden province."

"While it is an insulting term, from the point of view of protestant Canada, the fact that Quebec has not a single lay school, college or university for the French-speaking people, the fact that the place names are predominantly attached to Catholic saints and the fact that in the Catholic parishes the parish authorities can use the civil courts to enforce payment of church dues, is understandably going to make the 'anglo-saxon' people feel that the influence of the priest in the social life of the province is excessive," Scott wrote in his journal, summarizing the point he had made. "I might have mentioned the crucifixes in the court rooms, but didn't."

Scott, in fact, had a nuanced view of nationhood and the "two nations" theory. "Quebec is a unilingual, unicultural society, while English Canada is a unilingual, multicultural society," he observed to Laurendeau in November 1964, noting "Laurendeau agreed."

He developed this idea further in his confidential brief to the Commission in August 1965, which he entitled "A View of Canada." "The line of thought I have developed does not deny the existence of French Canada as a nation," he wrote. "I do not believe that every nationality has a right to total statehood . . . I do not believe that the rest of Canada apart from Quebec can properly be called a nation, since it is comprised of heterogeneous cultural groups, united only by the use of a common language and the desire to be politically united in a single state *which includes Quebec*. If Quebec is separated from them, they do not even live in a contiguous area. So I reject the two-nation [theory] without denying that French Canada can properly be called a nation." (Trudeau, in contrast, flatly described the two nations theory as "dangerous in theory and groundless in fact" – and argued in 1965 that French Canadians "must abandon their role of oppressed nation, and participate and decide to participate boldly and intelligently in the Canadian experience.")

The commissioners' travels across the country brought them dramatically in touch with the realities of the country. They found that attitudes in English Canada toward French and Quebec, let alone bilingualism, ranged from uninformed naïveté to outright hostility. And a reciprocal range of views was heard in Quebec. In Sherbrooke, a student said that he didn't care in the slightest about French-speaking minorities in the rest of the country; the only minority that mattered was the English-speaking minority in Quebec, and the sooner it left the better. "*J'y suis, j'y reste*," quipped Scott – I'm here and I'm staying – to appreciative laughter. (Two decades later, almost certainly coincidentally, the phrase became one of the No campaign slogans in the 1980 referendum.)

In Yarmouth, a former member of the Nova Scotia legislature told the Commission that French Canadians were fortunate to be living in a British country where freedom was equally extended to all. "This thing has gone far enough," he said. Scott noted in his diary, "He went on to explain that if you had a fractious child in the family you tolerated this for some time, but ultimately it was necessary to apply some discipline. A considerable clapping of hands followed this observation." Scott observed in his journal that the man was not trying to be offensive. "I think it was a tribute to the atmosphere we had created that this freedom of speech was possible; it was no more extreme than that of the young separatist in Sherbrooke who said that the only minority problem was that of the English minority in Quebec, and the sooner they went west the better."

Laurendeau didn't feel quite the same equanimity after absorbing hours of ignorance about Quebec and French Canada. "Faced with some anglophones, I feel an inner surge towards separatism: 'They're too dumb, they won't listen to anything but force,'" he wrote on February 22, 1964. "Back in Quebec, the separatists send me back to Canada: they are too naive, too far from political realities – or curiously fickle and superficial."

The catalyst for the Commission's decision to issue a preliminary report seems to have been the last public meeting they had in Quebec City on June 16, 1964. The meeting had been taken over by separatists in a calculated way. Looking for some papers he had left behind earlier, Jaroslav Rudnyckyj had stumbled into a room where they were planning their tactics before the meeting. The result left the commissioners shaken.

"Separatists completely took over the last informal public meeting of the Royal Commission on Bilingualism and

Biculturalism here last night," wrote Robert McKenzie in the *Gazette* the next day. "For more than two hours, they drew applause and cheers – and some jeers for the members of the commission as they rose one after another to outline the arguments to favour Quebec seceding from the nation." Michel Roy described it in similar terms in *Le Devoir*. "It was a tumultuous and stormy session Tuesday night in Quebec where the Laurendeau-Dunton Commission held its last regional session," he wrote. "Entirely dominated by militants of the RIN (Rassemblement pour l'indépendance nationale) who made 25 of the 30 statements, the meeting vehemently expressed with its noisy applause, with its cheers and boos, all of the resentment which the Commission inspired, all the hostility that it felt towards the Commission, all the bitterness it feels about the provocations suffered by French Canadians for 200 years." The headline in *Le Soleil* was "The separatists won the upper hand."

In his journal, Laurendeau observed wryly that for once, the newspapers hadn't exaggerated. "What struck me, is that there were at most one hundred separatists in the hall," he wrote. "However, they dominated the meeting, despite the relatively numerous presence of anti-separatists perfectly capable of expressing themselves, and of whom only three or four spoke, and very badly." Laurendeau was particularly saddened by the fact that a former Bloc Populaire member and old friend, Philippe Girard, had sat silently as he and Marchand were denounced.

Scott felt the same way. "It was painfully obvious that the separatists were anti-democratic, indeed fascist in their determination to force their views upon the entire assembly and to stifle all opposition," he wrote. "While they only used verbal violence, it was violence just the same."

Their internal meeting in Lac Beauport the next day was, Laurendeau wrote, "the fullest, the most moving, the most serious that we have had." He told his colleagues that he thought the separatists had created a revolutionary situation in which all other voices were silenced. "Hence it was obvious that things would get much worse as the tide surged their way," Scott reported, noting Laurendeau's observation that a former colleague of his had not had the courage or determination to speak against the prevalent opinion.

Then Rudnyckyj spoke up. Born in Poland in 1910, he had worked at the Ukrainian Scientific Institute in Berlin, and taught at the Ukrainian Free University, first in Prague from 1941 to 1947 and then in Heidelberg in 1947–48 before coming to Canada. He told them that he felt it was 11:45, with only fifteen minutes left before the crisis. He had seen identical situations in two European countries before he came to Canada, he said, and they both ended in disaster. "[He felt] that they were in the middle of a Greek drama which was moving inexorably to a climax," Scott wrote in his journal. "What kind of climax we don't know yet. We still have time to take some pre-climax action, not climax or post-climax action."

Frith was shaken by the meeting the night before. "I am an English Canadian, and I have come a long way," he said, according to Laurendeau's notes. "If I transpose my life to Quebec and imagine myself French, I understand the deep feelings of dissatisfaction of French Canadians. But as well, as a Commissioner, I know the mood of English-Canada: better disposed than I would have predicted, but a thousand leagues from understanding what is going on in Quebec, and certainly not prepared for the kind of negotiation which is required. . . . I believe that we are perhaps the best informed people on the state of mind of Canadians." Since they knew the situation was extremely dangerous, he argued that they had a duty to warn the public about it. "He wanted us to make some great declaration alerting all Canadians to the fact that they were headed for disaster," Scott wrote. "No-one else agreed with this tactic, though all shared his concern."

Scott was also worried that a consensus might form among the commissioners – at the expense of the English minority in his province, and a bilingual Quebec. "Father Cormier wants the French minorities included in the concept of French Canada; I feel Laurendeau and Lacoste want above all a powerful French Canada and are willing to pay a considerable price to get it," he wrote.

While few immediately agreed with Frith's idea, a consensus soon formed around the need for a preliminary report. In early July, the commissioners met with Pearson, who agreed to one, with a target date set for mid-autumn. The target was missed – but the process of reaching a consensus was a draining and difficult one.

"At the end of the morning, there was general agreement that this had been one of the best sessions we had ever held as a group, and that no matter what the report might do to other people, the writing of it had been an essential exercise for ourselves," Scott wrote in November. "We also came close to defining the nature of the crisis as being a kind of unavoidable tragedy."

But the debate was vigorous. At one point, Scott laid out what he called "a list of myths" that Laurendeau had not included in his account of the misunderstandings that existed in the country. Scott ripped off a series of them:

1. The French were the first in Canada – everywhere. Because they settled on the banks of the St. Lawrence, they are supposed to have some priority in British Columbia. They know practically nothing of the English exploration and first settlement in other parts of North America.

2. The English rights in Quebec come from the French and are the evidence of its greater generosity in the treatment of minorities. Actually, English rights in Quebec come from the English, from the time they controlled the entire Province. This is not the whole truth, since there have

been some further grants of separate school rights since
1867, but the basic pattern was set before that date.

3. The French are settlers in North America, but the English
    are invaders.

4. The French are a minority – everywhere. This leads them
    to think that their position is precarious and therefore
    they must become independent. Actually, the French
    majority in Quebec wields an almost indisputed sover-
    eignty over the vast area of Provincial jurisdiction. A
    corollary of the minority myth is that, being a minority,
    they are perpetually "dominated" by the majority and do
    not control its decisions on any important matter.

5. The French are willing to learn English, but the English
    won't learn French. Actually, the British element in
    Quebec is more bilingual than the French. Both races are
    the same in this regard; neither learns the other language
    unless it has to. Minorities always have to learn a little
    more than majorities all over the world.

6. Lord Durham was an evil monster. Suggestions of this are
    found even in Laurendeau's drafting of Chapter v. To the
    French, Durham was a great assimilator: to the English,
    he is a great decolonizer. Quebec pays no attention to
    'responsible government.' [...]

7. The constitutional rights of the French Canadians have
    been widely violated in Canada. There is a confusion here
    between constitutional and moral rights – which
    Laurendeau makes briefly.

8. The French Canadian is a second-class citizen. He means
    by this that he rarely occupies the top positions in the
    economic activities of the province. But he is supremely
    top in the religious activities of the province, still the most
    important, and in almost all of the professions, except
    those requiring technical training. He also commands an

ever increasing area of small industry and commerce as well as the Provincial political field. Thus it is more true to say that only in the economic area do the English have a privileged place. In those other activities, as well as in politics, it is a handicap to belong to the English minority.

9. There is nothing in common between the two cultures.

10. The English always assimilate minorities everywhere.

11. The corruption of the French spoken in Quebec is due to the proximity of the English. Actually, "joual" was found first in the Chicoutimi area where there are very few English. A N.F.B. film about a small fishing village in Quebec, absolutely remote from the English, beautifully made, was shown in France recently, and had to have French sub-titles added, or otherwise the speech of the characters would never have been understood. [He was referring to Pierre Perrault's film on Ile aux Coudres, *Pour la suite du monde*.]

It was a magnificent rant – and one can easily imagine Scott, in full rhetorical flight, delivering it. His line about Lord Durham appeared in the preliminary report; most of the rest of it fell away, but expressed his frustration as an English Quebecker and an anti-clerical anti-nationalist, suspicious of the role that the Catholic Church had played in Quebec.

One of Scott's concerns was what he saw as a movement toward French unilingualism in Quebec. His idea was a bilingual Quebec that could be a model for a bilingual Canada, and he saw that ideal slipping away. "It seems to me obvious, living in Quebec, that the whole trend there is towards unilingualism," he wrote, after noting that some members of the Protestant School Board had told commission staff privately that some Department of Education officials in Quebec City were refusing to reply in English to letters written to them in English. "If this can be done unofficially by a bilingual province, it means other Provinces can go bilingual officially without having much change from their present English unilingualism."

Scott argued to his colleagues that the English minority in Quebec was without representation. "I pointed out that even in Quebec the French Canadians have the St. Jean Baptiste Society. At this point, Jean-Louis Gagnon got into the act and shouted 'I'll trade you the St. Jean Baptiste Society for the Royal Bank of Canada any day!' I almost felt he believed that the Royal Bank spoke for the English-speaking minority!"

On February 3, 1965, the commissioners signed the final page of the preliminary report, and it was adopted. "I must say that I had no great feeling of exhilaration at this moment; while there is a great deal of interesting matter in the report, I do not feel it is likely to be widely read or to make any helpful contribution to the present situation," Scott wrote. He was dead wrong about that. In fact, the cry of alarm that it issued, the gap in understanding that it described, and the memorable phrase that Canada was passing through the greatest crisis in its history made a significant impact – probably as great as, if not greater than, anything else the Commission concluded or recommended.

The preliminary report was released on February 25 and, as Laurendeau noted, "made a noise from one ocean to the other." In *La Presse*, Vincent Prince praised the report, saying that it showed that "only radical decisions can prevent a rupture from taking place."

But there was skepticism in English Canada. The *Windsor Star* wrote that most English-speaking Canadians do not understand what is happening in Quebec, and that "the French-speaking people are too apt to blame English-speaking people for troubles of their own making." Similarly, the *Calgary Herald* complained, "The preliminary report . . . seems rather heavily weighted with sympathy toward the French-Canadian point of view, and tends to

make English-speaking Canada largely responsible for the strains
to which Canadian federation has been subjected during the last
two years." In a *Saturday Night* piece entitled "B and B's desperate
catalogue of the obvious," Peter Gzowski wrote that he couldn't
find anything in the report he disagreed with, adding, "Canada is
in trouble, serious trouble. The French Canadians aren't happy
with their lot and the English Canadians can't understand why.
But I *know* that. Lord Durham knew it 128 years ago. . . . We've
been served one of the most remarkable catalogues of the obvious
ever to see print in Canada."

To Laurendeau's annoyance, Charles Lynch of Southam News
concluded that the French-language commissioners prevailed
over the English-language commissioners, and should have been
signed "Laurendeau & Co." The Commission's research director
Neil Morrison told Laurendeau that Pearson's senior adviser, Tom
Kent, felt the same way. "This opens a pretty pessimistic perspective on the effect that a government would give one day to our
final report," Laurendeau wrote.

As it turned out, a better predictor of the government's final
reaction appeared in *Cité libre*, the small publication that Trudeau,
Pelletier, and a number of others had started in the early 1950s.
Under the title "Bizarre Algèbre," the Comité pour une politique
fonctionnelle – Albert Breton, Claude Bruneau, Yves Gauthier,
Marc Lalonde, and Maurice Pinard – signed eight commentaries
on the preliminary report. It was exceedingly critical: the
Commission had failed to meet its original mandate – but had
vastly exceeded it. They attacked its lack of sociological rigour, and
dissected the famous first questions of each public session ("These
two peoples, Anglophone and Francophone, can they and do they
want to live together? And under what new conditions? And are
they ready to accept these conditions?"), calling the second about
new conditions "the masterpiece of bad questions." They pointed
out that, after saying Canada was passing through the greatest

crisis in its history, the commissioners never define the term crisis, and produce no historical documentation to justify the claim. It was a cutting analysis, and while Trudeau – a member of the group – did not sign it, Marchand told Laurendeau later that Trudeau had worked on it. Marchand said he had told Trudeau he should not sign it, but Laurendeau was convinced he was the principal author, and Trudeau later confirmed to him his "partial paternity." He had no time or patience for the Quebec focus of Laurendeau's "*pages bleues.*"

Issuing a call of alarm and reporting on what they had heard was one thing; reaching a consensus on what should actually be recommended to resolve the crisis was something else. From the outset of the hearings, the commissioners had been stressing that it was neither their mandate nor their intention to get everyone to become bilingual. But if not, then what? In November 1966, the commissioners had a long discussion on what they meant by the term "bilingual country" – obviously central to their mandate and their recommendations. "Despite all the years spent together, it was still not clear in our minds," Scott wrote. "There was always the conflict between the notion of total bilingualism and the fact of a large degree of unilingualism, certain to continue for a long time, in many places. An example of this conflict: must every Federal Post Office have a bilingual staff?" Good question.

Their discussions were helped by a paper by one of the Commission's researchers, William Mackey, which laid out the principles of the bilingual state.

The first was that the survival of each linguistic group must be guaranteed. The second was that the state was founded not to promote bilingualism, but to protect the linguistic integrity of each group, meaning that the bilingual state must defend and even promote unilingualism for both. And the third principle was that the majority must not simply passively accept but must always help the minority to develop in order to maintain the bilingualism.

"In fact, there are fewer bilingual people in the bilingual countries than there are in the so-called unilingual countries," Mackey wrote. "For it is not always realized that bilingual countries were created not to promote bilingualism, but to guarantee the maintenance and use of two or more languages in the same nation."

At first, Scott was a bit taken aback. "In regard to this idea of promoting unilingualism, I confess that, perhaps lacking French logic, I could not see how a Commission appointed to promote bilingualism could end up by favouring the promotion of unilingualism," he wrote. "Gradually it dawned on me, and I think on the others, that what Mackey meant was that unless there was a strong degree of unilingualism in the bilingual country for each language, one would eventually dominate and assimilate the other. Promoting unilingualism, and having two essentially unilingual groups, did not exclude the possibility that individual members of each group might be able to speak the other language well."

The idea that a bilingual state depended on, and was obliged to protect, unilingual communities emerged as one of the themes of the Report. "Bilingual states were often developed to maintain or preserve the cultures and languages of their surviving national groups. . . . These unilingual nuclei form the great mass of the population of bilingual states; they are the centres around which each of the major language groups tend to cluster," the commissioners wrote. "The bilingual state is not intended as an instrument for the propagation of individual bilingualism."

This is the little-understood paradox of official bilingualism; it exists to serve the unilingual – who were then, and are now, the majority, both in English-speaking and French-speaking Canada. One of the important differences between now and then is that in the 1960s, Quebec's economy functioned largely in English, and bilingualism was a prerequisite for success for francophones. Today, Quebec's media and culture have thrived sufficiently that many of those who do speak English do not feel the need to do so;

they get their information about the country and the world in French. Outside Montreal and Gatineau, even the bilingual often don't speak or hear English frequently.

Unilinguals were certainly the majority, both in English Canada and in French Canada in 1961. There were 12 million unilingual English speakers, 3.5 million unilingual French speakers, and only 2.3 million bilingual Canadians – or 12 per cent. Thirty per cent of francophones were bilingual, but only 5 per cent of non-francophones. Indeed, Mackey's point was that if everyone in a bilingual state became completely bilingual, one of the languages would be superfluous. One would become dominant, and the other would disappear. "The bilingual state is characterized by a wide variety of bilingual institutions, designed to guarantee that citizens are not disadvantaged because they belong to a minority linguistic group." Laurendeau echoed this: "One is bilingual in North America if the possession of two languages is necessary or really useful," he wrote in his journal in August 1965. ". . . Bilingualism can only live if it is supported by two unilingualisms, without which bilingualism is a transitory situation which results in the unilingualism of the strongest and most numerous."

Scott's political differences with Laurendeau emerged occasionally over lunch. In March 1968, while Pierre Trudeau was running for the Liberal leadership, neither Laurendeau nor Frith thought he would win the leadership, or the election that would follow. "Laurendeau thought he would greatly injure Canada if he were chosen," Scott wrote. "I think he feared that he may be."

The tension that emerges from Scott's journal – between the emphasis placed by Laurendeau, Dion, and Lacoste on the requirements of French-speaking Quebec to thrive as a French-speaking community, and Scott's insistence that Quebec was a bilingual province that not only had constitutional obligations in this regard but provided a model for the country – can be seen running through Book I of the Commission's Report. Laurendeau wanted the report to use the definition in the mandate of the Commission – of an "equal partnership" – not only to define Quebec as "a distinct society" (which the Report does) but to ascribe more constitutional responsibilities to Quebec as a result.

Scott did not object to the idea of French Canada as a distinct society – he agreed, after all, that it was a nation – but dug in his heels on the issue of constitutional changes, going to see Pearson to reaffirm his view that this was not part of the Commission's mandate. Sometimes he joked about it. When there was a possibility that the Commission would not have its funding extended, he quipped that they should be the first Royal Commission to go on strike, and he would carry a placard saying "Unfair to Section 91" (the section of the Constitution that defines federal powers). But mostly he was dead serious.

Scott was clearly appalled at some of the things that Laurendeau was considering in terms of extended powers for Quebec, such as the suggestion that the federal government should be obliged to consult the provinces on all questions of money, banking, or credit, and that Quebec's diplomatic representation abroad should be extended. He wanted to avoid any constitutional change that would widen the gap between French and English Canada, and feared the emergence of what he called "the Belgian situation, where on one side of the line nothing is spoken but Flemish (English for us) and on the other side, French. I would prefer to see both languages recognized everywhere so that each language group can feel reasonably at home in any part of the country."

In his biography of Laurendeau, Denis Monière describes Scott's resistance to focusing attention on the constitutional issue as a "hijacking" and cites the decision to produce a series of reports based on the research rather than a conceptual report defining "a new philosophy of relations between the two founding peoples" as a great defeat for Laurendeau.

Laurendeau did write the famous "blue pages" of the Report, in which he eloquently described the relationships between language, culture, and identity, and the impact on individuals of having to work in their second language, and noted that the Commission "recognized the main elements of a distinct French-speaking society in Quebec." He began with a subtle description of the changing interaction of ethnicity and language, concluding that in a diverse and free society, where language can be chosen and ethnic background cannot, language should be a more important classification than ethnicity. It was a prescient analysis, foreseeing both the emergence of multiculturalism, and a future in which immigrants would join French-speaking as well as English-speaking Canada. "The problem of the first language must come first: it is vital; it is more important for the human being than questions about a second language," he wrote. "Therefore 'the existing state of bilingualism in Canada,' [a phrase from the Commission's mandate] in our opinion, means first the existing state of the English and French languages, each being first considered by itself. We must inquire whether each has, in a real sense, the means to live."

Laurendeau went on to spell out the psychological importance of language, which, he wrote, "is at the core of the intellectual and emotional life of every personality. . . . It is used for the trivia of [everyday] living, on the labour market, in professional activities, in several forms of recreation, in church, in clubs, in schools, and so on. We will mention later the difficulties, which may be dramatic in their intensity, faced by a bilingual person who must work in his second language – his sense of being diminished, the irritation which frequently results, and his loss of efficiency." Later in the blue pages, Laurendeau wrote, "We recognized the main elements of a distinct French-speaking society in Quebec" – using the phrase that would later emerge, famously, in the Meech Lake Accord.

Scott did not object to the use of the phrase "distinct French-speaking society," but he resisted any attempts to propose constitutional changes. "A serious debate arose on the proposal . . . about freeing Quebec from the obligations of section 133 (which required Quebec, like the federal government, to maintain both languages in the legislature and in the courts) if Ontario and New Brunswick did not agree to become officially bilingual," he wrote. "This idea I'm sure emanated from André Laurendeau, and had received no general Commission study before being drafted." As far as Scott was concerned, this was out of the question: "Quebec has an obligation to respect the language rights of some 600,000 people in its English-speaking minority, regardless of any good or bad action taken by any other province." Indeed, Laurendeau did think that if an English-speaking province had the right to refuse bilingualism, Quebec should have the right to declare itself to be unilingual French; respect for equality implied reciprocity.

"Laurendeau was the victim of the dynamic of compromise, which is inherent in all processes of informal negotiation in a limited group that operates according to the rule of consensus," Monière wrote, adding that the blue pages were "Laurendeau's political last will and testament."

The report had sweeping recommendations: that English and French be formally declared the official languages of the Parliament of Canada, of the federal courts, of the federal government, of the federal administration; that Ontario and New Brunswick declare themselves to be officially bilingual; that bilingual districts be established throughout Canada; that French and English education be provided in every province; that a Commissioner of Official Languages be established by the federal government and by every officially bilingual province.

The commissioners called for the creation of bilingual districts, based on the Finnish model. This involved a compromise between the purely territorial model adopted by Belgium and

Switzerland – where the "territorial principle" applied and language rights to services and education existed only within a specific boundary – and the South African approach, in which the "personality principle" applied, and citizens could use English and Afrikaans everywhere in the country. "The Commission intends to borrow and to adapt into the Canadian context an idea from Finland," they wrote. This was the concept of bilingual districts. "In the various fields and jurisdictions to be considered, and in conformity with what we hope will be the future spirit of Canada, we take as a guiding principle the recognition of both official languages, in law and in practice, wherever the minority is numerous enough to be viable as a group." Districts would be defined as bilingual if they had 10 per cent of the linguistic minority in the district. On the basis of the 1961 census, this meant one census division in Prince Edward Island, four in Nova Scotia, eight in New Brunswick, twenty-four in Quebec, eleven in Ontario, four in Manitoba, and one each in Saskatchewan and Alberta. The boundaries of the districts were to be negotiated between the federal government and the provinces. In addition, entry points to Canada and major forms of public transportation – Air Canada and Canadian National Railways – should provide services in both languages across the country, no matter how unilingual the region.

It was a broad consensus (marred only by a separate statement by J.B. Rudnyckyj calling for the recognition of "some extra privileges" for "Eskimo-Indian in the Northwest Territories and Yukon, German and Ukrainian in the Prairie Provinces, Italian in the metropolitan areas of Toronto and Montreal" and a technical quibble by Clément Cormier on the definition of official bilingualism) and a sweeping achievement. Laurendeau, however, was depressed and disappointed with the report. When Neil Morrison tried to cheer him up on the day it was published, saying Book 1 was very positive for French Canadians in the civil service, he replied bleakly, "It does nothing for Quebec."

Before the publication of the report on December 5, 1967, there were some unusual acknowledgements that the earlier criticisms of the preliminary report two years earlier were misplaced. The *Globe and Mail* had called it "unduly alarmist" but now conceded "perhaps the B and B Commission was right." Douglas Fisher and Harry Crowe, who shared a column in the *Toronto Telegram*, were more direct. "No one can now say, as was common stuff at the time, that the B and B Commission overstated the dimensions of the emerging crisis in its much-criticized preliminary report. The Commission was right. The rest of us were wrong."

The events of the previous few years, and the growth of the independence movement in Quebec, had had an impact on attitudes in the rest of Canada, the *Prince Albert Herald* noted. "What was hypothetical nonsense four years ago is reality today. The separatist movement is for real; French Canada's aspirations within Confederation are for real; de Gaulle's plea for a sovereign Quebec is for real."

When the report was released, the press reaction was generally positive, with some exceptions, mainly in small-town Canada. The *Pembroke Observer* said the policy "would be a disastrous one for Canada" which "would remove, at a stroke, any possibility of Canada achieving national greatness, and doom a large and growing number of Canadians to the status of second-class North Americans." The Brockville *Recorder and Times* lamented the passing of what it called "the British tradition," saying, "This has been a British country since 1759. And it has been the British tradition and institutions, not the French fact, which have made and kept us distinct and different from our friends and neighbours in the United States who speak the English tongue only."

But urban Canada embraced the report. *Le Devoir*'s Claude Ryan called it "an invitation to a superior form of civilized life," and predicted that it would remain one of the most concise and eloquent assessments of the Canadian experience in the previous century. The *Financial Post* wrote that "the realistic approach permeates the report," and the *Globe and Mail* approvingly called it "a first installment on the purchase price of a United Canada." Similarly, the *Toronto Star* called the recommendations "the price that Canadians should be glad to pay – if it would preserve Confederation." The *Star*'s Peter C. Newman was more explicit: "If English Canada rejects or even questions the commission's mild and eminently sensible conclusions, there'll be very little reason to believe that Canada can move very far into its second century."

But there was at least one note of concern about the prospect of requiring public institutions to offer services in two languages. The *Calgary Herald* pointed out that this would require employees able to know both languages. "This in effect would create an elite in our society. Admission to this elite would depend on one's proficiency in both French and English," the editorialist wrote. "Those Canadians who failed to make the grade would be relegated to the status of second class citizens. Is this a way of bringing about Canadian unity?" The *Herald*'s bleak analysis would be seized upon years later as either a prescient forecast, or a subtle attack on bilingualism. In retrospect, it was partly right and very wrong. Yes, there would be a bilingual elite; there would have to be if the federal state was going to serve two largely unilingual societies. But forty years on, there is no indication that unilingual Canadians have been "relegated to the status of second class citizens" – either in English Canada or in French-speaking Quebec.

Only a few weeks later, on May 15, Laurendeau suffered a serious stroke; on June 1, 1968, he died. The reaction was shock. Pierre Trudeau, then prime minister, wrote that Laurendeau had the fairest and most refined mind that he knew. "When I was still a student, he guided me with his advice," he wrote. "Later, he became an attentive, critical, generous friend." Claude Ryan wrote that one could feel him become, through the work of the Commission, more Canadian; as he came to know the diverse reality of the country, he understood and loved it more. "But at no moment did one have the impression that this experience was going to shake his Quebec convictions."

Whatever his differences with Laurendeau, Scott rose to the occasion; he wrote an eloquent tribute in *Le Devoir*, saying that the most striking thing about André Laurendeau was his unique mixture of passion and intelligence. "He believed deeply in the French culture and in French Canada," he wrote. "It would be perhaps fairer to say that his faith in human values was even deeper, but he knew that these values had to be expressed in a language and a culture, and for him, it was the French language and culture." Scott praised him for his fairness, and his ability to listen to the arguments of those with whom he violently disagreed. "I also profoundly admired André Laurendeau for his hatred of dictatorship and fascism," Scott wrote. "He is among the few public men who dared take a position on the Spanish Civil War, and show their sympathy for the republican government. Any sign of autocracy in the Quebec government led immediately to a reaction of opposition. He was the friend of liberty and equal justice for all." It was a comment that served as a reminder of the depth of Scott's own deep political convictions.

But Laurendeau's death did not change the dynamic of the Royal Commission. Paul Lacoste was named a commissioner, Jean-Louis Gagnon became co-chairman – and the essential debate over the nitty-gritty of the meaning of bilingualism continued. The next report was on the issue of the language of work.

Throughout the deliberations, the commissioners wrestled with the question of creating French-language and English-language units in the public service. How would they communicate with each other? Scott continued to feel that he was the only voice for a bilingual Quebec. The discussion concerning French as the language of work in Quebec – the issue that would ultimately lead Scott to write a dissent – inspired him to note, "It seemed to me that [Léon Dion] wanted all business to use French everywhere in the province. On being probed more deeply, he admitted he was talking about 'big business,' but where would the line be drawn?" As he was reading drafts of the Report, Scott wrote, "On reading this . . . I really felt they seemed designed to unilingualize Quebec and bilingualize the rest of Canada."

In May 1969, Scott spelled out his objections in a memo to his fellow commissioners: the recommendation that French should be the principal language of work in Quebec was "suffused with the territorial principle which the Commission had clearly rejected in Vol 1."; Scott felt this implicitly denied the "cardinal principle of equal partnership." There was no provision for firms moving into Quebec to use "their own main or exclusive language"; the recommendation "ignored the economic realities of Quebec industry" and "raised false hopes among those who now aspired to the top decision-making levels of business without knowing English."

In December 1969, Volume III on the language of work was published. The Commission recommended the creation of French-language units in the federal government and the military, an appropriate balance between anglophones and francophones in the federal public service, and that "in the private sector in Quebec, governments and industry adopt the objective that French become the language of work at all levels." Scott dissented, unswayed in his conviction that the effect would be a unilingual Quebec. When Scott saw the reaction to the recommendations, and speculation that they meant unilingualism in Quebec, he wrote grimly, "This is exactly what I knew would happen."

Disturbed by Scott's dissent, Gordon Pape of *The Gazette* saw a gloomy future for English Quebec. "The proposal raises the spectre of English-speaking Montrealers gradually being forced out of their jobs as more and more work units within a firm are designated as French-language units," he wrote on December 20. "Job opportunities for English-speaking people would decline accordingly, and in the end the English Quebecer would find himself in much the same position the French-Canadian is in today. If this vision of the future holds, the exodus of the English from Quebec to other parts of Canada appears inevitable."

This turned out to be a more accurate prediction than that of the *Calgary Herald* in 1967. Those English Quebeckers who were not prepared to live as a minority in a French-speaking society did leave; those who stayed overwhelmingly spoke, or learned, French.

The Commission slogged on for another year, and Scott grew increasingly dispirited with the results. Like Laurendeau, he had larger ambitions for the Commission than simply to fulfill its mandate – he wanted to stretch it. He had hoped that the Commission's last report on the mass media would deal with what he called "the steady decline of the public interest and the steady growth of control of programming and of prime time by commercialism." His indignation was undiminished. "Our Commission is bold enough to attack the English in Canada for their injustice towards French Canadians, but dare not raise a finger against the economic establishment."

When the Commission finally came to an end on March 31, 1971, Scott wrote a final note with the bitterly sardonic title "The End of the Affair."

"I will close on a personal note," he wrote. "It is astonishing and also frightening for me to watch Quebec abandon so many of its virtues and values in order to rush into the North American capitalist system with arms open for the embrace. The values of that system I learned to despise and reject in the 1930s. I had hoped that the Catholic tradition with its greater emphasis on social obligations would somehow mitigate the prevailing Protestant ethic of free enterprise. Now I am not so sure this can happen, though we did find by our research that in their attitudes towards business the francophones tended to think more than anglophones of their duty to society and less of mere profit making."

For an aging socialist who saw Quebec becoming both more capitalist and more unilingual, it was a bleak appraisal that was every bit as poignant as Laurendeau's gloomy assessment that the first volume of the Report had done nothing for Quebec. In the years ahead, Scott went on to fight a number of losing battles for bilingualism in Quebec, against Bill 22 which declared French to be the official language of Quebec, and against Bill 101.

Scott, like Laurendeau, had suffered from what Monière called "the dynamic of compromise"; both men had a sense of having failed. In both cases, however, their visions influenced others who both won and lost in applying a version of the language passions that the two men had brought to the Royal Commission. The debate between bilingualism and biculturalism, between individual and collective rights, would continue.

I have spent some time giving the details of these long-ago debates because I think they provide essential background to what followed. The tensions between Scott's vision and Laurendeau's have played themselves out over the last four decades, and their influences are still being felt in the country's varying language policies and initiatives. Canadians are still contending with some of the contradictory currents in bilingualism reflected in the thinking that Laurendeau, Scott, and all the others did on the subject – and with the language legislation and policies that flowed from that vitally important debate.

Two Friends,
Two Views

Si on me presse de dire pourquoi je l'aimais,
je sens que cela ne peut s'exprimer qu'en répondant:
"Parce que c'était lui, parce que c'était moi."

MICHEL DE MONTAIGNE

In December 1977, Pierre Trudeau was finishing a tour of provincial capitals, and came to Quebec City to meet René Lévesque, who had been elected thirteen months earlier. After their lunch alone, the two men came to the Salon Rouge to speak to the press and announce an economic development agreement that had been reached between their two governments. Sitting at a side table, Camille Laurin sat watching them, staring intently, smoking unfiltered Buckinghams to the end. Laurin was Lévesque's Secretary of State for Cultural Development – and his language legislation, known when it was introduced as Bill 101 (and still known that way to English-speakers almost thirty years later, even though it stopped being a bill and became a law on August 26, 1977), had been passed four months before.

When the news conference was over, and the two leaders got up to leave, Laurin approached Trudeau from behind and lightly touched his shoulder. Trudeau turned, and his face lit up spontaneously with pleasure, unfeigned testimony to their long-standing friendship. Indeed, they had been together at university, worked together at the student paper *Le Quartier Latin* and at *Cité libre*, and had fought Duplessis before taking different paths in the 1960s. Years later, Laurin said they had had "the same goals of modernity, declericalisation, the struggle for liberty against dictatorship, cynicism, immorality in politics."

Unaware of this relationship and quite surprised by the obvious warmth, I approached Laurin a few minutes later and asked him about it. "He is an old friend with whom I had the habit of exchanging ideas on the nature of man, the unconscious, authority, political life . . . and sports cars," he told me. "We have spent countless evenings chatting on the streets of Outremont or at home, at my place or at his."

Other journalists began to gather round, and one asked Laurin if he was displeased to see Quebec reaching an agreement with the federal government. "Not at all," he said. "In an occupied country, one has to deal with the occupying force." He said it without a smile. Coming only a minute or so after his nostalgic references inspired by a chance meeting with an old friend, the heavy-handed allusion to France's humiliation under the Nazi occupation during the Vichy regime came as a shock. Friends don't compare friends to Nazi occupiers.

The encounter always had a kind of symbolic importance for me. Here were two old friends who had made dramatically different political choices, and who were both committed to visions that were idealistic, dramatic, and transformative. Pierre Trudeau was deeply committed to the ideas that had been developed and articulated by his mentor, Frank Scott – a strong defence of Canadian federalism, a Charter of Rights, and official bilingualism. Camille Laurin was profoundly engaged in the struggle for an independent, officially unilingual Quebec, inspired and encouraged by André Laurendeau. At different levels, each man both succeeded and failed – and their success and their failure reshaped the country and its approach to language.

But the warmth of their encounter was further proof of the paradoxical nature of the ties that bound Quebec's post-war generation. Laurin had by then known Trudeau for almost thirty years; they had met in 1948, when Laurin had been involved, with Gérard Pelletier, Pierre Juneau, and Jeanne and Maurice Sauvé, in the Jeunesse étudiante catholique (JEC). In 1948, Laurin succeeded Pelletier as executive secretary of Entraide Mondiale (World University Service) and spent two years in Geneva before studying psychiatry in Paris and Boston from 1950 to 1957. He then returned to Montreal to work at the Institut Albert Prévost, where he became involved in a very public campaign on behalf of patients in Quebec's mental hospitals, which were then in a scandalous condition – a campaign in which he enlisted Laurendeau's support. When he clashed with the director of the private hospital and was fired in 1962, he hired a friend as a lawyer, Marc Lalonde, who succeeded in getting his job back.

Laurin was close enough to the circle of left-wing Liberals that Maurice Sauvé had approached him about joining Trudeau, Marchand, and Pelletier as a Liberal candidate in the election of 1965. Laurin refused without giving reasons; since 1961, he had felt drawn toward the independence movement. That attraction was only strengthened by his reading of the Bi and Bi preliminary report, and Laurendeau's analysis in the "*pages bleues*," and his description of the critical importance of language as being "at the core of the intellectual and emotional life of every personality." But in addition to Laurendeau's influence on Laurin's thinking, a more important factor was his own psychiatric, therapeutic model. He concluded, in his work as a psychiatrist, that the collective problem of French-speaking Quebeckers was that they had absorbed an internal colonialism – while those who had become *indépendantistes* were, in his words, "confident in themselves, joyous, capable of flourishing." His analysis was explicitly Freudian, suggesting that the *indépendantiste* had taken a step toward maturity while the federalist was emotionally backward.

When he was named to Lévesque's cabinet in 1976, Laurin set out to transform Quebec's approach to language policy. The result, Bill 1 – which became Bill 101 – was profoundly affected by Quebec's Civil Code, which was derived from the Napoleonic Code. It flowed logically and inexorably from a set of principles; once the principles were accepted, the terms of the legislation followed with irrefutable, almost Euclidian inevitability. Bill 101, which became La charte de la langue française, began with a dramatic flourish and a Cartesian declaration of principle: Quebec is French. Chapter 1, article 1: *Le français est la langue officielle du Québec*. Everything in it flowed from that assumption and from that declaration. And as a result, nothing in it could be challenged without challenging that basic assumption.

For Bill 101 was not just a law, it was a Charter of the French Language. It laid out not simply the right to communicate with government, but the right to work, live, and die in French, to operate inside a French-language visual environment. "The Quebec that this law prepares and announces will be a French country, educated, modern, which will take its place beside countries of the same size and which have already made their mark on the world," Laurin told the National Assembly on July 19, 1977, when the bill was in second reading. For Laurin, the language law was an act of liberation of a people, a gesture of defiance of the English-speaking North American majority, and a part of the groundwork for Quebec independence.

While Trudeau was friends with Laurin, Scott was his mentor and had a huge influence on his thinking. On April 16, 1982, the night before the Queen signed the proclamation of the new Constitution, Trudeau held a dinner for young Canadian achievers in Ottawa at the National Arts Centre. It coincided with a dinner for Rhodes Scholars, old and new – Scott later quipped that it was a dinner for young achievers and old deceivers – and Jean-François Garneau, a young Quebecker who had just been awarded a Rhodes Scholarship, was standing in line with an elderly gentleman whom he did not recognize while Trudeau led the Queen down the line, making the introductions. When they drew near, Trudeau's face lit up. He lunged in front of the Queen to greet the older man, in defiance of all the rules of protocol, and, to Garneau's astonishment, began literally to weep with joy. "Madam, if we have a Charter of Rights in this country, we owe it to this one man," he said. "Canada owes a lot to him, and I, for one, am in his debt. Everything I learned about the Constitution, I learned from this man."

Scott, who felt that Trudeau had conceded too much in the constitutional negotiations by accepting the so-called notwithstanding clause and had not defended English-language rights from Bill 22 and Bill 101, was both deeply proud of the recognition, and bitter that Trudeau had not done more. He would tell the story often, adding with a rueful flourish, "He didn't learn enough!" It was a revelation to Garneau, who was embarrassed that he had no idea who this person was, who was clearly so important to Trudeau. "I am perhaps one of the few Canadians who has seen Trudeau weep in public, and they were tears of joy, tears of gratitude," he told me after Trudeau's death. (While part of that gratitude was due to Scott's inspiration concerning a Charter, Trudeau biographer John English points out that it was also no doubt for Scott's unwavering support of Trudeau's use of the War Measures Act in 1970.) The emotions Trudeau showed on the eve of his greatest triumph were particularly revealing of a man who usually kept his deepest feelings to himself.

For Scott had been a tremendous influence. He was ten years Trudeau's senior, but for a young man who had lost his father when he was fifteen, he became an inspiration: intellectually rigorous, erudite, sensual, progressive, fiercely competitive. (Scott's impact on Trudeau, as a progressive and a legal mind, was a theme of the TV miniseries written by Wayne Grigsby and Guy Fournier, "Trudeau II: Maverick in the Making," broadcast by CBC in October 2005.)

As a student at Brébeuf and the Université de Montréal, Trudeau's friends were Catholic nationalists. In fact, some Quebec intellectuals argue that Scott was the critical influence that moved Trudeau from being an anti-conscription nationalist in the early 1940s to being a fierce anti-nationalist later in his life.

At some point, Trudeau – who had sought Laurendeau's advice on whether he should to go to Harvard for graduate school – began to seek out Scott instead. In 1943, Trudeau and his friend Charles Lussier had heard Scott speak in opposition to conscription at the Université de Montréal. When Trudeau returned from Harvard and went to work at the Privy Council Office in Ottawa, he was assigned to the Federal-Provincial Conference in 1950, which Scott attended on behalf of Saskatchewan premier Tommy Douglas. Trudeau was deeply impressed, and when he returned to Montreal, he would meet Scott at CCF meetings, gatherings of the Institut canadien des affaires publiques, and other gatherings of progressives in Quebec in the 1950s. (Scott, on the other hand, understood his protegé's tendency to procrastinate: he took him into his home when he was struggling to finish his major essay on the Asbestos Strike, and virtually held him captive until he finished the paper.)

In the 1950s, Trudeau had favoured a strict interpretation of federalism, writing a piece in 1948 supporting fascist Adrien

Arcand's right to sue the federal government for incarcerating him during the war, and in 1954, writing a brief that supported Duplessis's position that the federal government should not be funding universities.

But Scott's more centralist view of federalism ultimately had more impact on Trudeau. Scott abhorred nationalism. He remembered the riots in Quebec City during the First World War and the anti-Semitism of many French-Canadian nationalists like Abbé Groulx during the 1930s. And he hated what the Lords of the Privy Council had done to the British North America Act by reading in greater provincial powers to the Constitution than he felt were intended by the Fathers of Confederation. On the basis of what he saw during the Depression, Scott saw any devolution of powers to the provinces as, ultimately, a concession to big business, which could manipulate a provincial legislature much more easily than it could pressure the federal government. Scott was a strong advocate of the idea of entrenching a Bill of Rights in the Constitution – an idea that Trudeau adopted and made his own. "It's been from my contacts with Frank in his person and his actions that I absorbed most of my constitutional thinking," Trudeau told Scott's biographer Sandra Djwa, who noted that Trudeau, "always a little prickly on the issue of influence," once mistook a passage in one of Scott's articles from the 1940s as something he had written himself. She pointed out that Trudeau derived not only his constitutional vision, but also his famous phrase "a just society" from an essay Scott published in 1939.

So how did Trudeau and Laurin, the two old friends, approach the language question when they acquired the power to do something about it? First of all, language was not central to Trudeau's vision. It was a tool. There has been a tendency to talk and think about Trudeau's view of bilingualism as if there were an ur-text, a Martin Luther King "I have a dream"-like speech that laid out a vision of a bilingual country, coast to coast. "Trudeau seems to have dreamed of creating a country in which each individual would be bilingual," wrote Scott Reid, then a Reform Party researcher and now a Conservative MP, in his 1993 book *Lament for a Notion*. When he was working on his book on language policy, he searched for such a text, but had difficulty finding one. There were plenty suggesting that "the higher echelons of the civil service" and "men who call themselves intellectuals" should be bilingual – but Trudeau's emphasis was on the rights of individuals to deal with their government in the official language of their choice. (Reid did find an argument by Trudeau in 1965 that Canadians should have a right to a translator in their dealings with government, any government.)

From the observation that Canada was a multilingual and not a unilingual country, Reid writes, "Trudeau developed a Messianic vision of Canada as a prototype multilingual state that could serve as a model of ethnic tolerance in the rest of the world." Reid's supporting evidence for this is in an article Trudeau wrote in 1962, in which he wrote, "The die is cast in Canada: there are two main ethnic and linguistic groups; each is too strong and too deeply rooted in the past, too firmly bound to a mother culture, to be able to engulf the other. But if the two will collaborate *at the hub* [my italics] of a purely pluralistic state Canada could become the envied seat of a form of federalism that belongs to tomorrow's world. Better than the American melting-pot, Canada would offer an example to all those new Asian and African states . . . who must discover how to govern their polyethnic populations with justice and liberty." This, Trudeau argued, was an alternative approach to diversity and federalism to the American melting pot.

There are two observations to make here. The first is that Trudeau was talking about collaboration at the hub, at the centre – the federal government as the connector between French-speaking and English-speaking communities – not about some ideal Platonic country in which all Canadians were bilingual. The second is that in the four decades since Trudeau wrote that, his prediction has come to pass; diversity has become one of the defining characteristics of urban Canada. The Canadian attempt to combine official bilingualism and multiculturalism has not been some kind of utopian fantasy, but a domestic reality and an international asset.

Trudeau's focus, first and foremost, was based on the rights of the individual; language rights were part, but only a minor part, of that package. In fact, when he appeared before the Royal Commission at its first hearing in November 1963, his focus was on legal remedies to discrimination. He told the Commissioners they should concentrate on studying the barriers to power that exist for different ethnic groups. "There is an area, I say, where it is essential to do an inquiry . . . it is to find out how to ensure the equality in law of Canada's two languages," he said. "I don't mean that in changing laws we will succeed in changing the sociological or political reality – I don't think that's possible – but I think that the very source of French-Canadian nationalism is a defensive attitude towards an English-Canadian nationalist interpretation of the laws, of the judicial formulas." As far as other things were concerned, he seemed to shrug. "For the rest, my God, let the economic and social forces decide once the laws are just," he said, and then switched to English. "Let the consumer decide and let the investor decide what he is going to do within the framework of those laws." And, switching back to French, he continued, saying that the economic and human costs of bilingualism had to be established. "When we have established that, we will really know if the country can live, if it should continue to operate as a country."

Scott was not impressed by Trudeau's laissez-faire legalistic approach that day. "Pierre Trudeau seemed very uncertain about what he wanted to say, appeared to be thinking out loud rather than giving us some careful thought and was not at all impressive," he wrote disapprovingly. "He seems to have lost touch with what is going on in Quebec."

In his 1965 essay, as Reid points out, Trudeau realized that it would put a burden on public servants if the federal government were to play that role as a hub. "Absolute equality" between the two languages at the federal level would mean that officials serving the public in areas where both languages were spoken would have to speak both languages. In unilingual areas, unilingualism would suffice. If English were required at the top levels, so would French be. "It is obvious that if such rules were applied overnight, they would result in a great many injustices and might bring the state machinery grinding to a halt," Trudeau wrote. "But the introduction of such reforms must nevertheless be carried out by a fixed schedule set by law."

In his creation of a Messianic straw man, Reid quotes Official Languages Commissioner Keith Spicer as referring to "our linguistic New Jerusalem" to characterize Trudeau's vision. But Reid quotes Spicer out of context – he was referring to bilingual districts, the system which Reid himself argued should be adopted to reform the system. Trudeau's linguistic goals, as he put it to the Canadian Bar Association in September 1967, involved recognition of "the right to learn and to use" either of the official languages – a modest rather than a Messianic objective. Otherwise, every Canadian could not be assured of an equal opportunity to participate in the life of the country. "I venture to say that, if we are able to reach agreement on this vital aspect of the over-all problem, we will have found a solution to a basic issue facing Canada today," he said. Key to his position was a constitutional Bill of Rights. "A constitutional change recognizing broader rights with respect to the two official languages would add a new dimension to Confederation."

"The right to learn and to use" was a remarkably vague and limited way of expressing language rights. A few months later, Trudeau indicated that he saw official bilingualism as a way of defusing Quebec's collective demands for more constitutional powers – something that he, like Scott, categorically rejected. "What French Canadians want are guarantees of their language rights," he said in February. "That is what equality between two nations means."

In other words, language rights were individual, not collective. Bilingualism, not biculturalism. In fact, Trudeau objected to the word *biculturalism* in the name of the Royal Commission. (So did Pelletier, who wrote in his memoirs that he would always regret that the Pearson government had used "bilingualism" and "biculturalism" in the name of the Royal Commission. "Bilingualism" was too general and confusing, and even though he had approved the use of the word "biculturalism," he concluded that it suggested that no other culture in Canada had value.)

Similarly, when Trudeau tabled the Official Languages Act on October 17, 1968, less than four months after he was elected, he did so in a remarkably modest, low-key, almost diffident fashion, referring to a speech that Pearson had given more than two years before. In presenting the legislation he talked about how Canada's political theory and tradition had been inherited from Western Europe, where countries were relatively homogeneous in language and culture. Trudeau set out his policy as a rejection of uniformity and isolation. "We believe in two official languages and in a pluralist society, not merely as a political necessity but as an enrichment. We want to live in a country in which French Canadians can choose to live among English Canadians and English Canadians can choose to live among French Canadians without abandoning their cultural heritage." (That is perhaps the nearest echo one can find of King's "I have a dream" speech – and it is a very limited dream.) French Canada, he said, can survive not by turning in on itself, but by reaching out; English Canada should not "attempt to crush or expect to absorb" French Canada; all should take advantage of the fact that they live in "a country which has learned to speak in two great world languages."

With that odd mixture of high-mindedness and political prudence – there was no suggestion that actual citizens should have to learn another language, only that they should capitalize on the fact that they lived in "a country" which had learned two languages – Trudeau went on to frame the debate in terms of teaching public servants to speak French, and of "the language rights of citizens in their dealings with Parliament, with the federal government and with federal institutions, and the duties of those institutions toward the citizen in matters of language."

In the almost four decades since Trudeau gave that speech, there has been a lot of talk about his "dream" of bilingualism. Stephen Harper has written about bilingualism as "the God that failed," Scott Reid subtitled his book "The Life and Death of Canada's Bilingual Dream" and wrote about Trudeau having "dreamed" of a country in which every individual was bilingual. Richard Gwyn wrote about "Trudeau's dream, his impossible dream, of transforming a very ordinary sub-arctic country into 'a brilliant archetype for the moulding of tomorrow's civilization,'" implying that he had a fantasy of a bilingual country from coast to coast. But no. Like Reid, Gwyn quoted Trudeau out of context and misattributed the dream. Even a recent consultant's report in 2005 on the problems of language training in the public service talked about "Trudeau's dream." In fact, once in power, his goal was remarkably limited. Ensure that citizens could deal with the government in the official language of their choice. Create an institution at the centre that could engage with English-speaking and French-speaking Canada equally. Establish those as rights. That's it, that's all.

Trudeau's own bilingualism was so innate – he spoke to his sister in English and to his brother in French – that sometimes he took it for granted and underestimated the difficulty it could represent for others. He saw it as a necessary prerequisite to public service, and no more an uplifting dream than an engineer would see the fact that trigonometry is a necessary prerequisite to engineering as representing some transformative ideal. "He had no idea how difficult it is for an adult or near-adult to learn a second language," recalled Gordon Robertson, who dismisses the idea that Trudeau felt that every Canadian should be bilingual. "It was never his thought that they would or might or could."

Some immediately saw problems, even with that limited goal. Conservative MP Jack Horner, speaking in the House in the debate on the Official Languages Act, said that there were very few Albertans who spoke French and, as a result, public servants in the Department of Agriculture would be Quebeckers. Three decades on, this continued to be a theme from critics. In December 2002, when Official Languages Commissioner Dyane Adam agreed with a Quebec MP's suggestion that citizenship judges should be able to conduct citizenship ceremonies in both languages so as to project the bilingual nature of the country, there was an immediate response from MPs – not enough bilingual people for that in our province.

There was an element of pragmatism and *realpolitik* in Trudeau's approach. "We are dealing with straightforward political and social realities," he told the House of Commons on May 31, 1973. "If only because of the sheer force of numbers, either group has the power to destroy the unity of the country. These are the facts. . . . These facts leave Canada with only one choice, only one realistic policy: to guarantee the language rights of both linguistic communities." As political scientist Michael MacMillan observed in his book *The Practice of Language Rights in Canada*, "Language rights were conceived and justified primarily in terms of *political necessity*. They were *not* justified in terms of civil or political rights."

However, Trudeau had rejected Laurendeau's central idea of co-existing unilingual societies with bilingual districts. (The idea of bilingual districts gradually died when the Quebec government objected to Montreal being designated a bilingual district.) He found the concept of dualism – the idea that Quebec should be French and the rest of the country English – repugnant. As he said when he appeared before the Senate in 1988 in his attack on the Meech Lake Accord, "Bilingualism unites people; dualism divides them. Bilingualism means that you can speak to each other; duality means you can live in one language and the rest of Canada will live in another language."

In his book *Lament for a Notion*, Reid quotes Trudeau as suggesting in 1965 that it would be difficult to test cabinet ministers for their language skills – but unilingual ministers would be frustrated in a situation in which some decisions were taken in French and some decisions were taken in English. Interestingly enough, Trudeau never accepted the idea of simultaneous translation in cabinet. As a result, when Marcel Lessard, a former Alcan foreman and MP from Lac-Saint-Jean, was named Minister of Economic Expansion in 1975, he had to sit with a patient bilingual cabinet minister who was prepared to translate from English for him. Joe Clark introduced simultaneous translation in 1979 but he was defeated in 1980; back in power, Trudeau removed the translators – who returned with Brian Mulroney, and have remained.

Trudeau and Laurin had dramatically contradictory views about language, and about Quebec independence. They both succeeded to a remarkable degree – and both suffered significant failures.

Laurin set out to transform Quebec into an officially French-speaking society. By pushing the law as far as he could, he challenged his critics to force him to retreat. Almost thirty years after its introduction, despite a series of court challenges and a new Constitution, the framework that he created and the objectives he established remain intact. But the success of the legislation proved to be a setback for the independence movement. Rather than laying the groundwork, it has removed one of the major grievances that underlay the desire for sovereignty.

And that enabled Trudeau to succeed. The failure of the 1980 referendum gave Trudeau the opportunity he had been looking for to push for what had been his real dream: patriation of the Constitution and its amendment with a Charter of Rights. That was how he wanted to change the country – and he did. His failure was that he never succeeded in winning support for his vision of federalism in Quebec, as the overwhelming support for the Meech Lake Accord inside Quebec showed. And his victories over Quebec nationalists never diminished the power and appeal of Quebec nationalism. Two decades after he left politics and five years after his death, support for Quebec sovereignty remains solid.

Before leaving the two old friends and their conception of language behind and moving on to the application of their policies, it is worth taking a step back and looking at the unique convergence of events that began in Canada in the 1960s. To choose a metaphor that may seem excessive in light of the tsunami and earthquake tragedies of 2004 and 2005, Canada absorbed a generational tsunami that began following the earthquake that was the Quiet Revolution in Quebec. That event produced a political generation that swept through not only Quebec but the federal government as well.

In a number of ways, Trudeau and that part of the Quiet Revolution generation that followed him to Ottawa succeeded in transforming Canada. That they were able to do so is testimony to a unique series of events that produced an unusually talented generation with a remarkable amount in common. No longer young – Laurendeau had observed how the younger generation called Trudeau and Pelletier "*ces vieux messieurs*" – they had graduated from university during the Second World War, and had been forced to spend the fifteen years from 1945 until 1960 enduring the petty dictatorial conservatism of Maurice Duplessis. Some, like Trudeau, Lamontagne, and Michel Bélanger, had gone to Ottawa to work in the federal public service; others, like Pelletier and Lévesque, were in journalism or, like Jean Marchand, in the trade union movement. The sense of marginalization and frustration brought them together in various groups, beginning when they were students and active in the Catholic Action groups like the JEC, or later in various groups challenging the rigid conservatism of the Duplessis government in the 1940s and 1950s.

While Trudeau challenged Lévesque on the validity of nationalizing Hydro-Québec in their regular encounters at Pelletier's house with Marchand and Laurendeau, he shared the consensus that had been growing among the actors of the Quiet Revolution about the importance of the state as an economic tool. The rupture that occurred was not over economic ideology or the role of the state – but over which state should play the key role in the lives of Quebeckers, the federal government or the Quebec government. In 1965, despite all of the harsh things they had said about Pearson and his nuclear decision, Marchand, Pelletier, and Trudeau went to Ottawa; three years later, much of the activist and progressive element in the Quebec Liberal Party would follow Lévesque.

But Trudeau took to Ottawa the progressive Quebec consensus on the role of the state; the years of conflict between Ottawa and Quebec in the 1970s and 1980s that revolved around language and the Constitution tend to obscure that important commonality. The creation of Sidbec, a state-owned steel company, and a series of other state-owned enterprises in Quebec was matched by the creation of Petro-Canada in Ottawa; the National Energy Program reflected the expression of that Quebec consensus on the role of the state or, as the PQ was later to call it, *le modèle Québécois*.

In order to fully grasp the impact that Trudeau and those he attracted to Ottawa had on the country, consider how history might have been different. If Robert Winters, the former business-man and former cabinet minister, had won the Liberal leadership in 1968 against Trudeau – he was the alternative on the last ballot – the Liberals would have had trouble winning the 1968 election. Robert Stanfield, the Progressive Conservative leader, was a refreshing new face on the federal scene. Both he and Winters had similar qualities: both were rich businessmen from Nova Scotia with relatively conservative ideas. In fact, Stanfield was probably more progressive than Winters, and would have probably formed the government.

With Stanfield in office, a number of changes that trans-formed Canada would have been unlikely to occur, or would have taken very different forms. Consider the Constitution and the Charter of Rights and Freedoms.

The idea of a Charter is completely foreign to the traditions of British parliamentary democracy, but an integral part of the Civil Code tradition. As a result, during the 1960s and 1970s, Canada's English-language premiers watched, like spectators at a tennis match, the intense debate that was going on between Quebec Civil Code lawyers on whether or not a federal Charter of Rights was necessary or appropriate. At the time, it seemed to me as if half of the Quebec political elite had taught constitutional law to the other half. For a long time, constitutional law at the Université de Montréal was taught by two professors: Trudeau, who was deeply inspired by Scott, and Jacques-Yvan Morin, a strong nationalist who later became a minister in the Lévesque government. As a result, the constitutional debate that culminated in the patriation of the British North America Act and its amendment by a Charter of Rights and Freedoms was driven, in large part, by a debate between two groups of Quebec Civil Code lawyers.

As Kenneth McRoberts, author of *Misconceiving Canada: The Struggle for National Unity*, has pointed out, it is one of the great ironies of Canadian history that the Charter, which was completely foreign to the political and legal traditions of English-speaking Canada, has been embraced as a central part of Canadian identity – an embrace that helped doom the Meech Lake Accord in 1990. Nevertheless, it is almost impossible to imagine that a politician from outside Quebec would have fought to introduce the Charter. Indeed, eight of the ten provinces were opposed, and Trudeau achieved his success only by making the critical compromise of introducing the notwithstanding clause that would allow Parliament and legislatures to exempt legislation from some aspects of the Charter for five years – and by forcing the English-speaking premiers to choose between him and Lévesque, between two Quebec politicians, each one defending a made-in-Quebec solution to a problem that English Canada was slow to identify. But they were not prepared to fight a referendum with Lévesque, against Trudeau, in opposition to a Charter of Rights.

Quebec went on to play a critical role in the passage of the Free Trade Agreement in 1988. Without the strong consensus that existed in Quebec in favour of free trade, Brian Mulroney never would have succeeded in getting it through Parliament. Quebec's political strength endured, and could be seen in influencing Jean Chrétien's decisions to keep Canada out of the war in Iraq, decriminalize marijuana, and legalize same-sex marriage – decisions that have been retroactively endorsed by the Martin minority government. And Quebec's disenchantment with the Liberals over the sponsorship scandal in 2004 deprived the Liberals of their majority and at the same time ensured that Stephen Harper's Conservatives could not form a government.

How can Quebec's dominance over Canadian politics be explained – at a time when, as John A. Macdonald predicted, Quebec's demographic weight is shrinking rather than growing?

There are several factors. Canada, like Quebec, has enjoyed the effect of a particular convergence of events, which has resulted in the creation of a generation with an overabundance of political talent.

The fifteen years of the Duplessis regime from 1945 until 1960 produced a phenomenon that I have called "the greenhouse years"; a period that Pelletier in his memoirs called "the years of impatience." The rising generation of French-speaking Quebeckers were caught in a squeeze: on the one hand, they were highly educated, and frustrated by the nature of the society they were living in; on the other hand, most doors beyond medicine, the law, and the church were closed to them. As Donald Gordon had made clear, business and Crown corporations would not hire them. Duplessis controlled the universities, and the public sector was tiny. The narrow-mindedness of the Duplessis regime reinforced the solidarity of the generation, bringing nationalists and federalists, progressives and conservatives together – while the years of under-employment and marginalization sharpened their wits and their ideas. In that context, the election of the Quebec Liberals under Lesage in 1960 had the effect of a volcano or a broken dam. The explosion of energy in Quebec not only created a public sector in Quebec, it transformed the Canadian state. Suddenly, public life had a monopoly of talent.

And it was a substantial reservoir of talent – a generation born between 1919 and 1929 that included Trudeau, Lévesque, Marchand, Pelletier, Laurin, Jacques Parizeau, Marc Lalonde, Paul Gérin-Lajoie, and hundreds of others who were drawn to the enterprise of transforming Quebec. The strength and energy of this generation was such that, even when it divided on the issue of Quebec independence in the mid-sixties, the group that focused on Ottawa was able to transform the federal government.

A second generation, born in the 1930s and 1940s, was drawn to politics, inspired by their elders and their ideals. So, Jean

Chrétien, Bernard Landry, Pierre Marois, Louise Beaudoin, Serge Joyal, Louise Harel, Gilles Duceppe, and Claude Charron – among many others – were seduced by politics, entering young, either as a member of a minister's staff or as a young politician. But thanks to the reforms that they supported and helped implement, and the administrative experience that they received, this generation was liberated from the monopoly that the state had on Quebec talent. This generation was also divided – not only between sovereigntists and federalists, but also between those who remained in the public sector and those who chose to enter the business world. They are now everywhere: running large companies, in the financial sector, stockbroking, publishing, scientific research, high-tech innovation, and entrepreneurship. The monopoly was shattered.

But for almost three decades, Canada enjoyed – some would say endured – the effect of the monopoly of talent that public life enjoyed in Quebec. In many ways, to use an economist's phrase, English Canada was a "free-rider" – getting the benefits of the political leadership of this unique generation without contributing. In an odd way, this has added to further English-Canadian disengagement from politics; the fact that Quebec sent all of its best into public life, highly educated, engaged, and committed men and women, set the bar very high. The excellence of Quebec's contribution to federal political life acted as an obstacle for many of English Canada's best, who chose provincial politics or the private sector instead.

Politically, Pierre Trudeau won. He passed the Official Languages Act, and sidelined the notion of biculturalism; he won the 1980 referendum; he patriated the Constitution in 1982 and amended it with a Charter of Rights and Freedoms; he intervened so strategically and so effectively that he turned public opinion in English Canada, first against the Meech Lake Accord and then against the Charlottetown Accord.

But sociologically, Camille Laurin has been more successful on the language front. His language legislation remains largely intact, almost thirty years after it was introduced – and it has transformed the face of Quebec, and Montreal in particular. Ironically, the sense of security it created for French-speaking Quebeckers has been widely seen as one of the reasons that the independence movement lost its sense of urgency. The argument that Quebec needed to become independent in order to become a French-speaking society has been undermined by the fact that Quebec has, for all intents and purposes, become a French-speaking society within Confederation.

Camille Laurin's linguistic vision transformed Quebec society; Pierre Trudeau's vision of rights changed Canadian values and, as a result, Canadian society. But his view of language rights primarily affected government, leaving the linguistic face of Canada relatively unchanged.

chapter five

Ottawa Tries to Learn French

A smiling "one moment, please" in the client's language does not demand prodigious skill in language-learning, and it surely makes a short wait more tolerable than a sullen "I don't speak French (or English)." This seems a small point, but it is guaranteed to prevent future apoplexies and countertop replays of the Plains of Abraham. It also keeps telephone chats from becoming hot-line dialogues of the deaf.

KEITH SPICER, *Commissioner of Official Languages*
Second Annual Report, 1971-72

In 1966, just over a year after the Preliminary Report of the Bilingualism and Biculturalism Commission was published, Lester Pearson rose in the House of Commons to make an announcement on language policy. He did not want to wait for the Royal Commission to finish reporting before acting on one of the aspects that he had always considered important – a bilingual public service. "Many thought [the Preliminary Report] much too pessimistic and much too alarming. I did not," Pearson wrote in his memoirs. "I thought it exactly right. I wanted people to be shocked, and they were."

So he told the House of Commons that the government "hopes and expects that, within a reasonable period of time," the public service would achieve a position in which, as he put it:

(a) it will be normal practice for oral or written communications within the service to be made in either official language at the option of the persons making them, in the knowledge that they will be understood by those directly concerned;

(b) communications with the public will normally be made in either official language having regard to the person being served;

(c) the linguistic and cultural values of both English speaking and French speaking Canadians will be reflected through civil service recruitment and training; and

(d) a climate will be created in which public servants from both language groups will work together toward common goals, using their own language and applying their respective cultural values, but each fully appreciating and understanding those of the other.

This, remember, was in 1966 – two years before Pierre Trudeau became leader, two and a half years before the Official Languages Act was introduced, and three years before it was passed.

"I doubt if anyone at the time realized how ambitious a policy and program it was," Gordon Robertson told me. He was a strong believer in the need for a bilingual federal government; in 1965, as Clerk of the Privy Council, he been struck by the fact that Ottawa had found it very difficult to find an official who could negotiate with striking Montreal postal workers. "This episode epitomized perfectly one of the root problems we have in making the federal

government appear to be something other than an 'alien' government to the people of Quebec," he wrote to Pearson on July 26,
1965. "This is also the reason why almost no-one in Quebec con-
siders that the federal government speaks for him or Quebec; it
is the provincial government that is recognized as doing that
because it is a government that 'speaks French' and seems to
belong to the people."

Neither Pearson nor Robertson spoke French; nor did virtually anybody else in the senior public service, with the exception
of Marcel Cadieux, undersecretary of state for External Affairs.
With Pearson's agreement and encouragement, Robertson set up
a program whereby senior officials would spend a year at Laval.
"That program, for better and for worse, was worked out by
Pearson and me," he told me. "I remember sitting in his office
and talking about what could we do to make the government in
Ottawa more sensitive to the culture and aspirations of Quebec.
And we decided to send some senior people down there to
bloody well learn to speak French. We decided the best thing
would be to send families. We decided it was worth doing . . .
Mike was all in favour."

And, in the second year, in order to set an example, he went
himself – despite the strong objections of his wife and teenage
daughter. He found it extremely difficult to learn French, and
remembers thinking that forty-nine was no age to start learning a
language – although he succeeded in giving a speech to the
Quebec Board of Trade that resulted in his being called "*un
bilingue presque parfait*" in a local paper. However, his deal with
Pearson was that if there were a federal-provincial conference, he
would interrupt his studies and return. There was, and he did: "It
completely loused up my capacity to learn French fluently."

Nevertheless, with the blessing and encouragement of the
prime minister, the program continued; about twenty senior
officials a year spent an academic year at Laval, and the federal

government even bought houses for them to live in. There was considerable skepticism and opposition to the idea; Maurice Lamontagne told caucus that Robertson had received the highest scholarship that could be obtained in the world. Judy Lamarsh thought "we threw an awful lot of money away buying houses . . . and taking senior civil servants out of their positions for a whole year and sending them off to other parts of the country to learn the language." Lamontagne favoured the creation of an institute (as Pearson had discussed in his 1962 speech) that all those who became public servants after graduation would have to join. But the Quebec experience – which lasted a decade or so – was based on an important idea: that language was not simply an abstract code, but a means of communicating with people who lived in a society. Part of the point was not simply to teach middle-aged executives verb forms, but to put them physically into a very different community.

In the summer of 1968, after winning the Liberal leadership and then the election, Trudeau made it clear that he wanted to turn the 1966 policy statement into legislation. What Pearson had set as a hope and expectation was about to become law; what he had said should be "normal practice," "normally" done, and part of a new "climate" of appreciation and understanding would become a set of obligations and enforceable rights.

Trudeau asked his old friend Gérard Pelletier, whom he had first met in the late 1940s in Paris, to take charge of the language policy. The son of a railway worker, Pelletier grew up in Victoriaville. He was contemplative, wry, and both down to earth and worldly; his student activities and his work had brought him to Washington in 1939, to Santiago, Chile, in 1945, to Vienna in 1946, where, as a representative of the Catholic student federation Pax Romana, he delivered food and seven thousand pairs of shoes to Austrian students, and to Geneva that same year where he was executive director of Entraide Mondiale (World University

Service). He returned to Montreal in 1948 and became a labour reporter for *Le Devoir*, and covered the Asbestos Strike in 1949; in the 1950s, he was the editor of *Le Travail*, the publication of the Confédération des travailleurs catholiques du Canada, wrote a freelance radio column for *Le Devoir*, worked for Radio-Canada television and the National Film Board (NFB), wrote a radio series with his wife, and was one of the founding editors of *Cité libre* with Trudeau. "He made me think of a battery charged with electricity," wrote Geneviève de la Tour Fondue in 1952. "He was everywhere," recalled Gérard Bergeron in 1968. But urbane as he was, Pelletier had a stubborn sense of outrage at how French was treated as a second-class language in Canada, as a foreign language, not a Canadian language. In 1956, in London for an NFB documentary, he went to Canada House, the Chancellery of the Canadian High Commission, and insisted on speaking French. He was redirected to the French Embassy.

There was an element of chance in his career. A management shakeup at *La Presse* led to his being appointed editor in 1961. Had he not been fired as editor of *La Presse* in 1965 following a bitter strike, he would not have run for office with Trudeau and Marchand. When he came to Ottawa in 1965, he was taken aback by the Englishness of Parliament, above and beyond its British traditions. His constituents from east-end Montreal were greeted, often rudely, by unilingual security guards, and there were portraits of the prime ministers of England along the sixth floor of the Parliament Buildings, leading to the parliamentary restaurant.

Trudeau named him Secretary of State because he wanted him to introduce the new language legislation. But those who still imagine that bilingualism represented some kind of transformative patriotic dream as opposed to a utilitarian device to make a federal administration accessible and acceptable to French-speaking Quebeckers should read the third volume of Pelletier's memoirs. "To suppose that I have an emotional attachment to the Canadian political entity would be an error, because I feel none," he wrote. "My participation in the government of Canada was inspired from the beginning until the end, by reason and discernment rather than by emotion." Pelletier felt that he was bringing reason to Ottawa, and discernment to the language issue. When an Act Respecting the Official Languages of Canada was debated in the House on May 16, 1969, he tried to appeal to the spirit of renewal, saying, "With a minimum of common sense, of open-mindedness, realism and of good will, we can rejuvenate the face of Canada, enrich our society, make it more alive, more radiant and more just, in other words a better place in which to live for all who belong to it."

But he was promptly accused, along with Trudeau, of being "propagators of new faiths," and "narrow, fanatical and inflexible." Tory MP Jack McIntosh (Swift Current–Maple Creek) called the bill "bad law, bad politics and bad public relations . . . unconstitutional, undesirable, and in the light of the other grave problems confronting us, most frivolous." And Pelletier sat through hours of debate, which went on for weeks, in which the bill was denounced as dictatorial, unfair, discriminatory, illegal, and unconstitutional.

Toronto Telegram columnist Dennis Braithwaite summed up the position of the opponents of the bill in June. "We are not 'afraid' of any aspect of the language bill," he wrote. "We simply regard it as unnecessary, politically motivated, costly to implement, divisive, and, as it affects the non-English, non-French third of the population, wholly discriminatory."

Pelletier found these arguments enraging. He would respond to questions in the House by those arguing that unilingual public servants would be penalized by saying that he assumed that the Opposition MP was referring to unilingual French-speaking public servants. His questioners had a point, and Trudeau did not ease their fears at a news conference when the bill was tabled. Asked what would happen if an English-speaking civil servant said he was unwilling to learn French, Trudeau flippantly replied, "We'd say fine . . . we'll keep you running elevators where there are no French Canadians." (D'Iberville Fortier, a friend of Trudeau's, had had the experience in 1967 of working in a downtown federal office building in Ottawa with a unilingual elevator operator. Every morning, as a point of principle, Fortier would tell him his floor in French; every morning, the elevator operator – equally stubborn – would deliver him to the wrong floor. Fortier later became Official Languages Commissioner.)

Even before the legislation was passed, Trudeau made it clear that he saw his political future as intimately linked to its success. "If I don't think we can create some form of a bilingual country, I am no longer interested in working in Ottawa," he told the *Globe and Mail*'s Anthony Westell. "If I want to work as an English-speaking person, I'll look for a job in another country, or I'll go and work in Europe, or I'll look for a job in Washington. . . . What attaches me to this country is the belief that the French language can have certain rights. I think it's true for many French-Canadians who believe in federalism . . . it's the only view that can have any sense." Westell went on to add, "Trudeau's attitude on this issue should not be mistaken for what his critics allege, and his friends fear, is dilettantism. He is not really saying that if he cannot have his own way on bilingualism he will take his bat and ball to another country. Rather, his view that it is bilingualism or nothing for Canada is the measure of his determination to fight on this issue at the constitutional conference and after."

It was also a restatement of his *Cité libre* affirmation of 1962, that French and English needed to meet at the hub for federalism to function effectively. While he kept saying that the legislation did *not* mean that people would have to learn both French and English, he was also determined that it should be possible for French-speaking people to feel that Ottawa was their capital, that the federal government was their government, and that there was some recognition, both symbolic and real, that Quebec was not the only home for French in Canada. But even ten years later, the suggestion that Trudeau would leave Canada if it did not become "some form of a bilingual country" infuriated Tory author and commentator Dalton Camp. "That he could say this, much less think it, suggested he had no idea, or cared less, how such cavalier presumption would fall upon the ears of the English-speaking majority," he wrote in 1979. "But the presumption was a crucial one, for it served notice as to the internal reality of federal bilingualism, which was that the patronage links between the federal government and the unilingual sons and daughters of generations of English Canadians were now to be severed."

This was a very Tory view, one that was shared by many Conservatives: the idea that the legitimacy of the state was reinforced by "patronage links" and that there was an inherent right to work for government. The idea that working for the government at a senior level would involve the obligation to speak both official languages was seen as a deprivation of basic rights.

In the second reading vote on the legislation, sixteen Conservatives, led by John Diefenbaker, defied the Progressive Conservative leader Robert Stanfield and voted against the bill. Several continued to fight it to the end. "I speak for Western Canada," Calgary MP Eldon Woolliams told the House on July 2. "People in that part of the country demand justice. Westerners should have an equal opportunity in the Public Service of Canada." A few days later, Tory MP Don Mazankowski said the bill had "aroused unnecessary bitterness and controversy, and has seriously undermined the high degree of national unity achieved prior to its introduction."

In June 1969, Trudeau told the International Press Institute in Ottawa that the press had done a poor job of explaining the government's language legislation. In response, Canadian Press asked him to write a piece. So Trudeau signed an article produced by his office entitled "Why are they forcing French down our throats?"

which was issued by the wire service in July and subsequently published by the Secretary of State as a brochure. The article reiterated Trudeau's mantra: "Everyone in Canada will not be required to speak French, any more than everyone will be required to speak English." He stressed that "it is because everyone in the country is not expected to speak both languages, and never will be, that the federal government must be able to speak to Canadians in either French or English, wherever there are enough French speakers or English speakers to justify it."

The act would not prevent Canadians who speak only one language from working for the government, the Armed Forces, or the Crown corporations, "or from being promoted to important government jobs," he wrote, adding that through language training, "eventually it should be possible for anyone whose job requires a second language to be taught it as a regular part of their career." In the meantime, he said, "we are being careful not to handicap those who are already working for the government and who have not had an opportunity to learn a second language." It is "nonsense to suggest that the Commissioner of Official Languages" would be a "super snooper"; the Act does not violate the Constitution; and so on. Trudeau ended the piece by saying that "the very survival of our country depends on" the policy – but the benefits would not be reaped overnight. "That will require fundamental changes in attitudes and institutions which may take years, or even generations," he concluded. "In this historic process, the Official Languages Act is an important forward step."

It was a remarkably defensive document, reflecting the harsh resistance that had greeted the legislation. For despite the fact that it had been six years since the Royal Commission had been created, four years since the Preliminary Report, and three years since Pearson announced his language policy, somehow the actual implementation of the Official Languages Act came as a shock. Somehow, too, the policy was never trumpeted with pride and excitement; it was always presented apologetically, in terms of what it would not do rather than enthusiastically in terms of what it could do. That defensiveness may well have encouraged the opposition, and produced the conviction that there was some hidden agenda, some secret plan.

The legislation called for the appointment of a Commissioner of Official Languages, and the person who took on the critical job of being the first Commissioner was a thirty-five-year-old former editorial writer for the *Globe and Mail*, Keith Spicer. Spicer had the advantage of being imaginative, energetic, blunt, candid, outspoken, and a certifiable Toronto Anglo who spoke fluent French. Those strengths were also his liabilities. Spicer had criticized the powers of the Commissioner as a *Globe* editorial writer ("Justice unbalanced, however benign, however undeliberately, is but a euphemism for tyranny"), and had agreed to travel across the country to do a survey of editorial opinion on the Official Languages Act for Pelletier. Pleased with the report, Pelletier offered him the job, brushing aside his objections, saying, "No, we need a young man with energy, ideas, and the courage to speak out, and you're the man we want." Spicer was nothing if not energetic; beginning in February 1970, only a few weeks before his thirty-sixth birthday, he plunged in.

Despite Trudeau and Pelletier's vows that no one would be forced to learn French, within a few years it became clear that, if everybody had the right to remain unilingual and could deal with their government in the official language of their choice, someone would have to be there who could deal with them. That meant that some people who were unable to adapt to the new rules suffered. In a CBC report broadcast on February 28, 1971, Larry Zolf interviewed a civil servant who was photographed in shadow, so that he could not be identified. He had been a manager of thirteen people in a government department responsible for public relations; he had gone to two French-language seminars of three weeks each, but had failed to meet the French-language require-ments. As a result he had lost his position, and was now doing minor administrative work. "It leaves you with the feeling that you're a junior clerk," he said. "Now I'm relegated to the position of a junior, a junior person. It makes me . . . I feel I'm somewhat useless . . . useless and unwanted." He had spent thirty-one years in the government, and was now looking forward to retirement. After some prodding by Zolf, he acknowledged that, if it hadn't been for the support of his family, he would be contemplating suicide.

"Bilingualism has seriously upset the personal plans of hun-dreds of unilingual civil servants," wrote Erna Paris. "Those deputy minister posts they've been eying since they entered the service ten years ago have been redesignated 'bilingual,' and so have the inter-mediate positions that would have led to them." She wrote that in 1972, over thirty years ago. Three decades later, despite millions of dollars spent on French immersion in our schools, and millions more spent on teaching public servants how to speak French, the Canadian public service still has difficulty in meeting the standards required by the Act, and the requirements laid down by Treasury Board. This reinforces the argument that has been repeated by the critics of bilingualism – that the government's policy was restrict-ing senior jobs in the bureaucracy to a Central Canadian elite of those privileged enough to have grown up with two languages.

Some observers saw the federal government's bilingual policy as the root cause of a more profound shift of allegiance, and ascribed the unpopularity of the Trudeau government in 1972, and again in 1979, to a rejection of the government's bilingualism policies in English-speaking Canada. "The persistence and growing pervasiveness of bilingualism had alienated English Canadians from their federal government, turning them inwards to more familiar, compatible and nearer political jurisdictions in the provinces," wrote Dalton Camp in 1979. "The government of Canada had lost its constituency."

He was invoking a parallel situation that had existed in Quebec for years. French-speakers naturally looked to the Quebec government as theirs, the government that spoke and understood French and represented their interests. Camp was suggesting that the official languages policy was making the new Ottawa as foreign to English Canadians as it had traditionally been to Quebec francophones.

Richard Gwyn picked up this theme in his 1980 biography of Pierre Trudeau. Gwyn had a nuanced position, suggesting that "through bilingualism, Trudeau was able to keep alive 'The Canadian option within Quebec' . . . within Canada, he has kept alive the option of being able to speak French. In other words, he kept Canada going." Gwyn wondered "how could something so necessary and so reasonable (as Trudeau's bilingualism policy) have caused so much trouble" – and said that the *Calgary Herald* had come right to the point on the day after the passage of the Official Languages Act, saying that "for the more rewarding jobs, bilingualism is being made a practical necessity." He endorsed that view, suggesting that official bilingualism would not mean just the top jobs in Ottawa, but the middle-rank jobs that led to them, and jobs in national associations like the Canadian Manufacturers' Association and the Canadian Labour Congress, "on down the line to jobs in all companies which had dealings with francophones and to some provincial government positions. Eventually, unilingualism could mean a life sentence to job immobility." Trudeau, he said, "knew this all along. He fibbed about it as a necessary means to an end. . . . White lies like these are the acceptable tools of every politician's trade. Trudeau's difficulty was that the truth was bound to come out."

Gwyn's prediction was a stretch, even at the time; perhaps it should have turned out that way, but it never did. His was an exaggerated forecast that remains unfulfilled, and an unfair accusation of dishonesty.

This argument enraged Pelletier, who, ten years later, denounced Gwyn for serving up "the classic argument favoured by the most subtle opponents (of bilingualism)" and pointing out that the law had proven to be no barrier to English-Canadian unilingualism, which had continued to thrive for a decade after Gwyn's book. Gwyn responded with equal force, accusing Pelletier of calling him "a liar and a closet bigot." A decade apart, the exchange showed how bitter feelings could be on the issue.

Pelletier's view of the impact of the legislation seems more prescient than Gwyn's; twenty-five years after Gwyn's book and fifteen years after Pelletier's angry essay criticizing it, there are still few signs that the language requirements of the public service have spread to national associations or the private sector – with some recent exceptions, like the CBC's Ottawa offices. Unilingualism – certainly in English, and even in French – has hardly been "a life sentence to job immobility" except at certain executive levels of the federal public service.

Indeed, Gwyn and Camp were representative of a particular phenomenon. In the 1970s, the decade following the introduction of the Official Languages Act, none of the major columnists or commentators in the English-language media were comfortable in French. Charles Lynch and Allan Fotheringham of Southam News, Geoffrey Stevens of the *Globe and Mail,* Douglas Fisher of the Sun chain, all of them leading interpreters of the Ottawa political scene, like Gwyn and Camp, were uncomfortable in French and, as a result, uncomfortable with the new expectations, and the changing assumptions. While they rarely attacked bilingualism directly, they seemed uneasy at the growing presence of French in Ottawa, and several of them attacked Trudeau for his elitism and insensitivity to the concerns of ordinary Canadians. When Gwyn wrote about the "defensive-aggressive reaction to protect job security by middle-aged civil servants" and the "huge but inarticulate constituency of middle-class English Canadians, who realized that it was too late to learn French, and that their lives and careers would be constrained because of that lack," it is hard not to think that he was projecting his own anxieties as a no-longer young immigrant from England who was finding that new skills were required to understand the politics and government of the country.

As Trudeau and Pelletier and Spicer kept saying, again and again and again, the goal of the policy was to make the government capable of serving unilingual Canadians, not to transform Canadians into bilingual sophisticates. But even that limited goal was not an easy process. What it meant, in reality, was shifting the burden of bilingualism from citizens to the state, and sharing the burden between francophones and anglophones. But anglophones had a longer road to travel. Language training in the federal public service began in 1964; by 1972, twenty-two thousand public servants had taken language training, but only 10 per cent had acquired a working knowledge of French.

So a large part of Spicer's job was to be an enthusiast and a cheerleader, "lobbing Molotov cocktails mixing provocation, colour, common sense, irony, and a dash of wit," as he put it in his memoir *Life Sentences*, and "deliberately cultivating the image of a principled loose cannon, of a guy of thoughtful recklessness." He set out to be a kind of benevolent Pied Piper of language reform; when the village proved resistant, he set out to woo the children, leading them not to their deaths as in the folk tale, but to an interest in learning the other official language. His reports were provocative and amusing; he mixed his exasperated nagging with puns and jokes. But beneath the flippant style was a clear, unwavering commitment. His approach was based on a number of precise ideas. The government had to respect the law that Parliament had passed; it had to be sensible about it; this was a long-term rather than a short-term change – and at the same time, he recognized, as Laurendeau had stressed and as the Royal Commission had concluded, that the future of French would depend less on what was done by the federal government than on the degree to which French became what he called in his first report "the language of work and of general social use" in Quebec. This was a point he reiterated in his second, and again in his third, report. For French to be a working language in the federal government, its foundations had to be "solid and unshakeable" in Quebec. "There is no point trying to make French a useful working language in the federal administration until it is first well-established in the reality of Quebec."

As everyone else who talked about the policy had done, he reiterated that the government's policy did not mean that everyone had to learn a second language. "By federal law at least, Canada will remain a safe and comfortable place – or will at any rate leave plenty of room – for the citizen who knows, and only wants to know, one language," he wrote in his second report. But he felt compelled to remind federal employees of the basics of good manners, suggesting that anyone could learn how to say "One moment, please," or "*Un instant, s'il vous plaît.*"

In the early years of the Official Languages Act, not all of the reaction was negative. Some got into the spirit of the idea, determinedly taking language courses, gamely speaking French at meetings, sending their children to immersion. (One public servant remembers overhearing her six-year-old son, on learning that a classmate was going to be moved to an English stream, saying to him earnestly, "Don't do it, Jason! You'll never get a job!")

But not everyone took to it. At one point, Simon Reisman and his wife were taking French lessons, and Reisman was having difficulty with the conditional. Tell me, he asked the French teacher, what's the conditional for? Well, the instructor replied, it is to express uncertainty, doubt, and the hypothetical. "I'm the deputy minister of Finance!" Reisman rumbled. "I am never uncertain, I am never in doubt, and I never speak hypothetically! I don't need it!"

In an environment where power flowed from the top, example was everything. At one point in the late 1970s, I asked a senior federal official what language was spoken at meetings when, theoretically at least, the officials were bilingual. "How is the language chosen? That's easy," he explained, successfully keeping a straight face. "The civil servant of senior rank chooses the language." This was not, of course, what Laurendeau and Dunton had in mind. They wished to create an etiquette of "passive bilingualism" – where people would feel comfortable to speak their own language at meetings, and would understand the language spoken by others. Ideally, both languages would flow easily around the table. A decade later, that seemed to have gained ground in some areas, although one official in Brian Mulroney's Prime Minister's Office acknowledged that when French was spoken at meetings, there would be blank looks in some quarters, and some people would miss what had been said. The bilingualism of Ottawa, he observed wryly, was an overestimated phenomenon.

One former public servant recalled that in the heyday of language training, in the early 1970s, people would proudly emerge from meetings conducted entirely in French, smiling so hard their cheeks ached. The francophones had barely understood the heavily accented French of the anglophones, and vice versa, but everyone had smiled and nodded and been tremendously supportive, and everyone had felt a great sense of accomplishment. However, no one was sure what, if anything, had been decided.

"I only realized what was happening when I spent an exchange year in Paris," she recalled with a chuckle. "Then, when I said something people didn't understand, they didn't smile and nod – they gave me blank stares of incomprehension." She also discovered the limitations of her French. "I realized I had an intellectual level of about Grade 8," she recalled. "My analytical abilities could not go beyond my capacity in French – my ability to express my thoughts."

Nevertheless, for all of the flaws in language training and practice, some officials observed a transformation. Victor Rabinovitch, a Montrealer who came to government speaking French, entered the public service as an assistant deputy minister in 1982 after working for a commission of inquiry. He discovered that not only were some of the executives who reported to him not meeting the language requirements, one of them showed deep hostility to the idea, saying, "There's no damn way I'm learning that Frenchy language."

But other managers were keen. "One was from British Columbia, two were from Southern Ontario – and I noticed that these old core Anglo professionals were happy to get the opportunity," Rabinovitch recalled. What he then observed convinced him that there was a critical link between the official languages policy, and the then decade-old multiculturalism policy. For he saw the effect that language training had on ordinary English-Canadian bureaucrats who had grown up far from Quebec and had never come in contact with another language in any substantial way.

"All the inherited Orange reflexes and prejudices fell away; they all came back culturally renewed," he said, still marvelling at what he had seen, more than twenty years later. "They had a broader spirit of mind, a broader range of understanding of the country, a better grasp of the country's history. Call it a complete retooling of their sense of tolerance. A light went off for me: that's what the policy was about, the cultural retooling. Call it a cultural revolution; Mao destroyed with his, Trudeau built with his. It was a gestalt I had never anticipated – it made me a fervent supporter, when I had come into government a sceptic."

Rabinovitch put his finger on something important. Quebec nationalists have always argued, not without reason, that Trudeau's policy of multiculturalism was designed as a counterweight to bilingualism – not to mention as a sop to offended Ukrainian Canadians, German Canadians, and others who resented the "special treatment" given to French Canadians – and as an alternative to the dualism implied by "biculturalism." While that may be true in terms of political intentions, it doesn't take into account the psychological effect of a significant number of members of the majority trying to learn the language of the minority.

For the experience is a humbling one. It recreates the immigrant experience without leaving home. One discovers the awkwardness, the limitation, the handicap of being less articulate, less intelligent, less witty, and, at the same time, one experiences the unfolding reality of a world in another language. And even those Canadians who did not attempt the effort of learning French found themselves with a greater awareness that there was another language, another culture, another society within their country; accepting one otherness made it easier to conceive of a country of many.

But that process was slow, sometimes hard to recognize, and often drowned out by the louder sounds of resistance and resentment.

Spicer's first three reports were huge bricks; his annual assessments were followed by pages and pages of complaints that the law was not being respected. But as the years went by, he felt compelled to stress the same basic complaints.

"Nothing is more annoying than to call a federal government service only to find that it is impossible to communicate with it in one's own language," he wrote in his sixth, and last, report. "For example, a French-speaking person, already upset about his taxes, who telephones the taxation office for information and is told by the official, 'Sorry I don't speak French,' will be strongly inclined to add to the number of complaints we receive. However, if the officer answering the call had the presence of mind to say a simple phrase such as '*Un instant, s'il vous plaît,*' even in a broken accent, and then transfer the call to a colleague who could speak French, we would have a satisfied customer instead of a potential complainant, at least as far as language of service is concerned."

Spicer was responding to a rising tide of backlash from English-speaking Canadians, particularly in the public service. Tory MPs began to speak out against bilingualism – and received vigorous letters of support. "Wolfe defeated Montcalm, and flew the British flag on Quebec territory," wrote one. "The people of Quebec should remember that before they demand too much." Another wrote, "Canada is an English country and that should be the only spoken language, as in the past."

John Carson, chairman of the Public Service Commission, told a parliamentary committee that he was baffled by the complaints. "I cannot understand how people can complain, in 1972, about the requirement of bilingualism in the Public Service when, in 1966, Prime Minister Pearson mentioned 1975 as the target for Canada having a bilingual public service." But they did. They complained about the cost, they complained about the requirements, they complained about the implications, they complained about the classes, they complained about the implications for their careers. In 1971, Sandra Gwyn described this in the context of what she called "Twilight of the Ottawa Man" – the end of an era of unilingual Oxonian generalist mandarins, replaced by what she called "tough-minded problem-solvers."

"A full third of the newcomers are French Canadians," she wrote. "They either come in at the top, or move up quickly. Together with bilingual English Canadians, who themselves are predominantly from Montreal, the influx is shifting the geographic base of bureaucratic power." The ties to the West and the Maritimes were fraying: "There's no longer much room at the top for industrious but unilingual Scots out of Dalhousie Law

School or intellectual farmboys from United College [in Winnipeg] – the people who, from John A. Macdonald's day, pretty well ran the country." And yet, as she pointed out, the new francophone public servants could not, in fact, function in French in Ottawa. "'At any given meeting,' a man from Montreal told me, 'there'll always be at least two people who don't understand a word you're saying. So you have to speak English and the result is that after two hours you've had it for the day.'"

Spicer was not unaware of the problem. In 1975, exasperated with the apparently unending process of teaching middle-aged public servants to speak another language, he recommended what he called "the youth option": focusing more effort on teaching young people a second language. "Somehow, we must manage to produce a massive linguistic and attitudinal payoff for our children, thereby making it possible to phase out, or severely limit, costly (and, in its on-the-job use, distressingly underexploited) public service language training," he wrote. "Then we shall be doing more than exporting our own dreary tensions and hang-ups to still another generation of Canadians."

During the summer of 1976, the language issue seemed to be reaching a crisis. In June, Jean Marchand resigned from the federal cabinet in protest against the decision by Transport Minister Otto Lang to make concessions to the English-speaking air traffic controllers and pilots who sought to ban French-speaking pilots and controllers from speaking to each other in French. In August, a report by academic Gilles Bibeau found that the language-training policy was not working, that the anxiety level was high, the administrative social environment was not supportive of language training, and recommended a massive rethinking of the entire approach. In September, a packed Maple Leaf Gardens booed announcer Claude Mouton for speaking a few words of French at a Team Canada hockey game. When Trudeau complained that this was playing into the hands of the separatists, Toronto Maple Leafs owner Conn Smythe disagreed. "To me it is the other way around. Shoving French down other Canadians' throats is sure not helping the cause of bilingualism." And to make matters worse, Trudeau would lose ministers from both Quebec and Manitoba over the language issue.

The crisis in air traffic control began in 1975, when a Bilingual Communications Project (BILCOM) recommended to the federal Department of Transport that bilingual air traffic control services be extended in Quebec. The fact that the issue had emerged at all was testimony to growing affluence in French-speaking Quebec; ten years before, Dunton and Laurendeau never heard any complaints about air traffic control, because there were not enough affluent unilingual francophones who flew planes. But gradually, their numbers increased.

For air traffic controllers, the perspective was that bilingualism would become a job requirement. Suddenly, it became an issue of safety – it was claimed that it was a threat to air safety if English-speaking pilots overheard French-speaking pilots talking to the control tower in French. The suggestion that the skies were unsafe mobilized English Canada; in Quebec, what was at stake was the right of two French-speaking Quebeckers to speak to each other in French. There was another safety aspect as well. "I have been a controller for ten years, and at least once a day I have to deal with someone who doesn't understand what I'm saying in English," Noel Salomon, an air controller at Montreal's Dorval International Airport, told me in October 1976. "Sure, air control in one language is safer – provided everybody understands it."

But the Canadian Airline Pilots Association (CALPA) and the Canadian Air Traffic Control Association (CATCA) argued vehemently that extending bilingual air traffic control would put lives at risk. Under the cover of safety concerns, the government's bilingualism policy suddenly split the country; it was, in Trudeau's words, the worst crisis since conscription in 1942. French-speaking

pilots formed Les gens de l'air to represent Quebeckers in aviation. CATCA voted to go on strike on June 20 – just before the
summer holiday season and the beginning of the Montreal
Olympics. After a week-long illegal strike, Lang signed an agreement on June 27 which gave a major concession to the controllers:
a virtual veto over the introduction of bilingual air traffic control.

Marchand was appalled. After a passionate speech to caucus
and an equally passionate letter of resignation, saying that "it
would not be possible, in the circumstances, for me to respect the
rules of ministerial solidarity" and that he could not stay in a government that was prepared to negotiate bilingualism, he quit the
Trudeau cabinet.

It was a deeply wounding moment for Trudeau. Marchand
was not only a close friend, he had been a moral conscience. He
had made it a condition that Pelletier and Trudeau join him as a
Liberal candidate in 1965, but then he was the unquestioned star
of the trio. He was the only one of the three to be named to
cabinet and – prematurely, in the eyes of some – as Pearson's
Quebec lieutenant. But he was a pale version in Ottawa of the fiery
orator he had been in Quebec; his English was not strong enough,
and his impassioned style did not work well in the House of
Commons, although his emotional resignation speech hit the
Liberal caucus hard.

Spicer spent the day thinking that he should quit as well, and
told Trudeau, "This agreement is an intolerable affront to French
Canada, and risks eclipsing all our successes in advancing language reform. It saps the very foundations of the Official
Languages Act." Trudeau agreed, but said he could not risk crip-
pling the Olympics with a long strike. Spicer concluded that it
would be less damaging if he stayed – and that there should be at
least one anglo face defending French-speakers on French TV.

There was a spontaneous, massive, and multi-partisan reaction in Quebec. "I just can't understand the attitude taken by the

Minister of Transport or the Prime Minister," said Liberal MP Serge Joyal. "We either have a policy of bilingualism, where French Canadians have a right to speak French, or we don't." Federal Liberals and Quebec anglophones fighting Quebec's language law all joined Parti Québécois members, union activists, and celebrities like Maurice Richard in mobilizing support for the movement. "Their support comes from all sides, all walks of life, all political parties, provincial and federal," the late Pierre Deniger, then a special assistant to Otto Lang and later a Liberal MP, told me. "It's the first time it ever happened; it's just amazing." Historian John Saywell agreed. "Indeed, it is possible that there had never been such unanimity among Quebec Francophones in the history of Canada."

It was symbolic in a number of ways. The fifteen hundred members of Gens de l'air were the technological vanguard: pilots and air traffic controllers, they were highly trained professionals in a field where Quebec had traditionally been weak. (As Sandra Gwyn pointed out in an article in *Saturday Night*, Canadian aviation had its roots in the Royal Canadian Air Force, where French Canadians were virtually unrepresented.) Just as the Manicouagan Dam in the 1960s had become a symbol of national pride in Quebec, spawning a song and a continuous live television feed at Expo 67, the Gens de l'air represented the capacity of Quebeckers to engage in high technology activities in French. And the fact that this was being challenged, under the guise of safety issues, by English Canada, brought back an old concern: that French Canada's gains had been illusory, and could be wiped away by Western anti-French prejudice. (This fear was not helped by the fact that Otto Lang was from Saskatchewan.) There was a collective sense of outrage that, under any circumstances, it would be against the law for one francophone to speak to another in French.

Trudeau saw the backlash in Quebec as a threat to the idea of bilingualism, and argued in a TV address to the nation on July 9 that acceptance of bilingualism in the rest of Canada depended upon acceptance of bilingualism in Quebec. "From the moment Quebec says, 'It will be French in Quebec and English everywhere else,' I say from that moment it's the end of the country."

It was one of the bluntest statements he ever made summarizing what had become his position: the declaration that Quebec should be unilingual meant the end of Canada. He was wrong, of course; just over a year later, Quebec would do just that. In fact, paradoxically, the election of a Parti Québécois government determined to make Quebec an independent French-speaking country would momentarily silence the angry cries about the federal language policy.

Marchand was not the only casualty of the air traffic control language fight. After Trudeau told the Ontario caucus in Toronto in October that he equated bilingualism with "the salvation of the Liberal Party, and perhaps of the country," he lost Defence Minister James Richardson, who told Richard Gwyn that the air traffic control dispute proved "that the very policy designed to unify the country was the very policy that was dividing us." On October 13, Richardson quit, saying that he could not accept Trudeau's determination to have bilingualism entrenched in the Constitution. In December, he received a standing ovation in Winnipeg, his home town, when he said that Ottawa had encouraged separatism by putting too much emphasis in French-English cultural diversity.

Three years later, in a report submitted in August 1979, it was definitively established by a commission of inquiry that safety was not a concern and that French could be spoken between pilots and air traffic controllers. "It is clear that the air traffic control system finally has been able to accommodate the demands of francophone pilots and controllers to use French in Quebec, and has moved to a new equilibrium," concluded Sandford Borins in his book-length 1983 study of the conflict, *The Language of the Skies:*

The Bilingual Air Traffic Control Conflict in Canada. He predicted that the language patterns of Quebec air traffic controllers would resemble those of their counterparts in Switzerland and France, speaking French to French-speakers and English to others. "The new francophone controllers will be comparable to many members of the managerial and professional classes of Quebec Francophones, who are now working mainly in French, but who retain sufficient skill in English to be able to communicate with the English-speaking North American milieu. All told, the new status quo in air traffic control language is reflective of the linguistic status quo in Canada, in which there is not perfect equality between the two official languages, but in which the use of French (especially at the elite level) in Quebec has increased dramatically and in which there is greater, though far from perfect, availability of French services in the rest of Canada." New rules and air traffic techniques were established, and the issue is now almost forgotten, having fallen into that memory hole that exists for events that are too distant to be remembered clearly and too recent to be included in school textbooks.

But the political situation, and attitudes in English Canada, changed dramatically on November 15, 1976, when the Parti Québécois was elected. Suddenly, the mainstream criticisms of federal language policy were quieter. The French-speaking air traffic controllers sent their English-speaking colleagues a bottle of champagne the next day; their intransigence had helped make the victory possible.

The victory of the PQ was another defeat for Marchand; he had run provincially, and had been taunted by students as an Ottawa "*vendu.*" During the campaign, he told me in an interview that as a child in Trois-Rivières, he had been poor, and used to dive for nickels thrown from the decks of cruise ships. A true son of Quebec, he had studied in Quebec City, and had never moved to Ottawa. "If I endorsed separatism, I would be carried around on their shoulders," he told me bitterly. But he didn't; he was defeated by Claude Morin. Trudeau named him to the Senate, but he never really recovered from the events of 1976.

Early in 1977, English-Canadian hostility and paranoia were pulled together in a book by a retired lieutenant commander in the Canadian Navy, J.V. Andrew, *Bilingual Today, French Tomorrow*. Andrew argued that Trudeau's plan was to transform Canada into a French-speaking country, coast to coast; that there was a conspiracy of French Canadians to "hand Canada over to the French-Canadian race." Trudeau and Pelletier, he argued, based their strategy on one fact. "That one fact is that many, many French-Canadians speak English, while very few English-speaking Canadians speak French." Andrew argued that civil war was in the offing. "If Mr. Trudeau and Mr. Pelletier had really been concerned about unity in Canada, they could have, with the inge- nuity and resources they have spent on Bilingualism in the past eight years, convinced every single French-Canadian man, woman and child that the interests of all Canada would be best served if French-Canadians left their past behind and switched over to English." In the absence of that solution, which he considered to be the sensible one, Andrew concluded that there was only one way forward: "Divide Canada into two separate countries, one French- speaking, one English-speaking." He later claimed that his book went into ten printings and sold 110,000 copies.

For Trudeau's government in 1977, things looked bleak. The Lévesque government was extremely popular in Quebec, as was the preliminary version of its language policy. Patrick Gossage captured some of the federal unease after a lunch in early January 1977 with one of Pelletier's aides. "The insane manner of execut- ing institutional bilingualism in the federal civil service is his cross of sorts," Gossage wrote in his journal. "He gave me the headline that must *never* appear – one million a head for the 350 who got through language school training and were successful enough to use their newly acquired language skill." Gossage wrote that Trudeau had not been told the truth. "I hear him tell his francophone compatriots on his year-end TV interview that French units exist. They don't. Designated, yes, but not instituted," he wrote. "Bilingualism in the federal civil service, a keystone of Trudeau federalism, is crumbling sandstone."

Spicer presented his last report two months later, and issued his last, stinging criticism of the way the federal government had communicated its policy. "If it persists in ignoring the people's need to believe, or even to understand, the Government's reckless squandering of good will may sooner or later cost our language reform its vital, and newly fragile, support."

He identified three vices: first, legislative archivism (passing and then failing to explain the law). Second, the government's "minefield mentality toward language: its tendency to view Canadians as so explosively prejudiced that all talk of things linguistic must lead to apoplexies." Spicer identified the perpetual state of defensiveness the government had adopted from the beginning. "Getting off the defensive requires, for starters, that everybody stop the pitiful apologizing for 'not forcing French down your throats.' Instead, to those who allege they suffer from this complex of the Strasbourg goose, one could answer 'Try swallowing. It might taste good, and is rumoured to relieve constipation.'" Finally, he attacked the government for scattering responsibility across departments. "The idea underpinning all information efforts should be opportunity," he wrote. "No lasting progress in language reform can happen until Canadians change the value they assign to language: from pain in the neck to chance for growth."

Three decades have passed since those fateful events of 1976, and Spicer's criticisms of how the federal government handled its language policy. His successors were less flamboyant in their approach and less dramatic in their presentation, but Spicer's themes would recur. The bilingual bonus – eight hundred dollars given annually to all bilingual public servants – which was criticized by every Commissioner of Official Languages, remains in place, at a cost that has now risen to $60 million a year – money that could be dedicated to more effective purposes. The language training system of teaching middle-aged executives continues, despite the trenchant comment by Davidson Dunton in 1978 that "there were no recommendations for free language classes for Anglophone public servants [in the Royal Commission's report]."

Spicer's immediate successor was Max Yalden, a former diplomat who had worked with Pelletier at the Secretary of State's office in the elaboration of the language policy. His diplomatic training and bureaucratic experience did not disguise a profound commitment to the principles of the Act, and his exasperation at what he saw as "a combination of laziness and inattention," as he put it in the preface to his 1980 annual report. His concern was what he called "a certain lassitude or lack of staying power" on the part of the federal government. "The signs are everywhere apparent, particularly in the inclination to lecture others about language rights while paying relatively less attention to putting one's own house in order."

If Spicer's tone was an often playful teasing, Yalden – particularly as the years went on – showed a certain erudite exasperation. In 1980, he called the persistence of the bilingual bonus "folly"; in 1981, he pointed out that it had cost $40 million: "We still spent almost as much on a wasteful bilingualism bonus for federal functionaries as on grants to minority-language groups and youth-oriented programmes combined." In 1982, he noted acerbically that three things seemed to be lacking from the federal image of linguistic leadership: "consistency, imagination and sub-tlety." And his irritation at the refusal of Canadian universities to either require second-language proficiency or provide courses in a second language was obvious. "Naively, perhaps, we look to our post-secondary institutions to be in the avant-garde of both social and educational reform," he wrote. "It therefore comes as a bit of a blow to find them very sniffy about accepting any responsibility for the future quality of linguistic life in Canada." In his last appearance before a parliamentary committee as Commissioner, in June 1984, Yalden made a telling point: "Unless and until the French language in Canada achieves a broad-based and relatively unassailable security, the pressure toward linguistic polarization will persist."

D'Iberville Fortier, who served as Commissioner from 1984 until 1991, was also a former diplomat and, as the first francophone Commissioner of Official Languages, felt it would be appropriate to look at the English minority in Quebec. In his 1988 Annual Report, he concluded that English-speaking Quebeckers had been "humiliated" – which provoked a unanimous motion passed by the Quebec National Assembly denouncing the statement, and saying that the National Assembly had used its powers "always in a fully democratic manner so as to ensure the survival of the French collectivity and check the threat of anglicization." It was testimony to how sensitive the language issue remained in Quebec that even to look at the status of the English minority, let alone criticize its treatment, was grounds for outrage. His com-ments resulted in a unanimous motion of condemnation by the Quebec National Assembly. And while he was Commissioner during the period in which the new Official Languages Act was passed in 1988, he threatened to resign in 1989 in protest over the slowness of its implementation.

Victor Goldbloom, Commissioner from 1991–1998, was a pediatrician and a former member of the Bourassa cabinet. A gentle man, he was a natural mediator by temperament – but he soon acknowledged the frustration of dealing with the misinformation and myths that surrounded the Official Languages Act. "At the risk of sounding like a broken record, there is . . . an urgent need for the federal government itself to do more to explain in plain English (and plain French) what linguistic duality is all about," he wrote in the 1992 Annual Report. "People cannot be expected to support what they do not understand."

Dyane Adam, who has been Commissioner since 1999, is a Franco-Ontarian, a psychologist and former university administrator. In her first report, she was fiercely critical. "The picture . . . is clear: there is insufficient commitment and a flagrant lack of leadership by the federal government with respect to the full implementation of the Act," she wrote. "If the deficiencies and inertia are so widespread and persistent, it is because the government, at its highest level, does not provide the leadership it should to affirm linguistic duality. Yet this is the critical element for the success of Canadian federalism." Like her predecessors, she has been part cheerleader, part nag – constantly stressing the need to change the linguistic culture of the federal government in order to sustain a climate of linguistic equality.

But she was successful in helping the parties reach a consensus on the importance of making the federal government's commitment to minority language communities enforceable in the courts: a triumph in quiet behind-the-scenes diplomacy.

While the progress has been unmistakable, the pattern from one Commissioner's report to the next remains remarkably similar. Year after year, the same frustrations recur, and the problems that Spicer observed remain in place. And yet, over the three decades since Spicer's last report, much has changed.

PART TWO

Getting from There to Here

Montreal and the Changing Etiquette of Language Use

In Montreal, at the Second Cup across the street from the McGill University campus, I watched a trainee struggling a bit with the routine. A more experienced employee explained the terminology: the long double espresso that I had ordered to drink in the store was a "*double allongé planté . . .*" "It's a code," she said. "It just makes it easier if we all use the same terms." So, at Les cafés Second Cup, one English-speaking employee rattles off the in-house jargon for coffee orders in French while another employee, also English-speaking, pulls the levers and pumps out the orders.

It was the fall of 2002, and I was in Montreal to look at how, twenty-five years after the passage of Bill 101, language custom was operating in the city. I found my Second Cup experience repeated at counters and wickets all over the city; young people with name tags reading Jennifer and Matthew greeting customers saying, "*Bonjour, est-ce que je peux vous aider?*" English-speaking customers, if they didn't notice the name tag first, would often as not respond in French, ordering coffee or movie tickets in French from English-speaking teenagers.

Over the last four decades, through a combination of legislation, out-migration, education, and social consensus, French has become the social language, the language that most people use spontaneously in public, the default language of public intercourse.

English Quebeckers, once derided by René Lévesque and Keith Spicer as Westmount Rhodesians, are now much more bilingual than French-speaking Quebeckers: 67.2 per cent of English-speaking Quebeckers told the census-takers in 2001 that they could carry on a conversation in French as compared to only 36.9 per cent of francophones who could carry on a conversation in English. It has not been an easy or automatic process; hundreds of thousands of English-speaking Quebeckers have left Quebec – either because of greater economic opportunity elsewhere, or because they decided they would prefer to leave than adjust to their new status as part of a minority. One 1988 study showed that more left for a better job than because of politics or language – but the two factors were not unrelated, and leaving for a better job was a more socially acceptable answer.

Between 1971 and 2001, there was a net loss of 276,000 people with English as their mother tongue who moved from Quebec to other provinces or other countries. As Martha Radice put it in her fascinating 2000 book *Feeling Comfortable? The Urban Experience of Anglo Montrealers*, these departures "formed part of a collective absence that continues to mark the imaginations and actions of Anglo-Montrealers." (There is, interestingly enough, a net loss of 37,500 francophones during the same three decades – presumably moving for exclusively economic rather than linguistic reasons.)

But, despite the net loss, there continued to be a flow of English-speaking people from other provinces to Quebec. The number drops significantly after 1976 – but every five years after that, between 25,000 and 32,000 anglophones moved to the province.

Now, downtown Montreal restaurants and bars are an example of what Camille Laurin meant when he talked about institutional unilingualism and individual bilingualism: the signs, posters, and menus are in French only, while the staff – and sometimes the clients – flip easily from one language to the other. (I have surreptitiously watched what was clearly an office lunch in Montreal, and heard people switching from French to English and back, depending on which colleague they were talking to.)

It is not exactly the bilingualism that Frank Scott or Pierre Trudeau had in mind; in fact, it was precisely the model of a French-dominant workplace in Quebec that provoked Scott to write his dissent to the Royal Commission's report on the work world. But the transition to an environment of effective – as opposed to official – bilingualism has provoked me over the years to ask a whole series of questions that apply to bilingual situations, whether in Montreal or in the ranks of the federal bureaucracy. When two bilingual people meet, what language do they speak and how do they choose the language? How do waiters decide whether to address a customer in French or in English? How it is possible to be comfortable in a courtroom and lost in a *quincaillerie* (hardware store)? How did the public language in Montreal go through the change that so obviously occurred?

When I first came to Quebec and learned French as a student in 1965, I found it almost impossible to speak French in a public place and be replied to in French. Once my accent was recognized (in other words, as soon as I opened my mouth) the waitress or salesman would switch to English. On the rare occasions that this did not occur (in places like Quebec City), I would be questioned in cafeteria lines: "Excuse me, but where did you learn French?"

The very rarity of an anglophone speaking French at all became embarrassingly clear to me in the fall of 1965. While a student at the University of Toronto, I had attended a student convention at Laval in Quebec City, and had got a lift back to Montreal from an acquaintance. She stopped off at her parents' house on the South Shore to get something, and after introducing me, disappeared upstairs to find it. Her parents were close to retirement age; her father had worked for years in a minor position at the CNR. They were sitting in the living room playing cards with friends, and questioned me politely: Was my family French-speaking? No, my father spoke a little French, but that was all. My mother wasn't a francophone? No, she spoke no French at all. Had I grown up in a French-speaking neighbourhood? No, I had taken French at school, but I had really only learned it very recently. Finally, the penny dropped. An English-Canadian student from Toronto was standing in their living room, speaking to them in French. They became overwhelmingly effusive in their compliments: I spoke so well (I didn't), I had no trace of an accent (I certainly did). It was "*extraordinaire*," it was "*incroyable*" – and for me, it was really embarrassing. I realized that these four middle-aged people, living in Montreal, had never held a conversation in French with an English-Canadian before. It was a humiliating revelation of the relations between French and English.

I had another experience that brought home to me how English remained the dominant language in Montreal. As a student journalist in 1965, I had gone to meet a colleague, the editor of *Le Quartier Latin*, the student newspaper at the Université de Montréal. She was from a small town in Quebec and spoke no English. After our conversation, I suggested lunch at an Italian restaurant on Côte des Neiges, not far from the campus. The waiter did not understand French; I had to order. After lunch, she invited me to join her at a book launch she was going to. I accepted, and we hailed a taxi. The cab driver spoke no French; I had to give him our destination. My fellow student was twitching with rage.

It was an anger that reflected the conviction, articulated by demographer Jacques Henripin in 1969, that immigration was going to erode the French fact in Montreal, and the francophone majority would be seriously reduced, particularly in Montreal. "This would mean losing their only real power: that of making laws and electing governments," he wrote. The fear of French-speakers becoming a minority in Montreal because of immigrants adopting English as their language haunted Quebec politics in the late 1960s and early 1970s – and, despite all the changes caused by the language legislation, still exists.

Union Nationale premier Jean-Jacques Bertrand unleashed that anger when he introduced Bill 63 in 1969, which explicitly guaranteed the right of parents to choose the language of education for their child. The ensuing riots and demonstrations contributed to his government's defeat in 1970, and the election of Robert Bourassa's Liberals. Following the creation of a language inquiry, the Gendron Commission, Bourassa introduced Bill 22 in 1974, which established French as the official language of Quebec. Unfortunately, it also introduced a testing system for immigrant children entering school to establish if they had the right to go to English school or not. This process – the rigorous testing of six-year-old children – infuriated both French and English in Quebec. English Quebeckers hated the erosion of the right to English school; francophone Quebeckers loathed the spectacle of weeping children being tested, and being sent the message that those who passed entered the pearly gates of English school and those who failed were doomed to the hell of French school.

That failure not only contributed to the defeat of the Liberals in 1976, it laid the groundwork for Bill 101, and its Cartesian definition of Quebec as a French-speaking society. It left Bourassa deeply reluctant for the rest of his political career to do anything that might reignite the language passions that had helped to drive him out of office.

Technically, the term Bill 101 disappeared when the legislation was passed on August 26, 1977, and it stopped being a bill and became a law. However, the use of the phrase continues; in French, it is referred to as "*la loi 101*," but still, in English, as "Bill 101." Some Quebeckers argue that the persistence of the phrase in English, and the reference to the law as Bill 101 rather than as Law 101 or as the Charter of the French Language, reflects a refusal to accept the fact that it is, in fact, the law, and not simply a bill, which is merely proposed legislation, not yet law. The fact that it is a Charter, and referred to as such, speaks to the symbolic power of the law to francophone Quebeckers.

In my case, over the years that followed, I noticed that the visible shock at the spectacle of an English-speaking person speaking French, so common in the 1960s, gradually ebbed away. Little by little, French in Quebec was becoming a public language, and losing its status as a secret ethnic code, accessible only to the descendants of the pre-Conquest settlers. As a language, it could be learned and spoken; French with an English accent (or Italian, or Greek, or Haitian accent) was just that – a public language spoken with an accent, and not a cue for a switch into English. This process became accelerated with Bill 101, as French became, for the first time, a language that integrated immigrants through the school system. Those who draw quick conclusions about the supposed intolerance of Quebeckers toward immigrants perhaps forget that Quebeckers have had twenty-five years to learn what English-speaking North Americans have had 150 years to absorb: how to hear their language spoken with an accent.

But legislation did not establish custom or social ritual. At Expo 67, in Montreal, waiters and waitresses adopted a skilful technique for serving people who might be French-speaking or English-speaking. They would walk briskly up to the table, look the customers in the eye, smile warmly, nod their heads – and wait. In addition to choosing what to order, the customers had to choose what language to order it in. This, in itself, marked a dramatic change. Traditionally, it had been quite possible to live one's life in Montreal – and do so actively, with no sense of being part of a marginal community – without speaking a word of French. It was only the political activism and effervescence of the 1960s that eroded the younger edges of the affluent solitude (working-class anglo Montrealers never had the luxury of unilingualism; the higher the income level, the lower the rate of bilingualism in those days). But habits of a lifetime did not change. In the late 1970s, around the time of the passage of the language law, the late Henry Giniger, then the *New York Times*'s correspondent in Canada, invited a senior editor of the *Montreal Star*, then the leading English-speaking Montreal newspaper, and his wife to dinner with a well-known francophone Quebec sculptor and his wife. To his horror and embarrassment, Giniger – perfectly comfortable in French – discovered that the two prominent Montreal couples did not share a common language. He told me it was one of the most awkward evenings he could remember.

The introduction, passage, and implementation of the language legislation at first widened the gap between French and English in Quebec. Many French-speaking Quebeckers saw it as reassuring protection; many English-speaking Quebeckers saw it as authoritarian and vindictive. The inspectors for the Office de la langue française were known as the language police, or "the tongue troopers."

In 1979, William Weintraub, a Montrealer born and bred, wrote a satire, *The Underdogs*, portraying an independent future Quebec as a totalitarian state taking revenge on the few anglophones who had not fled. But his bitter exaggeration had much less impact than the attacks of his old friend, Mordecai Richler, who abandoned satire to launch a constant series of assaults on the language law.

Always an iconoclast, Richler hammered away at one of modern Quebec's most painful and repressed memories: the support given by Quebec's Catholic and nationalist elites for fascism and anti-Semitism in the 1930s. It was the breach of a taboo that made otherwise sensible people quiver with anger. One of his *New Yorker* pieces began, "I was brought up in a Quebec that was reactionary, church-ridden and notoriously corrupt – a stagnant backwater – its *chef* for most of that time, Premier Maurice Duplessis, a political thug – and even its intellectuals sickeningly anti-Semitic for the most part." He then went on to quote the anti-Semitic remarks of Abbé Lionel Groulx, *Le Devoir*'s founder Henri Bourassa, Laurendeau, and other nationalists of the 1930s – and the continued esteem in which Groulx was held in contemporary Quebec. But the remark that most outraged francophone Quebeckers was in his article published in *The New Yorker* in September 1991, in which he commented on the traditionally large Quebec families, writing, "This punishing level of reproduction, which seemed to me to be based on the assumption that women were sows, was encouraged with impunity by the Abbé Groulx, whose newspaper, *L'Action Française*, published in 1917, preached *la revanche des berceaux* [the revenge of the cradles]." "Sows" did not go down well.

Richler was picking at the scabs of Quebec's nationalist past, and the reaction was furious denial. Periodically, he would throw in a qualification to his condemnations, but there was always a barb. "René Lévesque was not an anti-Semite. Neither is Jacques Parizeau," he wrote. "All the same, Jews who have been Quebecers for generations understand only too well that when thousands of flag-waving nationalists march through the streets roaring 'Le

Québec aux Québécois!' they do not have in mind anybody named Ginsburg. Or MacGregor, for that matter."

Ironically, Richler was only known in French-speaking Quebec for his polemics; his fiction, known across much of the world, and which was to make him a household name in Italy, had not been translated, and there was little or no awareness that he had been just as sharp in his mockery of everyone else, including the Jewish community, which deeply resented his early fiction. He had been, as he wrote in the postscript to the book based on his *New Yorker* articles, "no less critical of WASP bigotry and English Canadian nationalism than I have been of Francophone follies."

Richler's 1992 book *Oh Canada! Oh Quebec! Requiem for a Divided Country* caused a furor; a Bloc MP urged in Parliament that it be banned, and that Richler be charged with hate literature. His own sense of pain from seeing "*À bas les juifs*" (Down with the Jews) painted on the highway to the Laurentians in the 1940s was masked by a deep and unforgiving anger. He argued in his book that francophones in Quebec "are still doggedly fighting against injustices that no longer exist"; others responded that the anti-Semitism in Quebec he was attacking no longer existed. Hugh Segal, then Brian Mulroney's chief of staff, was deeply troubled by the book. "My problem with the thesis that French-Canadian nationalism draws much of its roots from anti-Semitism is that I just don't think it's true," he told me, arguing that the roots of French-Canadian nationalism are much broader than that, and that the Union Nationale even funded Jewish schools. "You're looking at a guy who went to two levels of religious education in Quebec . . . up to Grade 11. That didn't happen in any other province in Canada."

Richler infuriated many Quebeckers not only because he spoke no French himself, but because his work encouraged the complacent belief in English Canada that Quebec is a harsh, intolerant society. For Quebeckers it also reinforced the sense that

English Canada seeks out examples of injustice in order to attack Quebec, while overlooking its own anti-Semitic past. In addition, there was great resentment at the fact that Richler was able to use the international platform of *The New Yorker* to vent his mockery and scorn, leaving them unable to reply.

When novelist, filmmaker, and publisher Jacques Godbout was asked to write a piece for the Sunday *New York Times* in September 2001, his anger at Richler, and his sense of finally getting a platform to respond, almost overwhelmed the article, ostensibly written about a Quebec arts festival in New York. What was intended as an essay on the development of Quebec culture kept returning to Richler, who had recently died, saying he had taken advantage of his fame as a novelist to embark on "a malicious campaign . . . in which he denounced, more or less honestly, the project for a sovereign and French Quebec."

But Godbout was clearly conflicted. Calling him "Quebec's greatest writer," he expressed regret that Richler had died before being able to attend the arts festival. "This man who never tired of denouncing the desire of Quebecers to exist in French could nonetheless have kicked off the New York festivities with a blast and could perhaps even have finally apologized, with his timid half-smile, for having described his French-speaking compatriots as raving fanatics." Unlikely as that might have been, as unlikely as a "timid" half-smile from Richler, there was something sadly poignant about Godbout's essay. His account of how Quebec had emerged from its clerical past kept swerving back to Richler, and the argument, which would have baffled most New Yorkers, was totally lost in the trauma of the events of September 11 – as was the festival.

In some ways, Richler was an heir to Frank Scott's fierce opposition to Quebec nationalism, and his long memory of its admiration for fascism in the 1930s. But while Scott also remembered Laurendeau's change of view and his opposition to Spain's

Generalissimo Franco, Richler never acknowledged Laurendeau's apology (although he quoted from other parts of the book where it was reprinted) preferring to rub salt in his own wounds, and stoke his anger.

But like many polemicists who are hated for what they say, Richler had an unacknowledged impact. Richler's articles – and his primary source for his polemics, author Esther Delisle's research on the links between French-Canadian nationalism and fascism in the 1930s – produced some dramatic results. Jean-Louis Roux was forced to step down as lieutenant-governor in 1996 after he was quoted as recalling that he had worn a swastika on his arm in medical school. (Later, in his memoirs, Roux apologized for his youthful idiocy.) And in December 2000, the National Assembly unanimously condemned Yves Michaud, a former Quebec politician, delegate-general in Paris, and friend of René Lévesque's, after he had repeated on the radio a sharp exchange of words he had had with Senator Leo Kolber in a hair salon (where he had suggested sarcastically that the Jews were the only people in the world who had suffered in the history of humanity) and vented some of his rage at suggestions that the Lionel-Groulx metro station should be renamed. Lucien Bouchard cited the support he found for Michaud inside the Parti Québécois as one of the reasons for his resignation in January 2001.

But even when those jagged edges were softened and the hot buttons avoided, the new linguistic reality created etiquette challenges. When two bilingual people meet, what language do they speak and how do they choose the language? The question seems silly, perhaps trivial – and, of course, without any single answer other than the obvious "It depends." But the ranges of circumstance influencing the answer are part of what makes the subject of culture contact so continually intriguing. For it can depend on

the language the relationship was established in, where the conversation happens, the presence of other people, the nature of the
relationship, and a whole series of other factors that can involve
shadings of power ("I'll pick the language here"), one-
upmanship ("I speak your language better than you speak
mine"), exclusion ("I speak my language only with my people –
and you're not one of them"), complicity ("We speak this
language and they don't"), solidarity ("I'm one of you" or "You're
one of us") – or simply convenience.

But because something apparently simple can be very complicated, a whole range of emotions can be provoked as people grope
to select an appropriate language. "The other day I walked into a
department store and had a conversation which made me feel
foolish," wrote Soma Day in 1978. "It was also frustrating. . . . It's
the kind of conversation I have an awful lot nowadays. . . . The
conversation always goes something like this:

"I walk up to the counter, intent on buying some socks.
'*Bonjour*,' says the woman, smiling. '*Est-ce que je peux vous aider?*'
'*Oui*,' I smile back. '*Je voudrais acheter des bas comme ça.*' I point to
some socks on display in the showcase. '*En beige s'il vous plaît.*' 'Yes,
of course, Madame,' she responds in English. 'What size?' 'Er . . .'
I pause, 'Nine and a half, please.'

"Our transaction continues smoothly and I thank her and leave
the store. But inwardly, the whole time this pleasant bilingual
woman is fishing my socks out of the showcase and putting them in
a bag and taking the money, I am cursing. Dammit, I want to say.
Dammit, lady, why do you always switch to English? . . . Does my
French sound so terrible that you'd rather not converse in it with
me . . . Do you recognize an anglophone . . . and presume I'd rather
use my own language? Could it even be that . . . you're telling me . . .
that you're a federalist? (This happened once, in such a conversation. I stopped in a garage and struggled to explain that my wind-
shield wipers were *congellé* and I wanted to make them *fonctionner*.

The man listened in mild amusement and then said 'You don't have to speak French to me, Madame. I'm not a separatist.')"

As Monica Heller, who quoted this passage, commented, "Something strange is going on in Montreal. Every encounter between strangers, especially in public places but by no means exclusively, has become a political act." One of the shrewdest observers of these encounters, Heller is a sociolinguist who brought a wry sense of irony and a careful ear to a changing environment in Montreal in the late 1970s and early 1980s. As she put it later, in 2002, "Language choices are power gestures." I found her insights invaluable in trying to describe and understand the subtleties and uncertainties of language contact. There was then no clearly understood etiquette of bilingualism, even in Montreal, where the language groups come into contact most often. Despite two hundred years of co-existence, there were few clearly understood and articulated rules, written or unwritten, or socially accepted rituals which are spelled out to explain how people do, or should, choose the language they speak.

Until very recently, the answer to the "which language" question was very simple: English. Until very recently, bilingualism went one way – and to a large extent, outside Quebec, it still does. (Only 7 per cent of English-speaking Canadians outside Quebec described themselves in 2001 as able to carry on a conversation in French.)

One more complex answer is: it depends on the language in which the relationship was formed. Language is a tool for communication, and it constitutes one of the key elements in the fabric of a relationship. Generally, bilingual people of different mother tongues establish a relationship in one language or another, switching only when the context requires it, or when other people join them.

But when relationships do not exist, the challenge is different. Just as francophones will sometimes agonize over whether to use "*tu*" or "*vous*," the bilingual find they have new, subtler problems with an equally high risk of embarrassment, awkwardness, and unintentional insult. For some people respond like Soma Day, insulted when the person they are talking to switches languages. Others are offended if they don't. One English Montrealer complained to me during the period between the election of the Parti Québécois and the 1980 referendum that he felt like a Ugandan Asian. When I asked him for an example, he told me that when he joined French-speaking colleagues at the bar, they used to switch into English; they no longer did this. It was an example that made me smile; fifteen years earlier, in the mid-sixties, I was struck by the pride with which my father recounted that he had joined a group of French-speaking colleagues at the National Press Club bar, and they had not switched into English. What was a gesture of exclusion for one was a gesture of inclusion for another.

To avoid the unintentional insult, people have been groping for a bilingualism etiquette, and that process itself creates a whole host of problems, complications, and often hilarious false steps. Getting into a cab, some Montrealers will glance to see what newspaper is on the front seat, or pause to hear the language of the car radio before choosing a language. Returning to Montreal for a visit from London, Canadian journalist Gwynne Dyer observed that one of the side effects has been that, in contrast with Londoners, Montrealers, uncertain of which language to use, do not spontaneously speak to strangers. Similarly, Montreal wit Josh Freed describes the increase in the use of "*allô*" as a greeting; neither "hello" nor "*bonjour*," it is language-neutral, enabling strangers to sort out which language to use.

This process has been occurring gradually for some time. "An etiquette of bilingualism is developing, but we don't know much about it," Université de Montréal anthropologist Gillian Sankoff told me in 1978. "What we've seen in Quebec in the last ten years is a big change in the meaning of the use of language in public situations."

Monica Heller watched this change closely – first using her experience in a part-time job at the outpatient's clinic at the Royal Victoria Hospital as material for her M.A. thesis in socio-linguistics, and then broadening her observations for a number of studies that led to her doctorate.

In her work, she described the process by which strangers and colleagues decided what the language of conversation would be, calling it "a curious dance" and a "negotiation . . . made up of implicit and explicit strategies" to figure out which language to use. In Quebec, by the mid-seventies, that language was increasingly French, but Heller saw an awkward waltz as people tried to manoeuvre to a comfortable consensus on how to communicate. She described one conversation between patient and clerk that switched back and forth from French to English several times, and then analyzed it.

"[The patient's] switch may mean 'She speaks English really, and I want to make sure she understands me, so I'd better speak English.' It may also or alternatively mean 'We can't have this conversation until I find out whether you are French or English.' If the clerk had persisted in speaking French, which also happens, the motivation would probably have been 'Nice of her to try to make it easier for me, but this will be easier and clearer if we do it in French.' (The clerk may feel it was genuinely nice, or she may feel it was snide.)"

She documented a subtle testing of the slippery ground of hierarchy, authority, power, and exclusion. There was an area of mutual suspicion, distrust, and need: clerks were supposed to be bilingual, which they were to a greater or lesser extent; patients wanted to make sure they were understood. The possibilities for misunderstandings were endless. Heller described one hilariously confusing encounter:

Clerk: May I help you?
Patient: [silence]
Clerk: *Est-ce que je peux vous aider?*
Patient: [confused look]
Clerk: *Anglais ou français?*
Patient: WHAT?
Clerk: MAY I HELP YOU?
Patient: Oh, yes, yes, I'm sorry. I'm just a little deaf.

Her observations at the hospital depicted the uneasy groping for advantage or survival or polite accommodation in a world where the linguistic rules were changing, where Quebeckers remained uneasy and uncertain of how to respond to French spoken with an accent, and where it was easier for a Torontonian to be accepted speaking French badly (it was taken for granted) than an English Montrealer (whose lack of ability in French was actively resented).

Other observers of bilingualism, like François Grosjean, have pointed out that bilingualism comes in many forms. Perfect bilingualism, or equilingualism (what one Ottawa official wryly calls "the linguistic hermaphrodites") is the rare exception: the vast majority of bilinguals have one dominant language, even though that dominant language can shift during one's lifetime. Moreover, someone can have a different dominant language for a different situation: be completely comfortable in French in court (as all Montreal criminal lawyers are, whether English or French-speaking), for example, and have no vocabulary in a hardware store; be much more accustomed to the business vocabulary in English, and speak only French at home. Paradoxically, those in the latter situation – middle-aged francophones who made their livelihoods in English-speaking companies – found the francization of business in the late 1970s a difficult experience.

Heller described this phenomenon when, a few years after finishing her fieldwork for her M.A., she returned to Montreal to watch the francization process that Quebec's language law set in motion in a major office in Montreal. She observed the following situation in a large Montreal-based company at a divisional meeting, which she described in a paper published in 1982.

Albert was a young French-speaking department head, recently promoted to replace an anglophone; Bob was a middle-aged unilingual Scot who would have got the job if it hadn't been for francization and *la loi 101*; Claude was an older francophone, used to working in English; and Daniel was a unilingual francophone recently promoted to a position originally slated for a unilingual anglophone. As chairman of the meeting, Albert was walking a very delicate line. On the one hand, he owed his job to the fact that French was officially the language of work, and he had at least one person at the meeting who spoke no English. On the other hand, the most experienced veteran in the department spoke no French.

"Albert has to balance expectations that he use French with courtesy to an older man whose job he has essentially usurped," she noted. "Bob must keep his dignity while showing flexible adaptation to new terms; and Claude must please both his new boss and his old colleague."

That transitional phase she described, one must remember, was taking place twenty-five years ago. The changes were not always steady; political tensions created their own social ripples, and some of the social equilibrium was achieved through the departure of a significant number of English-speaking Quebeckers. The new middle-class support for Quebec independence, which increased as the support for the Meech Lake Accord outside Quebec started to drop in the late 1980s, should be understood as taking place ten years after the francization of the private sector in Montreal began. The Alberts and the Daniels had ten years of fast-tracked success, bolstered by the continued economic growth of the 1980s and the tax-break-supported investments of the Quebec Stock Savings Plan to reinforce a sense of corporate linguistic self-sufficiency, and collective self-confidence. Increasingly, the new etiquette of bilingualism became a comfort zone for franco-phones. What was called Quebec Inc., the business class that emerged in part because of close ties between the new French-speaking business community and the Quebec government, had created a new phenomenon: French unilingualism in the Montreal business world.

However, the social equilibrium that resulted was maintained at a considerable cost. Robert Bourassa, who had returned to polit-ical life in 1983, promised to amend the language law before the 1985 election. The Liberal Party was committed to formal recognition of the English community's distinct status, specifically to allow the English community to use English-language signs, to administer its own institutions, to have fairer representation of anglophones in the Quebec public sector, and to receive an extension of English-language government services. After he was elected, a group of anglophone Quebeckers privately advised the government that they should take dramatic steps to bolster the French language – more money for immigrant classes, more money for libraries, films, and the recording industry – as the only way politically to do anything for the English community. But Bourassa was wary of reopening the language issue. Except for guaranteeing the right of an English-speaking person to receive health and social serv-ices in English, the promises were not kept. Bourassa decided to wait until the court cases challenging the language law were heard.

When the Supreme Court ruled in 1989 that it was unconsti-tutional to ban the use of other languages on signs, Bourassa – on the advice of Claude Ryan, his predecessor as Liberal leader and senior minister, and the man who, as publisher of *Le Devoir*, had denounced Bill 101 – concluded that he could not yet allow English on outdoor signs without stirring up unrest. When he used the notwithstanding clause in the Charter of Rights to exempt his legislation so that it could perpetuate unilingualism in signs, the result was twofold: on the one hand, fifteen thousand protesters filled Paul Sauvé Arena to denounce any dilution of Bill 101 – and, on the other, three powerful English-speaking cabinet ministers, Justice Minister Herbert Marx, Communications Minister Richard French, and Environment Minister Clifford Lincoln resigned – with Lincoln making a memorable speech in the National Assembly, in which he said that there were no inside rights or outside rights, that "rights are rights are rights."

"The signs issue is symbolically explosive," observed American urban historian Marc Levine in his 1990 book *The Reconquest of Montreal: Language Policy and Social Change in a Bilingual City*. "Many Montreal Francophones see anything short of unilingual French signs as a continuing legacy of the 'Conquest,' while Anglophones view bilingual signs as a symbol that Montreal is a 'social contract' between two linguistic communities. In short, the debate over Montreal's 'French face' revolves around antithetical visions of the city: Montreal as a fundamentally French city versus Montreal as a dualistic city."

The ensuing anger in English-speaking Canada over Bourassa's use of the notwithstanding clause contributed to the failure of the Meech Lake Accord in June 1990. When the use of the notwithstanding clause expired five years later, the Parti Québécois government introduced amendments to permit other languages on signs, provided that French had predominance. This met the requirements of the Supreme Court and there was little or no public outcry.

What occurred in the decade that followed the 1995 referendum was a kind of rebalancing. On the one hand, those anglophones who stayed in Montreal – and those who moved there, a small but observable phenomenon – did so in the recognition that French was the public language of Quebec. It was not always a happy acknowl-edgement. After two decades in Quebec public life, Reed Scowen concluded there was no place for the English in Quebec; that they were not wanted. "My strong impression is that there is no-one left in English Quebec today who believes that the community has a viable future," he wrote in a book, *Time to Say Goodbye*, pub-lished in 1999. "There are certainly many Anglophones who will continue to live in Quebec and enjoy it there. I am one of them. But it is virtually impossible to find a family whose children have remained, and intend to remain, in Quebec." (While this quote is graphic, dramatic, and reflects Scowen's experience, it is not nec-essarily – or perhaps more accurately, no longer – true. I can think of several families whose children have remained in, or returned to, Quebec.)

But at the same time, the effect of NAFTA, technological change, and an increasingly global economy meant that, after years of having the contact point between French and English move up the job pyramid, it was moving back down again.

Traditionally, in newly industrialized Quebec, workers had to learn English to become a foreman; no one in more senior posi-tions spoke any French. Quebec's language law – and the flood of Quebec university graduates in the 1960s – moved that contact point far from the factory floor. Quebec's language law meant that head offices moved to Toronto rather than operate in French, leaving their regional operations to function in French. Contact between the regional office and head office happened in English – but at the level of regional director or vice president. Until very recently, the workforce below that level operated entirely in French.

Stephen Harper's father worked at Imperial Oil, and anecdo-tally, Harper concluded from that corporate experience what he feels was the real impact of Bill 101.

"The company will deny this, knowing the management there, but what they essentially did at Imperial Oil was, as it became obvious there was a demand for the company to operate in French, . . . in the late '60s and early '70s, they undertook an extensive program to train their management to become bilingual and operate in French or in both languages," Harper said. "They actually concluded that that was not what the language policies were about. They then took any nationally oriented operations out of the Montreal office and moved them to Toronto. The head office was already in Toronto, but they moved what was left that was significant nationally out of Quebec. They made everything that was Quebec-centric operate in Montreal, and they moved out all the English people, even the bilingual ones, and replaced them with Francophones. They concluded that the policy was not about making Imperial Oil operate in French, they concluded that the policy was to displace existing staff with Francophones."

But the new economy did not respect this neat division of linguistic labour. English-Canadian and American firms bought Quebec firms; Quebec firms expanded into English Canada or the United States, or acquired companies from outside Quebec. When any of these things happened, suddenly people who had previously functioned in a French-only environment had to acquire English. Language schools began to thrive – teaching English to meat cutters and brewers, bankers and stockbrokers, purchasers and account managers.

One of the effects of the success of the language legislation was to take away one of the deepest emotional drivers for independence. It was no longer possible to argue that Quebec had to become independent in order to become a French-speaking society; it had done so within Confederation. "Bill 101 is probably the thing that did the most harm to the independence movement," observed Michael Goldbloom in 2002, then at the McGill Institute for the Study of Canada. (Ironically, one of the founders of Alliance Quebec, Goldbloom has become an example of economic migration himself; he is now the publisher of the *Toronto Star*.)

In one of his last interviews, shortly before he died in 2003, Pierre Bourgault acknowledged that the battle over French was finished. "We've won," he told Radio-Canada's Marie-France Bazzo. "I can't stand a revolutionary who doesn't recognize the revolution is over." Not everyone, however, recognized the victory. In December 2000, Yves Michaud appeared before the Larose Commission on the French Language and made an impassioned case for extending the school language requirements to the CEGEP, or junior college level, and asked for a law that would require the children of immigrants to go to French-language institutions.

"Why?" he asked rhetorically. "Because it is at that moment, when one is 16, 17, 18, 19, that one chooses one's partner, that one will probably have children who will speak English – and there are economic effects in all that – who won't open an account at the Caisse Populaire, who will not read *La Presse* or *Le Devoir* but will read *The Gazette* instead. So they will be assimilated by the 8 per cent of Anglo-Quebeckers who are comforted by the vast North American culture and the powerful neighbours of America." It was the fear of assimilation and dominance in its purest, most naked form, combined with a deep belief in the social-engineering powers of legislation. In June 2005, a group led by Michaud unsuccessfully made the same case at the Parti Québécois convention.

At times, these skirmishes produce Kafkaesque absurdities. Michael Parasiuk became entangled in one of them. Parasiuk grew up in Manitoba where his parents placed him in immersion French. As an adult, he moved to Ottawa to work for the federal government, and lived in Wakefield, some fifty kilometres north of Ottawa in Quebec, where his grandparents had lived. He and his wife decided to send his young son Cohen to immersion French in the neighbourhood school. But he was not permitted to do so; the Quebec authorities ruled that French immersion was part of the English school system, and Parasiuk was not eligible to send his

son to an English school because – wait for it – he had been educated in French. In other words, French immersion was French
education when it was outside Quebec – and English education
when it was in Quebec. The Parasiuks responded by home school-
ing their son for a year, and taking the government to court. In
September 2004, the Quebec Court of Appeal ruled that Cohen
could attend French immersion until the case was heard.

Shanning Casimir was in a similar situation. She had gone to a
French immersion program in Ottawa for Grades 1 and 2 when her
parents moved to Montreal in July 2000, and tried to enroll her in
an English-language school. The Quebec government refused her,
saying she had not had "the major part" of her education in English.
Her mother, Edwidge Casimir, took the case to court.

In March 2005, the Supreme Court ruled on the question of
what constituted the "major part" of a child's education – part
of the criterion for a child being able to transfer into English school
in Quebec. In a finely nuanced decision, the court, once again,
upheld the basic rationale for limiting access to English school as
laid out in section 23 of the Charter: a balancing act between concerns of the francophone minority outside Quebec, the English
minority in Quebec, and "the anxiety of a significant segment of
Quebec Francophones about the future of their language (which)
was a known fact, if only because of the upheavals it had caused in
Canadian politics, and even more so in Quebec politics."

But at the same time, the court endorsed the common-sense
position that French immersion, while it provides instruction in
French, is for English-speaking students – and has very little to do
with the French-language community. "Shanning Casimir was
actually receiving education for Anglophones," the judges wrote,
adding, "She has a stronger link with the English linguistic community than the French." So Shanning Casimir – and Michael
Parasiuk's son – were allowed to go to immersion school, on the

basis of both the Charter of Rights and Freedoms and the Charter of the French Language. At the same time, the court threw out the attempt by English-rights lawyer Brent Tyler to strike down the restrictions that prevented francophones from attending English schools. Tyler argued that the Charter of the French Language is discriminatory and contrary to the Charter of Rights and Freedoms. In the Gosselin case, issued the same day as the Casimir decision in March 2005, the Supreme Court issued a clear and unanimous decision. The practical effect of Tyler's appeal would be "to read out of the Constitution the carefully crafted compromise contained in s. 23 of the Charter of Rights and Freedoms. This would be impermissible." The carefully constructed arrangement establishing who had a right to minority language education in the Charter – which amended but did not strike down the restrictions on the Charter of Rights and Freedoms – was upheld. Common sense – and a finely honed respect for the intentions of the Quebec language law – prevailed, ending two of a number of lengthy fights.

Despite these occasional flashpoints, the word *equilibrium* kept recurring when French-speaking and English-speaking Montrealers talked about the language law on its twenty-fifth anniversary. "It was a revolutionary change," Goldbloom observed. "Like all revolutions, it went too far and has swung back to an equilibrium." Marcel Côté of the consulting firm SECOR said that the law propelled two already established trends. "It contributed to the establishment of French as a normal language – which would have happened – and it amplified the departure of Anglophones, who no longer felt at home."

Just as important, it favoured the integration of immigrants into the French-speaking majority rather than the English-speaking minority. According to Statistics Canada, 68 per cent of the non-French, non-English-speaking immigrants who came to Quebec before 1971 adopted English rather than French. For immigrants who came to Quebec between 1996 and 2001, however, those figures reversed: 73 per cent adopted French and 27 per cent adopted English. The result has been a dulling of the sharp edge of linguistic tension. "It is simply part of the statutes," Côté observed. "You don't see much discussion about it now. There is an equilibrium."

Some argue that the equilibrium has come at great cost and considerable injustice, and represents grudging acceptance or resignation by the English-speaking minority rather than support.

Nevertheless, a massive poll conducted in 2000 by the public opinion firm CROP of English-speaking Quebeckers found support for the Quebec language law – at least in principle. Half of those questioned agreed that it was important for the Quebec government to maintain laws to protect French. "'Made peace' is probably not the right expression, but there is a kind of accommodation that has taken place," observed Sarah Saber-Friedman of the Missisquoi Institute, which commissioned the study.

A kind of mutual tolerance had developed. In 2002, when violent storms in Montreal forced the cancellation of the Fête Nationale parade on June 24, the organizers of the Canada Day festivities offered a chance to participate in their July 1 parade. Guy Bouthillier, the president of the Société St-Jean-Baptiste, politely declined. It would involve a conflict in patriotisms, he said, adding that besides, two-thirds of the technical staff that had been booked for June 24 were also committed for the July 1 celebrations. Nobody underlined the significance of this at the time, but I was struck by it. In Montreal, ground zero of Canada's most historic, defining tension, most of the lighting, sound, and craft technicians engaged for the high point of Quebec nationalism were also booked, a week later, for the celebration of Canadian federalism. Not bad. As I watched the television footage of terrified Belfast children going to school through a hail of stones and curses two months later, I kept thinking about it. Canadians so take the health and ease of their intercultural and political relations for granted that no one noticed.

Not all francophones are comfortable with the renewed presence of anglophones in downtown Montreal. A friend was taken aback when a francophone filmmaker complained when the hip cinema Ex-Centris started showing films with English subtitles, saying that THEY have their own theatres where they can see their own films; this neighbourhood, and this cinema was OURS.

However, the policy dimensions of the language debate have shifted. In the spring of 2005, le Conseil supérieur de la langue française published a thick collection of essays, *Le Français au Québec: Les Nouveaux Défis*, which struck a very different tone from previous pronouncements on language. The challenge, as defined by the book's authors, involved capitalizing on Quebec's primary asset: not simply bilingualism, but trilingualism. Quebec, and in particular Montreal, were the most trilingual societies in North America, with some 50 per cent of allophones (those whose mother tongue is neither French nor English) being not merely bilingual but trilingual. "The day we drop this attitude of being 'threatened' linguistically, we will have reached the final stage of our process of collective self-confidence," wrote Christine Fréchette. "We should adopt a more serene approach in our relationships with English, and a more proactive strategy of development and promotion of Quebec's linguistic assets in the context of globalization."

In that new context, despite the cloud of a possible referendum in the future, which is likely to lead to a further acceleration of the Anglo exodus, thousands of English-speaking Montrealers have decided to stay, to remain part of what Martha Radice concluded is a comfortable minority. They like the sense of community, the diversity, the tolerant attitudes, and cosmopolitan qualities of the city. But, she found, there are limits to that sense of comfort. When politics intrudes, anxieties increase and the city is no longer as comfortable. People think and talk about leaving. "Feeling comfortable in Montreal is under continual renegotiation."

Fair enough. But that comfort level is very different from what Monica Heller observed and Soma Day recounted in the late 1970s. Université de Montréal sociolinguist Patricia Lamarre has observed a transformation of language skills in Montreal's West Island, historically English-speaking. She described how for the last few years, she has enjoyed shopping there, and switching from English to French with the young service personnel.

"After the 'hello, *bonjour*,' which is standard and announces a desire to serve clients in the language of their choice, they wait for my reply to determine the language of the interaction," she wrote in an essay published in 2005. "And voilà, the game begins. I cruise from one language to the other to see what they will do . . . and they follow me, without raising an eyebrow and without hesitation. Sometimes, I end up identifying their first language, and other times I remain ambivalent. Some quickly understand my game and when I ask them, laughing, 'OK, what is your first language?' they reply by laughing and saying with a certain satisfaction, 'If you can't tell, I'm not going to tell you.'" These, she writes, are the children of mixed marriages and immersion schools; one-way bilingualism is a thing of the past, and the level of bilingualism among Quebec anglophones between fifteen and twenty-four reached more than 80 per cent by 1996.

Some of the departures, paradoxically, have been related to the increasing bilingualism of the Montreal English-speaking community. Those who graduate from university with a working knowledge of French find that they are competing with fellow graduates whose first language is French, and who are thus more effective in a French-speaking environment. In Ottawa, working for the federal government, the relative bilingualism of the Montreal Anglos gives them a competitive advantage they do not have in Montreal. So, like other bilingual members of Canada's linguistic minorities – Acadians, Franco-Ontarians, Franco-Manitobans, and Fransaskois – they are drawn to the nation's capital.

Talking about Montreal, consultant Marcel Côté argues that French and English live in different bubbles – not solitudes, because there is now much better communication between the two communities – but bubbles. This linguistic insulation, he argues, has limited Montreal's potential as a business, deal-making centre – but dramatically increased its standing as a creative and pro-duction centre. The fact that many francophones are reluctant to leave Quebec was once seen as an economic liability; now, with an increasingly educated, high-tech workforce, that reflex means a lower rate of turnover for high-tech employers. Côté sees a com-plexity that the rest of Canada does not understand, adding, "We have to learn how to live with these linguistic cultural dualities."

But there are limitations to the new connections between French and English in Montreal. Côté observed, "I am bilingual, and my English is pretty good – but 95 per cent of my friends are francophone. [My colleague] in the next office to mine is bilin-gual, and his French is pretty good, but 95 per cent of his friends are anglophone." If this is true in Montreal, it is even more the case in Ottawa.

chapter seven

The Federal
Capital – and
David Levine's
Ottawa

Can ye not discern the signs of the times?

MATTHEW, 16:3

Every day, there is a noisy procession that is as symbolic, in its own way, as the formal march that the Speaker takes along the main corridor of Parliament to open each day's sitting of the House of Commons. A great line of blue buses queues up along Wellington Street during rush hour, and lines of passengers, many of them carrying the French-language paper *Le Droit,* step on to be taken across the river to the French-speaking suburbs in Gatineau. Two and three blocks south, on Albert and Slater streets, even longer lines of red buses pick up crowds of passengers, many of them carrying the

English-language newspapers *The Citizen* or the *Ottawa Sun*. The daily rush-hour ritual suggests that Ottawa is as segregated along language lines as Washington is segregated along racial lines – where commuters on the south side of the platform at the Metro Centre metro station headed southeast are largely black, while the commuters on the north side, headed northwest, are overwhelmingly white. It is not an entirely fair image, as some of the Ottawa suburbs have become increasingly French-speaking, but it is a suggestive one. In Montreal, Marcel Côté says, colleagues get along in one or the other of the official languages, or switch back and forth; friendships, however, generally occur in the mother tongue. Similarly, there is very little bilingual social life in Ottawa; francophones and anglophones rarely meet socially – except at office parties, official receptions, or at French Embassy events.

In 1970, the Royal Commission on Bilingualism and Biculturalism published its fifth report on the federal capital, which included the eloquent statement that a capital is a symbol of the country. "It should express, in the best way possible, the values of the country as a whole, its way of life, its cultural richness and diversity, its social outlook, its aspirations for the future," the commissioners wrote. "A capital should serve as a meeting place where persons of different languages and from different parts of Canada may, in a very general sense, live and work together." How does Ottawa meet that test, thirty-six years later?

Signs, as any semiotician will tell you and as Camille Laurin understood, matter. They are the public face and voice of a city, the presentation of self, the visual representation of the character, class, style, language, ethnicity, and discourse of an urban community. Standing in front of the War Memorial in Confederation Square in Ottawa in the spring of 2005, it was possible to think that Ottawa is not only bilingual, but playfully so. Looking to the southeast, there was a large sign on the National Arts Centre saying ORCHESTR followed by a maple leaf. Above the sign, it reads

National Arts Centre . . . and below, Centre national des arts. The maple leaf served triple duty – as a national symbol, as an a (for the English word *orchestra*), and as an e (for the French word *orchestre*).

Unfortunately, this linguistic flourish is almost unique in Ottawa's visual landscape. In most cases, bilingual signs in Ottawa are a requirement for federal buildings, and relentlessly uniform, or are an indication of Franco-Ontarian ownership – a notification that French is a private code that can be used on the premises. Walking on the streets of Ottawa, shopping in its stores, eating in its restaurants, or dealing with its public institutions, one hears French often. But Ottawa's streetscape, its visual environment, its commercial face, is overwhelmingly English Only.

Imagine, for a minute, that you are one of the almost 4 million unilingual French-speakers in Quebec. You are part of a signifi-cant group; if unilingual French-speaking Quebeckers constituted a province, it would be the second-largest in Canada after Ontario – as large as British Columbia (3.9 million), larger than the rest of Quebec (3 million), Alberta (2.9 million), all of the Atlantic provinces together (2.5 million), Manitoba (1.1 million), and Saskatchewan (978,000). You live off the island of Montreal, which means that you live in a part of Quebec where only a small minor-ity of the population speaks any English at all – in Quebec City or Saguenay or Trois-Rivières or Sherbrooke. You are a business person, a provincial or municipal public servant or a technician, a community college teacher or a farmer, a contractor or a factory worker. You are active in your community, you watch television, read books, go to movies, take courses – in French.

This is the group that Lamontagne and Laurendeau were thinking of when they considered the importance of a bilingual federal government, and when Trudeau talked about collabora-tion at the hub of a pluralistic state. What has changed since the 1960s is that in addition to the unilingual French-speakers there are now many francophone Quebeckers who can speak and read

English, but rarely use it: they work in French, watch television in French, read newspapers and books in French, and have little contact with a unilingual English environment.

Imagine that you go to Ottawa – to discuss a problem with your member of Parliament, to meet officials in a government department, as a delegate to a political convention, as a student or just as a tourist. Visiting Parliament is not a problem for you; there are now bilingual security guards, guides, and signs, and there is simultaneous translation for the debates in the House of Commons and the Senate, and the parliamentary committees. Visiting the National Gallery, the Canadian Museum of Civilization, the War Museum, the Museum of Science and Technology, the National Arts Centre, the Museum of Nature – none of that is a problem.

But walking south from Parliament Hill, crossing Wellington Street, the situation changes. At the corner of Metcalfe and Wellington, there is a small open square where the Rideau Club once stood until it was destroyed in a fire. Facing the street is a modern façade with a sign reading Capital Infocentre de la capitale, a tourist information centre operated by the National Capital Commission. On the right is a sign for the Parliamentary Pub. Farther south, on the east side of Metcalfe, is the New Windsor Cigar store and O'Shea's Market Ireland at the corner of the Sparks Street Mall. Opposite O'Shea's is Canada's Four Corners, with signs advertising Canadian Handicrafts and Canadian Souvenirs. Heading east on the Sparks Street Mall, the signs read O'Shea's Celtic Shop, Château Fine Pastry and – at the entrance to the building where the Privy Council Offices are – Édifice Blackburn Building, with Édifice in a different typeface, obviously an afterthought. Beside that, The Snow Goose, Canadian Crafts, Barristers Restaurant, Doxon Jewellers, Patrick McGahern Books and The Astrolabe Gallery, La Mode Hair Studio and Day Spa, Sparks Sports – with "sports souvenir cadeaux" underneath – I.C.L. Language Institute, Federal Government Levels A-B-C, Institut canadien des langues, CS Co-op, and the Post Office. The words *Post Office* are carved into the wall; underneath, on the bronze door frame, *Ministère des Postes.*

All of these buildings are owned by the federal government; all the businesses are tenants of the federal government. The buildings along the Sparks Street Mall are owned by Public Works and Government Services Canada and, as the Royal Commission recommended in 1970 should be done, most of the leases specify bilingual service and bilingual signage. Yet there is little in any of the windows to suggest that these storefronts are any different from those in, say, Victoria, Edmonton, Winnipeg, or Toronto. With a few exceptions, menus are in English only. There is barely a visual clue for a tourist or visitor that this is a capital that welcomes French-speaking visitors, the capital of a country that defines itself as officially bilingual.

At times, this negligence seems almost wilful. Ottawa announced in the spring of 2005 that it was going to ramp up a campaign to attract tourists, starting with Toronto – a five-hour drive away. Montreal, a two-hour drive away, is for later. And yet, according to the Ottawa Tourism and Convention Authority, in 2001, Ottawa received an estimated 1.5 million French-speaking visitors, and in addition, a share of the 200,000 French-speaking visitors who came to Ontario – spending an estimated $270 million in Ottawa. The numbers are on the increase – from 1997–99, a study for the Ontario government estimated that 1.1 million Quebeckers visited Ontario, and spent at least one night there. But you wouldn't know their money was welcome by walking the streets of downtown Ottawa.

Christina Spencer, who surveyed the state of commercial bilingualism for *Ottawa City* magazine in 2003, found a series of excuses from service people. "Joan Colbourn works behind the counter at The Astrolabe Gallery, which sells maps and prints. She once lived in France but doesn't use the language now," Spencer wrote. "'Most people who come in have a smattering of English . . . people will persevere because they have no choice.'" So Jacques Legendre, an Ottawa city councillor, no longer bothers attempting to be served in French. "Success is so infrequent, you stop even trying." In fact, one of the paradoxes in Ottawa is the substantial number of stores in Ottawa that are owned and operated by francophones that give little or no indication in their signage that French is, in fact, the language of work behind the counter. (There are some honourable exceptions to this, like Letellier, a shoe store that is very visibly bilingual, and Lapointe, a fish store.) This is a relic of the traditional reticence of Franco-Ontarian society, which used French as a private ethnic code rather than as a public language.

Dalhousie Street and Murray Street, a ten-minute walk north-east of Confederation Square, can be considered as close to the heart of what remains of Ottawa's original French quarter, on the edge of the ByWard Market, not far from Notre Dame Cathedral, De la Salle school, and the Élizabeth Bruyère health centre, all institutions with an important history in the franco-phone Ottawa community. There are some indications that this is a historically French-language neighbourhood. Just to the east is a municipal parking garage, with all the signs carefully identical in French and English. Across the street, and a hundred metres farther east, there is a historical plaque marking the site of L'École Guigues, now a day recreation centre for the elderly. The plaque tells a story of the ancient fight around French in Ottawa. The school was the centre of resistance to Regulation 17, the directive issued by the Ontario government in 1912 forbidding the use of French in the classroom past elementary school. In the course of the resistance by the Ottawa separate school board, the board closed down the school and the Ontario government withheld funds, dismissed the elected board, and imposed a commission. The disenfranchised board fought back and regained control of the school in 1916. Finally, in 1927, fifteen years after Regulation 17, the Ontario government recognized bilingual schools.

Here and there on Dalhousie, Murray, St. Patrick, St. Andrew, Guigues, and Bruyère streets – streets near the ByWard Market – it is possible to see occasional hints of bilingualism. On closer examination, they are almost always commercial establishments run by Franco-Ontarians: Brisson, the original pharmacist; Lapointe, the fishmonger; Letellier, the shoe-store owner. There are Franco-Ontarian professionals who announce themselves in both languages: Financial consultant/Conseiller financier Jean-Paul Bélanger and Richard G.J. Chatelain, avocat-notaire/lawyer-notary on St. Patrick Street, across the road from Éditions Vermillon; Antoine Taillefer, Designer/Couturier. But these are mere hints in a visual landscape of English signs: The Design Place, Royal Thai, Chinese Treasures, The Swarma Place, Laundromat, Cleaners, Mellos Restaurant. This is the core of what was once a thriving French-Canadian community – and bilingualism is almost entirely restricted to Franco-Ontarian businesses. There has been an attempt to address this – in 2001, the federal government reached an agreement with the city to provide $2.5 million over five years to help translation, language training, and business assistance – which produced a Business Assistance Plan to help small businesses provide services in both languages, particularly in the ByWard Market. By 2004, a study showed some improvement, but there is still less visible French here than there is visible Chinese in Toronto's Chinatown, or Italian in Little Italy.

The semiotics are clear. English is the language of commerce in an English-speaking city; French is visible only when the proprietor is French-speaking, or the service is, in fact, being offered by the federal government. And this reflects a certain commercial reality. An ambassador from a French-speaking country told me that he quickly learned not to start a conversation in French with a salesperson in Ottawa because it quickly became embarrassing. The embarrassment has even proven to be international: during his visit to Ottawa in May 2003, then French prime minister Jean-Pierre Raffarin publicly expressed the wish that Ottawa be some day declared a bilingual city.

"On a daily basis, when we work in Ottawa, we are in a minority," explained mathematician Charles Castonguay of l'Université d'Ottawa, who has made a specialty of examining language statistics. "If you affirm your Frenchness too much, you are looked at severely. So you adopt the behaviour of Franco-Ontarians, the policy of *bonne entente*, so as not to annoy the English. This is full bilingualism, experienced as a sublimation of assimilation."

Symbols matter in a capital. One of the many extraordinary things about Washington as a capital city is that it lays out, in graphic physical form, the history of the country. The Washington Monument and the Jefferson Memorial project the founding myth; the Lincoln Memorial and the Vietnam Memorial mark two of the national tragedies. A visitor to Washington, whether a student, a tourist, a foreign visitor, or a recent immigrant, can grasp the history of the country simply by walking around. And each monument functions on several levels: a purely symbolic level, and a more detailed intellectual level; each monument, for example, includes a bookstore with a range of material from guidebooks to academic studies and biographies. Ottawa does not play the same role for Canada. In fact, it sends a number of mixed messages as a capital city.

I was born in Ottawa, and lived there until I was fourteen, returning at the age of forty. The community I grew up in reflected some of those mixed messages about French. On the one hand, thanks to pressure from parents, the public school I attended introduced French in Grade 1, when we learned to count the paper tulips on the wall. Ottawa is now and was then a government town; I can remember one classmate being sent to a French-language boarding school in Montreal for a year, in 1957, because his parents thought it would be important for him to speak the language. But on the other hand, those people who actually spoke French in Ottawa were seen as remote, slightly foreign, even faintly hostile. For us, the kids who lived in Eastview, a French-speaking municipality in Ottawa, were "the Frenchies": they were seen as rough, tough, scary. Michael Ignatieff, who spent his childhood in the same neighbourhood as I did, recalled our fears in his book *Blood and Belonging*: "They were tough Catholic kids and they had slingshots. . . . Everyone at school knew that they pulled kids off their bikes and rode away on their wheels. They were bad kids, it was common knowledge."

Eastview — which became Vanier and has now been absorbed in the new City of Ottawa — was not the only French-Canadian community in Ottawa. Lowertown, which stretched from the Rideau River to the ByWard Market (since cleared for urban renewal) and Sandy Hill were like French-Canadian villages, tucked into the fabric of an English-speaking Ontario city. Remnants can be seen today: small brick houses within walking distance of the parish church, or medical service centres that were once hospitals run by nuns, their distinctive stone walls making them look like convents.

Parliament was an important employer for Franco-Ontarians, and many of the service jobs on Parliament Hill — the cafeteria and restaurant jobs, the clerks and security guards, the support personnel — have been held by Franco-Ontarians. (Don Boudria, the former minister, began his career in Parliament as a busboy in the parliamentary restaurant.) But Ottawa was also a refuge for Quebec intellectuals who felt unwelcome in the province's universities if they were not practising Catholics. In his novel *L'Écureuil noir*, Daniel Poliquin — himself a translator and parliamentary interpreter – refers to "those Quebec intellectuals of the last century who fled their ultramontane and intolerant country by becoming Parliamentary translators, becoming anonymous inhabitants of a town where no one asked them if they went to mass on Sunday, free to read forbidden writers." This phenomenon continued well into the twentieth century. In the late 1940s, when Pierre Trudeau and Marcel Rioux were both working in Ottawa for the federal government, they would refer to potentially sympathetic fellow French Canadians as "Greeks" in conversation, for fear of being overheard. And in 1954, as previously recounted, Maurice Lamontagne left Laval University when his book on federalism was disavowed by the rector of the university because Duplessis didn't like it – and came to Ottawa to become a public servant.

In their look at Ottawa in the 1960s, the Royal Commission on Bilingualism and Biculturalism received a considerable amount of testimony, as they put it, "that the language and culture of English-speaking Canada predominate there; that a Francophone resident or visitor from Quebec cannot feel 'at home' there; that the federal capital is like a foreign territory to a substantial sector of the Canadian population." The briefs they received listed off several examples to illustrate this: the refusal of Ottawa City Council to permit traffic signs in French, the predominance of English signs on federal public buildings; the difficulties of obtaining service in French in the shops; and the obstacles to testifying in French in local courts. Some of these realities were underlined in 1969, when the government introduced the Official Languages Act; that day, several Créditiste MPs had been stopped by an Ottawa police officer unable to explain in French what they had done and why he was stopping them.

At an institutional level, much has changed since the 1960s. Ottawa's street signs are now bilingual, the Ontario government's French Language Services Act – Bill 8 – introduced in 1988, has provided French-language services where numbers warrant, so that driver's licences and health cards are in English and French, and can be obtained and renewed in both languages. The federal public service has, by and large, succeeded in delivering services to Canadians in both official languages. But there is also a silent recognition of the fact that the language of signs is perceived, not as a matter of marketing to potential customers or welcoming fellow citizens to the capital of their country, but as an issue of power. Any move to increase the visibility of French in Ottawa is greeted with reactions ranging from suspicion to outrage.

For unilingual francophones, coming to Ottawa is a shock. "I have had students come here from Chicoutimi, and they are stunned. They feel as if they are in a foreign country," Linda Cardinal, a political scientist at the Université d'Ottawa told me. "When they go home, they go to work for the Bloc. Or, if they stay here, they volunteer for francophone organizations." For there is little consensus among the people who live in the capital about sustaining an active bilingual character to the city. "There is a healthy level of discord among the people who live here and share the space," observed Graham Fox, who grew up in Ottawa, the son of an English-speaking father and a French-speaking mother. "The workable peace is workable, but still fragile."

Sometimes the friction leads to bursts of anger that can be correlated to events on the national stage. In 1989–90, in the months that led up to the collapse of the Meech Lake Accord, there was a dramatic increase in overt anti-French remarks and gestures in Ottawa. Living in Ottawa at the time and writing about the tensions that were growing through the last months of Meech, I began to collect anecdotes that suggested that the tensions were not simply between governments and political leaders, but were being translated into incidents on the street. A well-dressed woman emerged from Holt Renfrew in a shopping concourse in downtown Ottawa, a stone's throw from Parliament Hill. A fran-cophone woman was walking by and inadvertently bumped into her. "*Pardon*," she said in French. The well-dressed woman turned and snarled, "Frog bitch!" A bus driver on Ottawa's No. 1 bus, which then went from downtown to Rockcliffe Park, an affluent, leafy neighbourhood of embassies, large stone houses, and elegant gardens, said in a strong French-Canadian accent, "Please move to the rear of the bus." Another passenger said loudly and sarcastically, "Yes, move to the back and make room for French Canadians!" Public servants and political aides noticed that, when staff took phone calls from the public on politically controversial issues like Via Rail cuts and the Goods and Services Tax, a noticeable French accent provoked additional abuse.

This was during the period when the Bourassa government used the notwithstanding clause in the Constitution to suspend Charter rights in order to postpone any permission for English signs, the period when angry Anglo rights activists in Brockville trampled on a Quebec flag, and when, in response to Ontario's Bill 8, the French-language Services Act, a number of Ontario municipalities, in particular Sault Ste. Marie, declared themselves to be English-only. They could be countered by incidents in Quebec: francophone students in Rock Forest chanting, "Go home! Go home" in English when their team fell behind in a game with an English school, and vandalism and graffiti on an English church.

Sadly, this pattern of bitter response in the context of the larger tensions stimulated by the debate over Meech Lake and Bourassa's use of the notwithstanding clause was the same as what occurred in Canada a century earlier, in the 1880s and 1890s, when a similarly negative escalation took place. First, the hanging of Louis Riel in 1885 began a cycle of anger and resentment, and more outspoken nationalism in Quebec, which provoked anti-French responses in other provinces. Then, when the Jesuit Estates Bill was passed in Quebec in 1888, it led to the creation of the Equal Rights Association in Manitoba, which successfully lobbied for the elimination of French and Catholic schools.

Meech Lake died in June 1990, support for Quebec independence soared, and the federal and Quebec governments became entangled in ultimately fruitless efforts to rescue some form of constitutional amendment. Every so often linguistic flashpoints occurred in Ontario, and in Ottawa. When the Ontario government moved to introduce bilingual highway signs, 116,000 people signed petitions in protest. Clearly, a solid base of resistance to – and resentment of – the public presence of French remained, regardless of the political tensions. When Ottawa's streetscape is resolutely unilingual in English, no one seems to find it unusual or inappropriate. But if anyone other than a restaurant owner slips in the other direction, the reaction can be virulent.

In the fall of 1997, Tasc Management Inc. of Montreal bought the Ottawa bus station from Voyageur Bus. In the spring of 1998, Tasc embarked on a renovation of the station, and put up a sign reading "Station Centrale." "Does this unilingual francophone sign bug me, as an anglophone?" wrote Earl McRae, an outspoken columnist in the *Ottawa Sun*. "Damn right it bugs me. And it should bug you, too, if you're an anglophone with an ounce of common sense. Does it make you a bigoted, braying, brain-dead, anti-francophone redneck to be bugged by this unilingual francophone sign on the outside of the Ottawa bus terminal? No, it sure as hell doesn't."

Perhaps not. On the other hand, it might make you just a bit more sensitive to the sense of exclusion that francophones feel in an Ottawa where bilingualism is restricted to federal buildings and street signs. (The Ontario Press Council found that McRae's comments on September 24, 2000, "stray beyond what constitutes acceptable discourse" when he attacked federal funding of the Francophone Games, by calling them the Frankenweenie Games attracting athletes from "francophoney countries around the planet." McRae told me he had thought it was "simply over-the-top, black humour" but then added, "Reading it again from the distance of four and a half years, I guess it is pretty rough and unsophisticated humour. But there was certainly no racist motivation on my part.")

In May 2001, a city committee held a meeting to discuss the bilingualism policy of the former City of Ottawa, prior to its expansion through amalgamation. The comments of the members of the public were revealing: "The objective [of the bilingualism policy] is to replace our anglophone majority with our francophone minority in all positions of power and influence," said one. "English gave Canada democracy, the common law, the legal system, education, choices to live as we wished and freedom of speech," said another. Others commented, "French gave Canada large families with many children" and "[The policy] is the antithesis of British democracy and something that is practised by totalitarian societies that have a supreme contempt for the citizenry."

In the spring of 2003, Senator Jean-Robert Gauthier discovered that he could not even get French on a menu at restaurants that leased their space from the federal government. Frustrated after decades of complaints, he called for an amendment to the Constitution to make the capital officially bilingual. *Ottawa Citizen* columnist Ron Corbett was beside himself. "Maybe what the city does on this issue is – what's the phrase I'm looking for here; it's right on the tip of my tongue; oh right – none of his business," he sneered. "Mr. Gauthier's sense of entitlement is so profound it wafts around him like Paris cologne, and one day – after he has finished changing the Constitution, made every menu in Ottawa bilingual, taken Air Canada down a notch or two, he may well decide what Canada needs is a new Canada." Corbett's visceral reaction spooked the city's officials; the Business Assistance Program was thrown on the defensive, and one employee told me that the senior officials were suddenly much more concerned about attacks from the critics of bilingualism than about helping businesses to serve French-speaking residents and customers in French.

(Gauthier did succeed in a significant change in minority language rights. In November 2005, Liberal MP Don Boudria succeeded in getting Gauthier's bill, S-3, through Parliament. The bill amended the Official Languages Act and makes the federal government's obligation to promote minority language communities enforceable in the courts. It was the last political act for both men; Gauthier had already left the Senate and Boudria had announced he would not run for re-election.)

On January 10, 2005, the rural municipality of Clarence-Rockland, east of Ottawa, which is majority French-speaking, passed a municipal bylaw requiring new businesses to post signs that give equal prominence to French and English. Not French only, not French predominance – but equal prominence to both. The reaction of the *Ottawa Citizen* was to make this a banner six-column headline across the front page: "Our French Revolution." It is hard to imagine a more graphic metaphor for the sensitivities of the English-speaking majority in Ottawa, which is encouraged by its local English-language newspapers to see bilingualism, even when restricted to signs, as a revolutionary threat to the established order of things.

One of the ironies of the application of federal-language policy has been that former Montrealers have been both the most supportive – and the most resistant. It was a commonplace observation that the constituency that most strongly supported Pierre Trudeau's political ideas was English Montreal. As English Montrealers became more bilingual, many were drawn to the federal government in Ottawa. But, at the same time, as the language of work requirements of Quebec's Charter of the French Language began to take effect, many of those who felt uncomfortable, and left, moved to the Ottawa area. Thus, paradoxically, Quebec's success in transforming Montreal into a city that functions in French has made it difficult for Ottawa to be effectively bilingual – because many of the anglophones who were unable or unwilling to learn French and adapt to a French-speaking working environment moved to Ottawa, and were horrified at the prospect of seeing Ottawa's institutions become bilingual.

The perfect example of this dual migration occurred after the creation of the new Ottawa Hospital from the merger of the Ottawa Civic (traditionally an English-language hospital) and the Ottawa General (created by a French-speaking religious order, and a functionally bilingual hospital) into a single institution. As part of the merger, required by a commission established by the Harris government, it was stipulated that the new hospital president should be comfortable in both languages. That stipulation automatically shrank the number of possible candidates, and when the selection committee chose a bilingual Montreal hospital administrator named David Levine, the decision revealed a vein of nasty, deep-seated fear and hatred in the community.

David Levine was a professional hospital administrator. For ten years, he had been the head of the Verdun Hospital, and from 1992 until 1997, he had been the director-general of the Notre Dame Hospital in Montreal. He had served a term as president of the Canadian Association of Teaching Hospitals. He also had political experience. As a young man, he had worked on the staff of Bernard Landry, then Quebec's Minister of State for Economic Development and became a good friend of his. He ran as a Parti Québécois candidate in 1979, and worked for the Yes campaign during the 1980 referendum. When Levine lost his job at the Notre Dame Hospital after the hospital was amalgamated, he was appointed as Quebec's delegate-general in New York.

On May 1, 1998, the *Citizen* reported that Levine had been selected to head the new Ottawa hospital in a front-page story that began, "A former political candidate for the Parti Québécois is poised to become the president of the new amalgamated Ottawa

Hospital." That story was the beginning of a saga that led to wild public meetings where citizens shouted down hospital board members, heated radio phone-in shows, and even picketing of the homes and boycotts of the businesses of members of the board who had chosen Levine and stuck by their decision. Levine was attacked as "a traitor" and "an enemy" in letters to the editor, and there were dire predictions about the fate of English-speaking patients. "How soon can we expect qualified anglophone staff to be replaced by less qualified francophone staff?" asked George Potter in a letter to the newspaper. "And how much of the overall service will be in French for the majority anglophone patients?"

The incident led to demagoguery by provincial and local politicians, inflammatory rhetoric by columnists and radio hosts, and an outpouring of bitter anger and resentment: of Quebec, of French, of separatism, of Levine, of bilingualism. It was an astonishing hint of the emotions that would be seen if Quebec ever did vote in favour of sovereignty, and of the hostility and fears that clearly lie not far beneath the surface in Ottawa. As Carleton philosophy professor Randal Marlin put it in his book *The David Levine Affair: Separatist Betrayal or McCarthyism North*, the Levine appointment hit a series of sensitive subjects in Ottawa: separatism, bilingualism, resentment over the fee differentials between Quebec and Ontario, concern that acceptance of Levine despite his political connections would imply acceptance of an independent Quebec, and fears about the erosion of medical care in the region and in the province.

In March 1997, some ten thousand Franco-Ontarians had filled an arena – what was described as the largest rally in their history – as part of an ultimately successful mobilization to save the only French-language teaching hospital in Ontario, Montfort. The combination of the merger of the Civic Hospital, traditionally English, and the traditionally bilingual Ottawa General, the implication that bilingual service would be required throughout the new hospital, and the fight to save Montfort all fuelled fears among unilingual anglophone hospital staff that language requirements would be imposed.

But that underlying concern – expressed most vehemently at one of the public meetings and in letters to the editor by some anglophones who had left Montreal for Ottawa because of the language requirements in Quebec – burst out in expressions of hatred and rage. On May 19, at one meeting, people chanted, "Resign!" and "Shame on you!"; Ottawa Liberal MP Mauril Bélanger (who, ironically, was one of the organizers of the pro-federalist rally in Montreal before the 1995 referendum) was denounced as a separatist when he told the crowd that it would be discriminatory to dismiss anyone because of their political beliefs. The meeting itself was a shock for many people in Ottawa. "Had it been in the 1890s, people would have been lynched," observed a shaken board member, Pierre de Blois. *Citizen* columnist Janice Kennedy said that a "howling mob of self-proclaimed patriots . . . took over a meeting intended to answer questions about the controversial hiring of David Levine." Later, Intergovernmental Affairs Minister Stéphane Dion called the conduct of the crowd "inexcusable," adding, "This is the type of intolerance which must be put to an end. Mr. Levine is the best candidate, so he should manage the hospital."

Some of the more rabble-rousing commentators were unrepentant. In the *Sun*, Earl McRae urged his readers to keep the heat on – and called for a boycott of Bell Canada, pointing out that the chairman of the hospital board, Nick Mulder, was the president and CEO of Stentor Telecom Policy, a lobbying arm of Bell Canada. But other critics of Levine's appointment were shocked by the rage and hatred they had witnessed. There was a noticeable shift in tone in the public comments, and some of the commentary in the *Citizen* took an abrupt shift. The board stuck to its guns, Levine kept his job, and began work on the problem that was much more difficult than language: the hospital's massive deficit.

W. Anton Hart, publisher of *Healthcare Quarterly*, noted approvingly that Levine chose a unilingual anglophone as his chief of staff. "Rather than impose bilingualism he obtained agreement from board and staff that its reality can only be achieved in the context of the hospital's noble cause: excellent patient care," Hart wrote in the winter 1998 issue of his magazine. "He says this approach has worked well. In effect, the priority of bilingualism is measured in terms of its contribution to the hospital's ability to deliver its services. This has de-politicized the issue and put the policy in the proper perspective."

Ironically, Levine's term as president came to an end, not because of the language issue but because of the hospital's deficit – which, according to some at the hospital, was inevitable because of the low level of provincial funding at the time. In 2001, the Ontario government dissolved the board and imposed a new management on the hospital; Levine was asked to stay on, but left in October 2001 when he felt the terms of the agreement were not being respected. Then, some of those who had supported Levine felt a sense of betrayal when he was named to Bernard Landry's cabinet – and ran in a by-election for the Parti Québécois in 2002, where he was defeated.

Four years later, Levine – a natural enthusiast, now the president and CEO of the Montreal health authority, named by the PQ and kept on by the Quebec Liberals – looked back on his Ottawa experience as a very positive one. "I loved the experience," he told me. "I wanted to merge a hospital – I had left the delegate-general job in New York with a house, a chauffeur, and a chef, my wife and kids thought I was crazy – and I enjoyed it greatly."

In fact, he found that the initial controversy had a bonding effect. "There was a kind of rallying around; it allowed me to get some things done, like saving the Riverside as an ambulatory centre. I got a lot of support inside; it almost caused the whole organization to coalesce more than would have happened otherwise."

But the controversy left the community feeling as if it had lived through a bitter family squabble, ruefully aware of how deeply ingrained its hostilities and tensions were below the surface of an apparently placid government town. The incident was also proof that, fundamentally, Ottawa had not changed a great deal as a result of language legislation.

Various attempts to make the City of Ottawa officially bilingual, despite pressures from the prime minister and the Commissioner of Official Languages, have met constant, unyielding resistance. Despite his election promise to make Ottawa bilingual, Ontario premier Dalton McGuinty introduced much weaker legislation that only obligated the new amalgamated city to respect the language regulations established twenty-five years before by the old City of Ottawa. Mauril Bélanger, now Minister Responsible for Official Languages, observed to me that he has found more resistance to French in Ottawa than anywhere else in the country. Certainly, the English-language newspapers are strident in their treatment of the language question. The reason is not surprising. Those in Ottawa who do not speak French usually do not see bilingual signs and services as an effective tourism marketing tool or part of the obligation that comes with being a capital city in exchange for the privileges of having more parks, galleries, theatres, and museums than a similarly sized city could afford, along with the presence of thousands of public servants who are well-paid, well-educated taxpaying citizens – but as a threat. For them, language services are seen as a zero-sum game; if French "wins," they lose.

One of the effects of this environment has been a high rate of anglicization of francophones in the City of Ottawa. Going through census material, Charles Castonguay concluded that in

1971, 27 per cent of the young adults between twenty and twenty-five who had French as their mother tongue had switched to speaking English most often at home. This pattern accelerated in the years that followed. The rate of anglicization moved steadily upward, from one census to the next: 15.6 per cent in 1971, 23 per cent in 1991, 24.7 per cent in 1996, and 27.4 per cent in 2001. And in the area that became the new City of Ottawa, the rate of anglicization of francophones almost doubled from 1971 to 2001, moving from 16.4 per cent to 30.5 per cent.

In an essay for the magazine *Inroads*, Castonguay describes what happened in Hull, the Quebec city (now renamed Gatineau) across the river from Ottawa that had its downtown core torn out by the invasion of federal office towers. Its gradual transformation into an English-speaking town halted abruptly with the introduction of Quebec's language law, which restricted access to English-language schools. Comparing the two communities on either side of the river, Castonguay points to the different results of the two different approaches to language. "The capital region can be seen as a testing ground for language policies aimed at protecting Canada's French-speaking minority – the federal linguistic free-trade approach versus Quebec's moderately territorial policy favouring French," he wrote. "Trends on either side of the river offer a small-scale model of language trends in Quebec compared to the rest of Canada." In contrast with the ballooning rate of assimilation that Castonguay found in Ottawa, French remained stable in Gatineau, with its assimilation rate dropping from a very low 1.7 per cent in 1971 to an even lower 0.1 per cent in 1996.

Castonguay summed up the situation this way: "A quarter century of Canadian bilingualism has not improved the picture regarding French in the capital one iota," and ended his essay by quoting the Royal Commissioners: "If the capital of a bilingual country is to command the respect and loyalty of its citizens of both official languages, it should not reflect the domination of one language over the other."

It is hard to challenge Castonguay's closing observation: "The only reasonable conclusion is that the Commissioners' recommendations on how to realize that goal have failed. It is time to rethink Canadian language policy."

chapter eight

Talking to
Ourselves

> Learning languages can show up people's
> craziness in dramatic ways.
>
> ALICE KAPLAN

For three days in April 2005, thirty-four high-school students
from across the country gathered in Ottawa for the eighth annual
"French for the Future/Français pour l'avenir" conference. It was
a project initiated by John Ralston Saul in 1998; as a writer who
had first caught international attention when he took the research
for his Ph.D. thesis and turned it into a political thriller that he
wrote in French, he had long been a believer in the importance
of bilingualism. Over the years, Saul became convinced that one of
the problems with immersion education is that the students do
not have any contact with other immersion students – or with
adults for whom speaking French has been an important part of
their personal or professional lives. He concluded that immersion
students in Canada get little encouragement, have little contact with
other French-speakers, and have little sense of how the language

skills they are acquiring connect with a larger Canadian world. So he decided that one way to make French real for these students, many of whom had been in immersion classes since they entered school, would be to organize an annual conference with a video link to conferences in other cities, in which immersion students could meet, talk, and hear from bilingual English Canadians about what French had meant to them. So, over the years, immersion students heard from people as varied as novelist Russell Smith, Major General Andrew Leslie, then journalist Michaëlle Jean, Justin Trudeau, columnist Paul Wells, and a number of other bilingual Canadians prepared to talk about the experience.

At the Ottawa conference in the spring of 2005, there were at least two students from every province and territory, with a wide diversity in background. Some had Scottish, English, or French surnames; others were from Middle Eastern, South Asian, Chinese, or African backgrounds. Some were geeky; others were jocks; some wore plain blouses or sweaters and sensible shoes; others wore tight T-shirts and spiked heels. The subject under discussion was whether or not Canada is a generous society – and some had clearly prepared and others had not. Some complained about taxation and argued that Canada should concentrate on problems at home before sending money abroad, while others argued that Canada is a rich country and does not give enough. The group – and the discussion – reflected the diversity of style, ethnicity, and opinion that now characterizes Canadian secondary schools. What the students had in common was that they were all from immersion programs, and all the discussions were in French.

The quality of French was as varied as the students were diverse. Some of the students had clearly spent time in Quebec, and reeled off colloquial expressions with ease but stumbled over more conventional words; one girl from Montreal, making the argument that tax money was wasted, said that road conditions in Quebec were "*dégeulasse*" (a word considered extremely vulgar in France, more commonly used in Quebec, meaning disgusting) – but had to be prompted for the French word for "recognition" (*reconnaissance*). Others rattled away fluently, but sounded more as if they were speaking English than French. And some made crude grammatical errors (*"J'ai allé"* instead of *"Je suis allé"*) or spoke in what might kindly be called syntax-free sentence fragments.

Invited to speak to some of the workshops, I came early to watch some of the discussions, curious about the quality of French that I would find. My previous experience with immersion, as a parent, had been mixed. During the seven years we lived in Quebec City, our older son had done all of his primary education in French, and when we moved to Ottawa he was appalled at the quality of French spoken by his classmates in immersion. I was a little taken aback myself when I discovered that, in high school, the book being studied for French literature was not a French novel (no Stendhal or Balzac) or even a Quebec novel (no Blais or Beauchemin) – but a novel written by a Sudbury writer. It occurred to me that possibly French immersion was being seen as much as a cultural support and job-creation program as it was regarded as an education system. However, in the years that have passed since my sons graduated from high school, I have been struck by the number of their former classmates who are now living in Montreal or Paris – or, having learned a third language, Berlin. Clearly, something worked.

What I observed at the "French for the Future" conference would have provided fodder for both the supporters and the critics of immersion French. These teenagers were poised, comfortable, and relatively articulate while engaging in a free-flowing discussion about generosity, charity, taxation, and foreign aid – in French. On the other hand, most of them had clearly learned their French from hearing other English-speaking students, and routinely made mistakes that no native French-speaker would ever make. It was a discussion that was sometimes naïve and sometimes shrewd and sophisticated – like many discussions of public

policy by teenagers – being carried on by English-Canadian students from across the country talking to each other in French. It
was fascinating, inspiring, and a little odd – revealing both the
strengths and the flaws of a particularly Canadian innovation in
second-language learning. That combination of fluency and inac-
curacy is no accident; it is part of the nature of Immersion French,
and is at the core of the academic debate that has continued since
the program was introduced.

The central idea behind immersion is that young people can
learn a second language at the same time as they are learning
an academic subject matter; that, at a relatively early age, they can
absorb both. This is a dramatic shift from the traditional classroom method of second-language teaching, which involves
teaching the grammar, structure, and vocabulary of the second
language as an academic subject – a method which, notoriously,
produced high-school graduates who could barely ask for
directions or listen to the television news, let alone carry on a
conversation, but could regurgitate large memorized sections of
French novels. (*Le Notaire du Hâvre* by Anatole France was the
novel assigned when I was in Grade 13, and I can remember learning whole pages by heart that I could reproduce in response to
relatively predictable questions; my French teacher managed
to pick 80 per cent of the questions on the exam, I memorized the
passages that represented the correct response, and got a mark of
80 per cent. My conversational ability was extremely limited; I
only learned French as a means of communication later on.)

René-Étienne Bellavance, an immersion teacher, professor of
immersion teaching techniques, and passionate supporter of French
immersion, was at the "French for the Future" conference, and
after the last meeting, chatted about his experience. He observed
that education operates through revolutions rather than evolution. "Today, the emphasis is on production, on communication,"
he said. "Students are being told 'Speak, you will learn by speaking.'"

In the past, it was the reverse: 'Learn the rules of grammar, and don't speak until you've got them right.'" He is very conscious of the fact that students are learning French in the company of other English-speaking students rather than through a genuine immersion among those whose mother tongue is French, and he works on strategies to teach teachers how to correct the typical mistakes that inevitably occur. But, regardless of its shortcomings, he remains an overwhelming enthusiast for immersion, and is only occasionally exasperated by what he sees as continuing public ignorance. "For thirty-five years, French immersion has been functioning in Canada, and for thirty-five years parents have been asking 'Will my child's ability to read and write English suffer?'" he said, citing studies that show that French immersion students actually do better in English than non-immersion students.

French immersion has been called "the most evaluated program in the history of Canadian education." It has been praised as "a quiet language revolution" and "the most successful language program ever recorded in the professional language teaching literature." Equally, it has been criticized for producing a patois of ungrammatical French: French words pinned together with English syntax. It grew from an experiment conducted by Wallace Lambert in 1965 in the South Shore Montreal community of St. Lambert. The experiment grew out of a series of informal meetings by English-speaking parents. As author Fred Genesee put it, "These parents felt that their lack of competence in French contributed to and indeed was attributable in part to the two solitudes which effectively prevented them from learning French informally from their French-speaking neighbours. Their inability to communicate in French, they felt, was also attributable to inadequate methods of second-language instruction in the English schools."

As Genesee pointed out, the goal that the parents had in mind was not just improved second-language teaching and acquisition. "Rather, it was intended to be an intermediate goal leading to improved relationships between English and French Quebecers and thus ultimately to a breaking down of the two solitudes." In Quebec, as was described in Chapter Five, it can be argued that this goal was, in fact, achieved. English-speaking Quebeckers are now one of the most bilingual groups in Canada – and French immersion played a significant role in achieving that. Yet it was very easy for immersion students in Quebec to communicate with native French-speakers, and to hear French spoken. This is not the case in the rest of Canada.

However, from the experimental beginnings in St. Lambert, French immersion soon spread across Canada. Parents would camp out overnight to sign up their children for immersion programs, and demand soon outstripped supply. In the mid-seventies, immersion was offered in three school districts in British Columbia to about 1,000 students; by 1987, thirty school districts were providing immersion French to almost 21,000 students. Across Canada, the trend was similar: by 1986, there were 177,824 students in immersion, an increase of 369 per cent since 1978. This was related in part to the enthusiasm with which parents from across Canada greeted immersion and in part to the dramatic increase in federal spending on second-language education; between 1970–71 and 1978–79, nearly one billion dollars was spent on bilingual education by the federal government, and more than two-thirds of that went to French immersion programs.

Immersion has not been without its critics. In a memorable article entitled "Speaking Immersion" published in the *Canadian Modern Language Review* in 1987, Roy Lyster wrote that when he started teaching Grade 8 in a French immersion program in 1982, he was surprised at the quality of French his students spoke after seven years, having expected them to have acquired native-like proficiency. "My students' ability to communicate almost any message they tried to express reassured me that French Immersion was indeed an effective means to develop students' communicative competence, especially when compared to results achieved through the regular Core French program which I also taught," he wrote. "Nonetheless, I had expected my immersion students to be able to communicate much more accurately. I consistently heard errors like *Je suis douze* and *Ça regarde bon* [literal translations of "I am twelve" and "That looks good," incomprehensible in French] and was very puzzled to hear students after eight years of French immersion say sentences like 'Sur samedi j'ai allé à le magasin avec mon mère' [a transliteration from the English of "On Saturday I went to the store with my mother," but with every element of the sentence grammatically incorrect in French]. I wondered if it was possible that no one had ever corrected them. However, after reviewing some basic material with my students, I realized that they still made the same errors anyway. No matter how often I tried to correct the errors, they seemed incorrigible. The immersion language had fossilized."

Part of the problem was that children were learning from each other, as well as the teacher. A friend remembers that her daughter spoke beautiful French in kindergarten and Grade 1, but by Grade 2 was speaking the flat Anglo-influenced patois of immersion. She observed to her daughter that she used to speak differently. "Oh, you mean like this?" she said, and spoke a sentence in the native speaker's accented French she had been speaking the year before. "Everyone thinks you're showing off if you talk like that."

The phrase "fossilized errors" entered the language of French immersion education. But the criticisms – later made even more strongly by Simon Fraser linguistics professor Hector Hammerly – had little impact. In 1989, André Obadia of Simon Fraser University predicted that if the increase continued at the current rate, there would be a million students in immersion by 1999. But that continued expansion did not happen; enrolment in immersion plateaued at about 300,000, where it has remained for several years.

In our conversation at the conclusion of the "French for the Future" conference, Bellavance pointed to an explosion of interest in immersion in Alberta over the last few years – and, at the same time, a stagnation in Ontario. He suggests a possible – and unconscious – political motive: parents were sending their children to immersion, he suspects, not because they were committed to the idea of their children learning French, but because they wanted to please Quebec. As they stopped wanting to do that, or felt that it was having little or no impact on the attitudes of Quebeckers toward the rest of the country, enrolment in immersion stopped increasing in Ontario, while in Alberta, there has been an increase in interest in second-language learning generally.

After watching the students in "French for the Future" perform, I went to Kingston – two hundred kilometres south of Ottawa – to get some sense of how immersion was working in an ordinary school. I chose Kingston for a number of reasons: it is not Ottawa, so students are less conscious of political or employment imperatives that might encourage them to study in French; and it is a university city, with two universities that pride themselves on producing national leaders: Queen's and the Royal Military College.

Kingston Collegiate Vocational Institute (KCVI) is the oldest high school in Ontario, founded in 1792; a red-brick building, it is tucked into the Queen's University campus in downtown Kingston. It has a strong academic tradition, a little over 1,000 students, and about 50 per cent of its Grade 9 students are in immersion. The way immersion works in secondary school in Ontario is that eight credits are required to get a bilingual certificate – and at KCVI, in addition to French literature, courses in geography, history, physical education, business and technology, and career civics are offered in French: about 10 per cent of the classes offered in the school.

The principal, Ian McFarlane, organized a meeting for me with two teachers, Jennifer Bailey and Christine Armstrong, and two fifteen-year-old Grade 10 students, Lauren de la Parra and Catherine Lukits, who had both been in immersion since kindergarten, and were both enthusiastic. "I like it; it's good, you learn a lot more," Lauren told me. "With English at home and French at school, you get different perspectives in the way you think." They had both gone to different public schools, but noticed some of the same characteristics: immersion attracted the smart kids, those that were less likely to get into trouble; their parents were better informed about what immersion meant and more involved in the school; there were some rivalries between the children in immersion and those in the English stream ("We were the Frenchies and they were the English muffins," recalled Catherine somewhat nostalgically). But they were aware of some problems; Lauren remembered when her school had trouble hiring immersion teachers. She was in a class of thirty-six one year, grades were put together, and classes were given in portables. They also confirmed that, as they advanced in school, boys were more likely to withdraw from immersion than girls. "There have always been more girls than boys in my classes," Catherine said, with a grin of exasperation.

"I really notice it in my Spanish class; boys are more embarrassed to be talking in Spanish in front of their friends," said Lauren. "In French, it's not so bad, because they've been doing it all their lives. It's a 'cool' thing" – meaning that sounding foolish in another language was not cool. She paused and added, "I don't want to sound sexist, but girls just tend to be better. Boys don't get the marks that they want."

Ian McFarlane interjected with a useful point. "The key decision points [concerning whether to continue in French immersion] are at the age of twelve and fourteen," he said. "There is no point in life when the gender differences are as great. If the key decision points were at age six and sixteen, the results might be a little different."

The girls had both travelled – Lauren to France, and Catherine to a music camp in Charlevoix, Quebec – and were pleased at their ability to understand and be understood. But they retained a certain hesitancy about speaking French. "Definitely, my parents – it kind of bothers them, because when we go to Quebec, they'll want me to go speak in French, or ask directions," Catherine said. "I find I'm really self-conscious doing it because of the Quebec accent, and their way of speaking is faster, and different. And I feel it's so obvious that I'm from French immersion, because everybody from French immersion speaks the same way. I've met kids from Vancouver and you can immediately tell, you speak French exactly the same way. . . . You can always tell the accent of someone who has gone through French immersion as opposed to someone who was brought up in Quebec, or someone who has done late immersion. You can tell the difference."

She had put her finger on one of the inescapable realities about immersion; in hearing more French spoken by their English-speaking classmates (and often an English-speaking teacher who has learned French as a second language), immersion students have produced a distinct accent, a version of French that is almost a dialect or creole.

After they left, Jennifer Bailey expressed some disagreement with Catherine's comments, saying that there are all different levels of verbal ability in her classes. "Catherine speaks French; she has obviously been taught young by someone who is a native speaker, and has duplicated a lot of the intonations and pronunciations," she said. "But there are kids that you'd swear started learning French yesterday." And Catherine's observations about her own self-consciousness were no less exasperating for being familiar. "I don't know what that is," Bailey said. "My own daughter is exactly the same way; my daughter was a very high achieving language student – the language courses she took here were French, Latin, Spanish. Great marks getting into McGill. She doesn't like to speak French. She feels self-conscious. She feels people will laugh at her, make fun of her. I don't know why so many kids feel like that. Oftentimes, I think it's the most high achieving students; they're the perfectionists. They want to be right."

Christine Armstrong has been teaching in Kingston since 1989, and, at forty-one, has spent almost twenty years in a classroom including the time she spent as a student teacher. She has lived in Quebec, lived in France, taught at a lycée and an elementary school in France, and she went to a bilingual university campus, and worked in Quebec. "I've had a language base from multiple sources," she said. "What struck me when I first started teaching my very first year here in Kingston, in 1989 – I started right away with extended French classes – right away I was struck . . ." She interrupted herself to say that she wanted to be very careful to make sure that she wasn't implying that she had all the answers, or that her French was much better than that of her colleagues. ". . . But I was really struck at how poor their writing was," she said. "Not the oral so much. In the domains of reading, listening, and speaking, the comprehension and the passive aspects are so great and so strong and so deeply developed in those students, I'd say that they are really close to commensurate with native language. Say anything, hear anything, videos, movies, radio – it's very close to 95, 96, 97 per cent of the time they'll get it all. Comprehension is good . . . aural, auditory input comprehension is excellent to superb, across the board. Reading comprehension is very good, to let's say almost excellent. Oral production is good."

But she started to have some questions in her first year of teaching, and has been developing them into a thesis. She stops herself to say she doesn't want to put down any aspect of immersion; she has a huge personal investment in it. It is her job, her passion, her education, and her personal commitment: her children are in immersion. "I love it! And I want to make it better!"

There is an unspoken "but" the size of a moving van in everything she is saying. And the "but" is her continuing frustration at the weaknesses in her students' ability to write proper French, largely because of "fossilized errors," the mistakes that were learned young and have become ingrained in the speech and writing patterns of immersion students. "These students have spent – how old are they when they graduate? Seventeen? Used to be eighteen? – thirteen or fourteen years of instruction and they are still writing with the infinitive? What happened with those hundreds of hours of formal instruction? Why is there the break or the disconnect between the how many thousands of words that they have read of accurate authentic input?" Ian McFarlane interrupted. "You're not going to like my answer. My answer, as a former teacher of English, is that English teachers make the same observation."

It was an intriguing conversation: bright, engaging students, passionate, well-educated, and deeply committed teachers, and a supportive school principal, all giving a candid assessment of the immersion system. "What I see are kids and teachers who love what they're doing," McFarlane concluded. "It's not about political stability, it's not about careerism . . . they see it as personal and intellectual growth. I know that doesn't sound like high-school students, but that's what I've observed."

Christine Armstrong, despite her deep commitment, has a more critical view, which she is developing in her M.A. thesis. "French immersion philosophy . . . there was a very, very lofty theoretical philosophical goal and belief that ultimately, by going through immersion, the children would have a parallel native language acquisition experience, that they would become almost like native speakers or just native speakers – and it ended up never happening," she said. "But the plan got put out there, the notion got established, the lofty, heroic, aren't-we-wonderful, this-is-the-greatest-thing-since-sliced-bread notion has remained, but nobody did a catch-up reality check."

On the question of immersion French, her conclusion is clear. "They end up not speaking French like a native speaker. There's a number of language-acquisition-related reasons, and then just real-life-human-being-limitation reasons." Among them: it is impossible for a single person to provide enough feedback to twenty-five to thirty kids at a time; there are not enough native French-speaking teachers in the system; too many of the teachers make mistakes themselves and pass them on to their students; children spend several years listening to their mother tongue being spoken by many people before they start to speak, while immersion children are encouraged to speak almost immediately, without enough time spent listening to the language as it is spoken by native speakers; they are reinforced in their accent and their errors by their English-speaking classmates; and there is a tendency to gloss over any potential problem by teachers, parents, and academics for fear of undermining public support for the program.

She did not mention some of the other problems mentioned by Canadian Parents for French in their annual reports: a generation of French teachers is retiring and not being replaced, and enrolment in French classes is slipping. "I think immersion needs an overhaul," Armstrong said bluntly.

And yet. It provides a solid basis for those who want to build on what they have acquired, and many do. Catherine and Lauren say they plan to go to McGill because they want to be in Montreal and use their French; a significant number of graduates from KCVI have gone to the University of Ottawa, presumably drawn to the university's bilingualism. Jennifer Bailey says proudly that two of her students have been accepted in the House of Commons's pages program where bilingualism is a prerequisite; their French got them somewhere. "We let them know that the onus is on them," she says. "We've given them the basics – more than the basics – but they've got to do more themselves."

Immersion continues to be debated as either the ultimate solution or an experiment which has failed to meet expectations. There is no question that immersion graduates do not have the fluency of native speakers. And, in many cases, the errors that are part of immersion patois become ingrained. But it provides an invaluable building block that has enabled hundreds, if not thousands, of immersion graduates to operate in a French-language environment that allows them to acquire that fluency. And study after study has shown that immersion students acquire better, not worse, first-language skills than their non-immersion contemporaries.

On balance, French immersion has been a terrific success – there are three hundred thousand children in immersion in Canada, and as one official put it, the brakes on its expansion are a problem of supply, not demand. A recent test in Alberta found that immersion graduates met the top-level requirements of the federal government's language testing. But as my observation and conversations with students and teachers confirmed, it is not without weaknesses. Perhaps the most obvious is that, with some (even many) honourable exceptions thanks to dedicated teachers who do much more than is required or expected, French immersion doesn't connect to a French-speaking reality. Its curriculum is usually the Anglo curriculum in translation, and, in contrast with the original St. Lambert experiment, there is little communication with French-speaking students, whether contemporaries in Quebec or in the local French-speaking minorities. Immersion students acquire a code, which means they are most comfortable talking to other immersion students. As Catherine noted, you can tell an immersion student anywhere, as soon as she (as they are predominantly girls by the end of the program) opens her mouth.

It is an important stepping stone toward true mastery of the language, and many of those who are now entering journalism or the public service after having graduated from immersion are able to get up to the level they need to to interview politicians or serve the public without nearly the time, effort, or emotional strain required of their older colleagues.

Indeed, traditionally there are tensions between immersion and minority French-language education; francophones have viewed immersion with suspicion, either as a competition for scarce resources – money and teachers – or as a competing school system that will lead to the assimilation of the minority French-speaking community.

But regardless of its weaknesses, immersion is part of the solution, not part of the problem. And paradoxically, just at the point that governments – federal and provincial – began to pour money into teaching French as a second language, the universities stopped requiring it for admission, and the high schools made it optional. "Most Canadian universities had once required knowledge of a second language as a prerequisite to admission," wrote Matthew Hayday in his Ph.D. thesis, "Bilingual Today, United Tomorrow: Canadian Federalism and the Development of the Official Languages in Education Program, 1968–1984." "Throughout the 1960s, several major universities dropped this requirement. Accordingly, a major reason for students to continue with the study of French, the most widely available second language, had disappeared by the late 1960s."

By the mid-seventies, this began to have an impact. As Richard Gwyn pointed out in *The Northern Magus*, "Since no one needed to learn French any longer to get into university, fewer and fewer students spent time on the subject." Between 1970–71 and 1977–78, outside Quebec enrolment in French dropped from 56 per cent of students to 40 per cent. Jean Chrétien, then Trudeau's Minister of Indian and Northern Affairs, succeeded in persuading the cabinet to consider withdrawing grants from universities that did not require French as an entrance requirement. However, Gwyn noted, the cabinet decided "political discretion was the better part of bilingual valour."

Dropping French as a university prerequisite was only one of the problems affecting the teaching of French as a second language. Canadian Parents for French (CPF) has documented in its annual reports on the State of French Second Language (FSL) education in Canada the evidence of teacher shortages. In 2001, the organization found that the quality of French second-language teaching was undermined by inadequate teaching materials, a lack of qualified teachers, and a high drop-out rate. In 2002, CPF pointed out that "it is unclear which national policies on FSL education are in place," and "There is no national policy ensuring access to FSL learning." It found that 96 per cent of school districts were expecting shortages of substitute teachers, 80 per cent expected shortages of elementary teachers, and 89 per cent expected shortages of high-school teachers. There are other factors that have converged to reduce the numbers of students studying French – for, despite, the continued growth in immersion, CPF found what it called "a universal decline in core French enrolments across all jurisdictions." Core French – where French is taught as a subject, between twenty and fifty minutes a day – remains the way most Canadian students study French. And, as study after study has shown, it remains inadequate; according to one CPF survey, almost half of those who had passed Grade 12 French in Ontario felt they could not understand spoken French. And the drop-out rate from core French in Ontario is striking: in its 2003 report, CPF found that enrolment in core French dropped by 25,000 between 2000–2001 and 2001–2002. From 129,173 in core French in Grade 6, the enrolment dropped to 12,372 in Grade 11 in 2001–2002.

In March 2003, the federal government released the "Action Plan for Official Languages," which called for a doubling of the proportion of high-school graduates with a functional knowledge of the other official language – from 25 per cent to 50 per cent – by 2013. To achieve this, it dedicated $137 million over five years. But so far, there is little indication of how the goal will be achieved. CPF found that there was little encouragement for students to stay in French; 77 per cent said that they had received no such encouragement to continue. "All too often, the French teacher is alone in advocating for students to stay in French."

Despite these findings, James Shea, executive director of CPF, remains optimistic. "What I'm optimistic about is that regularly and consistently and across the country, non-francophone parents are choosing to have their children educated in two languages," he told me. "We still see a pioneering spirit." But there are still petty bureaucratic barriers; school boards that set arbitrary limits on how many applications are required to start a program, or that refuse to start early immersion programs. And there are interprovincial barriers as well. Incredibly, it is much easier for teachers to go on exchanges with teachers in other countries than with teachers in other provinces.

"We have international teacher exchanges – a teacher can go to England or Australia," Shea said, pointing to programs where teachers literally swap jobs (and homes) with colleagues in other countries, and do not lose their job security or their pensions. "But we don't have interprovincial exchanges." When you think about it, it is stunning that it is easy to organize an exchange of jobs for a year or two between a teacher in Ontario and a teacher in Australia – and impossible between a teacher in Ontario and a teacher in Quebec. He argues that teachers should be actively encouraged to move from French-language to English-language schools and vice versa in exchanges; instead, there are obstacles.

Similarly, there are obstacles for students who would be interested in continuing in French. Presumably, guidance teachers would advise students that if they wanted to go into engineering, they should not drop algebra or trigonometry and if they wanted to go into medicine, they should not drop physics or chemistry. Presumably, too, a student who wants to study political science or journalism or public administration will be advised to keep studying French. Well, no, actually. There are several reasons for this, the most striking being that most English-language universities treat French as a foreign language – just like, say, German or Spanish – rather than as a critical skill or a Canadian language of instruction. I wanted to see if my assumption about this was correct at the university level.

Across the street from KCVI is Queen's School of Policy Studies. For generations, Queen's has prided itself on its reputation as being the source of the best and the brightest for the federal public service. It could be argued, in fact, that academics from Queen's founded the federal public service – with a little help from some University of Toronto graduates like Lester Pearson, Escott Reid, Wyn Plumptre, R.B. Bryce, Hume Wrong, and Louis Rasminsky. Jack Granatstein wrote that "the modern civil service had its founder in Oscar Douglas Skelton." When he left Queen's in 1925 to become Undersecretary of State for External Affairs, he carried with him the belief, Granatstein observed, that "the government of Canada could be improved only by regular infusions of bright, talented young university graduates." In 1932, he recommended his former student Clifford Clark to Prime Minister R.B. Bennett as the best person to write a paper on monetary policy for the Imperial Economic Conference; Clark stayed to become Deputy Minister of Finance. Other notable Queen's contributions to the federal public service included W.A. Mackintosh of the Department of Finance, and John Deutsch and Alex Skelton of the Bank of Canada. Of the current generation of Ottawa players, Queen's has produced Paul Martin's chief of staff Tim Murphy,

Foreign Affairs deputy minister Peter Harder, House of Commons Speaker Peter Milliken, Liberal parliamentary strategist Jerry Yanover, *Globe and Mail* columnist Jeffrey Simpson, former Natural Resources Canada deputy minister George Anderson, Power Corporation vice president – and Chrétien loyalist – John Rae, former *Globe and Mail* bureau chief and now senior Foreign Affairs official Drew Fagan, and a host of lesser known journalists, bureaucrats, and political activists.

Since 1988, the School of Policy Studies has specialized in diploma and graduate degree programs aimed at those interested specifically in public policy. Given the degree to which bilingualism is now a prerequisite for promotion to the senior ranks of the federal public service, I wanted to see how French had become part of the preparation and training of public servants at Queen's. I asked Keith Banting, a professor of public administration and former director of the school, how it responded to the fact that there were three hundred thousand students in immersion – and there are increasing requirements for bilingualism in the senior ranks of the public service. It seemed to me that a school of public service that prepares graduate students for work in government would ensure that they met the language levels required for senior executives. Not so.

"The bottom line is that the school has no language training," he told me. "The basic structure of the program focuses exclusively on the skill side – the analytical, the knowledge-based side, but in the definitions of skills we have never included language. Occasionally a student will take a course in French as an elective. It's not all that easy, because these are graduate courses because it's a graduate degree. The problem is that basic conversational French doesn't qualify. Sometimes we've been able to get the graduate school to bend, but it's not part of the curriculum of the school."

The last time the issue was discussed, he told me, was when the school considered making the degree a two-year program instead of one calendar year. One of the arguments in favour of extending the course was to facilitate, for those who wanted it, a period of French immersion during the summer between the two years. However, the conclusion was that making the program two years would significantly increase the costs for students, who usually have to work during the summer anyway to handle the expense. It remains a one-year program. "So we don't know the answer to your question. I don't know how well most of these kids speak French," Banting told me. "They know about the expectations in Ottawa; many of them, as you would anticipate, have done immersion. But I'm always struck by the number of students who end up aiming for the Ontario public service as much as the federal public service. The idea that Queen's is a pipeline to the federal level . . . historically that may have been true, but I bet as many of our students end up at the Ontario public service."

That has to do partly with the attraction and the scale of Toronto, with the greater likelihood of partners or spouses getting jobs there, Banting said, adding, "But some of it may be language." He observed sardonically that if the federal government said that bilingualism would be a requirement for hiring, "there would be meetings," and the school would respond very quickly to meet that requirement.

Interestingly, further research suggested that some of the students are ahead of the institution where they are enrolled. David Elder, a former senior public servant and a fellow at the School of Policy Studies, told me that twenty-eight of the fifty-two students in the program had organized French instruction with the Queen's French Department on their own initiative.

It is one of the great, stupid Canadian paradoxes. In 1960, as one federal official pointed out to me, every university in Canada required a second language as a prerequisite for admission – and, in most cases, that second language was French. Over the next forty years, as primary and secondary schools embraced French immersion, universities dropped their language requirements. At the vast majority of Canada's English-speaking universities, French remains a foreign language, just like German; it is taught by French departments, which are departments of literature; their students are being prepared to be French teachers. There are few indications – at least at the oldest, most established universities, the ones with the best reputations – that French is recognized as a Canadian language, and necessary for communicating with other Canadians; or that knowledge of the language is a prerequisite for national leadership.

The result has clear statistical consequences. Through the investment of literally billions of dollars, Canada has succeeded in enabling English Canadians outside Quebec to reach their peak of bilingualism between the ages of fifteen and nineteen. From then on, their skill tapers off steadily, dropping every five years.

The news is not all bad. Some of the newer, smaller, or more innovative universities are trying to do something about the problem. The most dramatic example is the University of Ottawa, which has been working to define itself as "Canada's University." David Mitchell, the university's vice president for university affairs, responsible for development, alumni affairs, and marketing, was hired away from Simon Fraser University in British Columbia. Before coming to Ottawa, he spent five weeks in immersion in Jonquière so that he could function effectively in an institution that, while bilingual, often functions predominantly in French. He did not emerge completely bilingual, but he became comfortable operating in French. "On a day-to-day basis, I was able to work and live and celebrate and play in an environment that is impressively bilingual," he told me. "Not in a false manner, as the Public Service of Canada can be, but in a genuine way, where people speak both of Canada's official languages interchangeably. At any meeting on this campus, you will hear both languages being spoken."

In fact, because of the traditions of the institution, and the concern that French is now in the minority in what was a predominantly French-language university for many years, he suggests that there is a greater effort made to ensure that French is spoken, and it is often used more than English at meetings. Traditionally, the university was a Catholic institution run by the Oblate Fathers. There was a French-speaking and an English-speaking part of the university, and both parts were about the same size. Connecting the two elements of the university – and the broader community – was part of the mandate of the institution, and it was a requirement that every French-speaking student take some courses in English, and that every English-speaking student take some courses in French.

For years, the university attracted a significant number of students from Quebec – particularly in the years prior to the late 1960s, when their only way to get into a French-language university in Quebec was to have gone to classical college, the elite private institutions run by the Church. By contrast, the University of Ottawa accepted students from secondary school, and provided a transition year. In addition, as the one post-secondary institution in Ontario providing any French-language instruction (until 1960, when Laurentian University was created as a bilingual university in Northern Ontario), it was a key institution for the francophone minority.

Two things changed that equation. Tuition fees in Ontario went up significantly, while those in Quebec remained frozen – $1,700 in Quebec compared to $4,500 in Ontario for undergraduates – which had the effect of turning off the tap from the pool of French-speaking Quebec that used to provide a steady stream of students to the university. Shortly afterward, perhaps to make up for the drop in enrolment, the university decoupled the two programs. When it was no longer a requirement to take at least some courses in French, enrolment in the English side increased significantly. This was particularly noticeable following the arrival of the so-called double cohort in Ontario when Grade 13 was eliminated. Now two-thirds of the student body is English-speaking and only one-third is French-speaking.

As a result, the university has now embarked on a unique effort to attract immersion graduates to the French-language courses being offered at the university. It has created a program of tutors to encourage students to take courses in the language that is not their mother tongue, providing an hour and a half of tutoring for every four and a half hours of courses – and allowing students to write essays and exams in their preferred language. The intention is to provide extra support and coaching to overcome the reticence that many immersion graduates feel about taking university courses in French – and to build on the assets that the university has.

"The federal government hires our students, certainly more than any other university in Canada, because of the likelihood of language competency," Mitchell told me, saying that the university is introducing a certificate of second-language competence. "The competitive advantage that the university has and the distinguishing characteristic it offers students oftentimes is the fact that students can study in a bilingual environment and learn Canada's other language. It's a bit of a leg up."

However, the language issue remains contentious, as the university tries to balance the conflicting pressures between its desire to grow and its mandate to ensure that it remains a healthy bilingual institution.

In September 2005, Gisèle Fortin-Dion wrote a memo to the university staff who were to attend the Ontario Universities Fair: "Also, be sure to speak English at all times," she wrote. "This is an English fair. We will meet a couple of French students throughout the weekend (and don't hesitate to address them in French), but we do not want to scare those English students (who probably already think that they need to be bilingual to attend our university)."

· When the memo was leaked to Denis Gratton, a columnist at *Le Droit*, he was outraged. "Is that the way they promote a bilingual university?" he wondered in a column entitled "Speak White." By hiding the fact that it is . . . bilingual? By hiding the fact that French-speaking students are welcome? Or are they still?"

The column set off an uproar at the university. Senior administrators were quick to respond, pointing out that in raw numbers, there were more francophone students at the university than there had ever been. Robert Major, the academic vice-president, responded to Gratton's column the next day, saying that it was a matter of basic courtesy for French-speaking administration staff to respond to English-speaking students in English.

"The extension of this principle of basic courtesy applies for the presence of the University of Ottawa at the Universities Fair, in Toronto," he wrote. "When the university visits CEGEPs (junior colleges) in Quebec, when it visits French-speaking or immersion schools in Ontario and the rest of Canada, it does so in French. But it happens that the fair in Toronto is an English-speaking fair.

Major went on to say that if parents and would-be students came by the kiosk and only heard French, they would have the inaccurate but widespread view that the school is a French-speaking university. In fact, it has always been a bilingual institution. But the proportion of French-speaking students dropped from 64 per cent in 1958 to 32 per cent now. For many years, the university required that all students, English-speaking and French-speaking, had to pass a test in their second language in order to graduate. That requirement was abolished in 1992.

But the debate did not subside; graduate students in political studies, concerned that the university was tilting too far toward an

English-speaking clientele, organized a day-long study session on the subject.

Mitchell was philosophic about the ongoing controversy, telling me that it showed that the university, like the country, is a work in progress. "I think that's healthy."

But the University of Ottawa is not alone. In the 1960s, Glendon College at York University was established with the goal of providing a bilingual environment. It was the dream of former diplomat Escott Reid, who, while he did not speak French himself, believed – as his friend and former colleague Lester Pearson had – that it was essential that the universities produce bilingual graduates. Kenneth McRoberts, the principal of Glendon, has been devoting a lot of energy to reinvigorating Reid's vision, and the college is developing an M.A. in public administration that produces bilingual graduates.

More recently, other universities have been following the example set by Ottawa and Glendon. In 2004, thanks to a five-year grant from the federal government of almost $6 million, Simon Fraser established a program designed to attract some of British Columbia's thirty-five thousand immersion students and enable them to get a degree entirely in French. As part of that, the university hired Yolande Grisé, previously director of the Centre for French Canadian Culture at the University of Ottawa, to be the director of the Office of Francophone and Francophile Affairs – a title that expresses the goal of bringing together members of the French-speaking minority (francophones) and immersion students (francophiles). The program started with eight students enrolled in political science in French; Grisé's immediate goal was to triple that, and to develop partnerships with universities in Quebec and in France. Her dream is to have francophone and francophile students camping outside the university's admissions office, trying to get into the program – as so many of their parents lined up, years earlier, to get them into immersion.

There are other efforts under way as well. Bishop's University is developing a relationship with the Université de Sherbrooke, and Mount Allison is developing joint programs with the Université de Moncton. Gradually, forty years after the Royal Commission, some universities are coming to terms with the fact that French is not a foreign language in Canada, that it is a pre-requisite for leadership in the national public sector, and that there is a pool of three hundred thousand potential students in French immersion. But French remains in every sense a foreign language for most English-language Canadian universities and for most English Canadians – unless they have ambitions for leader-ship in public life.

PART THREE

Trying to Make It Work

chapter nine

Bumping Together, Drifting Apart

> *To be a Canadian officer, you must be able to*
> *communicate, not just talk. Communicate in the*
> *language of the soldier. Because no longer will*
> *the soldier die in the language of the officers.*
>
> *ROMÉO DALLAIRE*

As we have seen, Canada's English-language universities treat French as a foreign language whose literature should be studied by those preparing to be French teachers, while our schools treat it like catechism, something to be absorbed before the age of twelve and then neglected. So it is not surprising that there continue to be language-based communications problems for national organizations in Canada. For the reality of the country is that there are relatively few ways in which English-speaking Canadians outside Quebec and French-speaking Canadians and Quebeckers come into contact, even in areas where such contact might be expected: the academic world, for instance, voluntary associations, non-governmental organizations, national sports teams, or social movements.

Different national institutions respond in different ways to the language divide: by creating French-language units that are provided a certain amount of autonomy, by separating into a French-speaking and an English-speaking organization, by hiring a bilingual staff that can act as intermediary between English-speaking and French-speaking participants (often leading to what political scientist Richard Simeon has called "asymmetrical bilingualism"), or by making competence in both languages an absolute requirement for advancement. It is worth taking a look at how a variety of national institutions have dealt with the language issue.

i: The Military

In 1978, fifteen years before he was assigned to Rwanda in 1993, Roméo Dallaire was given the command of an artillery battery in Val Cartier, outside of Quebec City. He found it to be an ineffective, not particularly efficient group, and he was determined to change that. "I pushed for some reforms, chiefly the ability to give orders in French," he wrote in his memoirs. "Almost 11 years after the Official Languages Act had been passed, we were still fighting those stupid regulations and as a result we were never reaching our potential as an operational artillery regiment." With the support of his superiors, he embarked on a translation project, converting the lexicon of technical artillery terms into French. "When the troops were able to fight in their own language, there was a positive surge in morale and effectiveness," Dallaire wrote.

This was only one of a series of struggles he had engaged in from the time he enrolled in the Collège militaire royale de Saint-Jean in the early 1960s. The college had only been established in 1952 after complaints about the small number of French-speaking officers in the Canadian Forces. As Dallaire put it, "The numbers enlisting from Quebec were embarrassingly low; potential recruits from that province were repelled by an armed forces that

was English-dominant and highly intolerant of French Canadians."
(Indeed, one of the formative experiences of a young officer in the
early 1960s was being told "Speak English, Lt. Landry! That's an
order!" That was Bernard Landry, future leader of the Parti
Québécois.)

Traditionally, the military had been an English-dominant, if not
an English-only institution. "When you're a minority, you have to
struggle every day," Dallaire told me in September 2004. "The bilingualism exercise was done as a crisis exercise. Remember? Bombs
were flying in Montreal and everything else. So bingo, they throw
this thing," he said. "So in the unsophisticated way that it was, the
first thing you do is find every damn French Canadian that you
can, look at him, and if he's promotable, promote him, and start
building up quotas. Creating quotas. Then you start putting in
draconian measures like 'Listen, you're an EX-3, we want to
promote you to an EX-4, but you won't get it unless you take a
French course.' So you get a forty-seven or fifty-three-year-old
bureaucrat going a year, for Crissake, on the language course,
which he may never use much, because the whole operation is still
in English, but he's got the numbers now to be promoted. You
create this incredible tension amongst the structure in this regard
because of very unsophisticated, inept methodologies to meet
quotas, established by politicians, or by bureaucrats with the
politicians, so that they can look good. That's why it's taken thirty-
five years."

The pressure to deal with the French fact in the Canadian
Forces runs though the history of the military, as successive military leaders tried to reconcile the need to recruit francophones
with the English-only nature of the Armed Forces. In 1914, the
Royal 22e – the Vandoos – was created, first as a battalion and then
as a regiment, and in the Second World War there were four
French-speaking infantry units. But the infantry remained one of
the few areas of the military that had French-language units. "The

Forces remained English in language, tradition and outlook," wrote Jean Pariseau and Serge Bernier in their two-volume history *French Canadians and Bilingualism in the Canadian Forces*. In fact, it was so widely understood in Quebec that to join the Canadian military meant losing one's French that "Parc des Braves," a Radio-Canada television series broadcast between 1984 and 1988, set during the Second World War, had one of its characters, Col. Tancrède Rousseau, speaking with a slightly English accent. It was not an unfair portrait of the times.

Mackenzie King's nephew, Capt. Horatio Nelson Lay (clearly born for a naval career), was the commanding officer of HMS *Nabob* in 1944, which had a largely Canadian crew, including one hundred French Canadians – who provided 50 per cent of the cases of insubordination. Lay made a formal suggestion that was prescient, foreseeing Dallaire's observation: French Canadians should be assigned to ships with French-Canadian officers. In 1952, at the urging of Defence Minister Brooke Claxton, the Collège militaire royale de Saint-Jean was established. In 1959, when Queen Elizabeth presented new colours to the Royal 22e Régiment, all of the commands at the parade square ceremony were given in French – despite orders to the contrary from higher up. It was a small but significant victory for French-speaking soldiers in the Canadian Forces; it was the first time this had happened in Canada since 1759.

But the real impetus for change in the Canadian Forces came with the appointment of General Jean-Victor Allard as chief of the defence staff in 1966. Allard had strong views about the fate of French Canadians in the Canadian military. "To enlist at the age of 18 in the Navy or Air Force was almost equivalent to abandoning one's culture and language for good," he wrote in his memoir. Allard had fought for the rights of French-speaking soldiers, submitting his resignation in March 1965 when it looked as if plans for unification would eliminate the Vandoos. He was chosen to implement National Defence Minister Paul Hellyer's plan to unify the three services. But before he accepted Hellyer's offer, he made it a condition that he could establish a study to look into the conditions of francophones in the Canadian Forces. The inquiry found that francophones made up 16 per cent of the Canadian Forces. On the basis of that study – and his own experience as an officer – he decided that French-language units should be established. He felt that the record of the Vandoos spoke for itself; the French-speaking regiment had produced more generals than any other regiment in Canada, proving to his satisfaction that being able to work in one's mother tongue was more conducive to building successful careers than spending the early stages of one's career in a second language.

But the idea of creating French-language units that would be based in Quebec disturbed some of Pearson's advisers. Marc Lalonde, then a Pearson aide, wrote to him on December 5, 1967, when he heard about Allard's idea.

"We should avoid very carefully the concentration of these French-speaking Forces inside Quebec. . . . We have to think here of the problems that such a concentration would cause in the event of a serious political uprising in Quebec," he wrote. "I don't want to sound unduly pessimistic but we should avoid providing the Government of Quebec with a ready-made Army at its disposal." Similarly, on March 12, 1968, Michael Pitfield, also a Pearson aide, wrote that the French-language units were "one of the most potentially dangerous decisions the Federal government could ever take." He added, "I submit that . . . unilingual French-Canadian units concentrated in Quebec could – in the circumstances of our times, and with the trends that are likely to become even more powerful in the future – irrevocably lay the groundwork for an exceedingly dangerous situation."

But to no avail. As a result of the changes that Allard started, bilingualism became the military's policy. In 1970, four goals were established: to provide bilingual services, to reflect the linguistic and cultural values and proportional representation of the country, to create a climate in which all military personnel could seek to achieve common goals while using either official language, and to provide instruction in both languages. This meant introducing language skill as part of the military personnel file of every member of the Canadian Forces, increasing the number of francophones, promoting more francophones, and setting requirements for language skill in senior officers. The military being the military – despite deep resentment in many quarters – it was done. By 1987, the proportion of francophones had gone from 16 per cent to 27 per cent, and by 1997, functional bilingualism was a requirement for promotion to the rank of lieutenant-colonel and above.

By 1991, Jocelyn Coulon could report in his book *En Première Ligne* that francophones were happy with the progress that had been made, and were taking the place they should, demographically, at every level of the military. But he acknowledged that English Canadians would pay a price for this. "The young English-Canadian from Moose Jaw who joins the army at 17 and eventually becomes an officer will never be able to master the second language as a Francophone does," Coulon wrote. "Despite the French courses and hanging out with French-speaking colleagues, if he is not assigned to a French Language Unit for a few years, which certainly won't happen, he won't master the language. Once an officer, and bilingual on paper, he will only be able to work in the language with considerable effort."

The process of adjustment was not easy or pleasant. As Desmond Morton put it, "From being a virtual Anglophone monopoly, the Canadian armed forces came, for a time, to resemble the country they served: two mutually resentful solitudes." And today, military historian Jack Granatstein suggests that there are three armies: the army of Quebec, the army of Ontario, and the army of the West – each with a different culture reflected in the differences of the Princess Patricias, the Royal Canadian Regiment, and the Vandoos.

Certainly, despite the changes, some tensions remain. "Bilingualism was never sold as a fundamental premise of Canadian officership," Dallaire told me. "It was sold as 'French-Canadians need a break in order to be able to work and do their initial competencies in French, and you Anglos, if you want to go somewhere, you better get your numbers up in French in order to get promoted.'"

That being the case, it is not surprising that there was some hostility to the moves to make the Canadian Forces bilingual. It introduced new factors for promotion, there was a scramble to promote francophone officers (known informally in the Canadian Forces as "the Franco by-pass"), and the creation of new French-language units led to new competition for talented officers. At this point, after a career in the military, Dallaire observes a number of continuing problems.

"There is a core – much, much fewer – of those who have no intention of learning French, still; who have been able to avoid it, and thank God for it," he said, identifying those who will not make an effort to improve their language skills unless they get a formal, obligatory course of instruction. "They'll enhance their skills in karate, nights and weekends, but they won't do it in French." But the majority of members of the English-Canadian officer corps, he suggested, is sensitive to the issue, and has varying levels of skills and knowledge in the language, if not the culture. Those officers feel that not being able to communicate with the French-speaking soldiers in French is a shortcoming and a disappointment. "So it's not like before 'We're the majority, why do I have to?' No, it is 'I should be able to.'"

Others are not so generous in their appraisal. Michel Drapeau, a retired colonel and military analyst and critic, is more severe, arguing that the language of work is English. "That leaves two choices for Francophones: conform to the majority, or insist on spending their career at the bases at Val Cartier or Saint-Jean, thus limiting their chances of advancement," he wrote. "During my military service, I quickly learned that promotion depended largely on the fact that a French-speaking senior officer must master the English language perfectly."

Dallaire says he has observed a significant improvement in the language skills of the young officers, both English-speaking and French-speaking, coming into the Canadian Forces. "The question that arises is still one of the culture," he said. "When they closed the military college in Saint-Jean, they destroyed the recruiting of the best potential candidates that are French Canadian. And that has not been replaced to the scale it was." But he feels that a more serious effect has been that English-Canadian officer cadets have lost a valuable immersion in Quebec, and French-language military culture – an experience that cannot be re-created at the Royal Military College in Kingston. Nor is it easy for English-Canadian officers to get posted to French-speaking units. "I tried to get posted to Val Cartier my entire career," one lieutenant-colonel told me.

Canada's French-language regiments, it turns out, are notable not only for language differences, but cultural differences as well – including different styles of leadership. "The French-Canadian regiment's style of leadership is far more intimate. It's nearly touchy, sort of thing," Dallaire told me. "It's very much body language. It requires considerable communication, all the time." By contrast, he said, in an English-Canadian regiment there is more of a structure to the leadership. "There is more independence of the individuals and a protection of their independence from the leadership. There is just as much devotion to good leaders and to the cause, but it's got to be presented in a fashion that is more detached, and more structured," he said. "While in a French-Canadian regiment that is not the fact. It's intimate, on the highest plane of intimacy. And in that case, it requires close links. Not that you become overly friendly with your troops, but it requires a very human presence of that authority. And you have to see it and sense it."

Dallaire's and Granatstein's observations about cultural differences within the Armed Forces are confirmed in a 2005 study, "Canadian Soldiers: Military Ethos and Canadian Values in the 21st Century," a draft of which was obtained by Stephen Thorne of Canadian Press. The study, based on a survey of 1,700 of Canada's 19,500 full-time soldiers, found that Quebec-based troops rated disaster relief and search and rescue in Canada as the first and second priorities for the army – while soldiers in the three other areas in Canada rated combat operations to defend Canadian territory first, and combat operations to defend Canadian citizens at home and abroad second. For Quebec-based soldiers, combat operations were rated fourth and fifth in priority.

The survey also found that Quebec-based soldiers are more concerned about ecology and social responsibility than their fellow soldiers in the rest of the country – but more intolerant of foreigners. "This might lead to a preference for 'in Canada' disaster relief operations rather than foreign war-fighting operations," the study's authors observed. "[Quebec-based] personnel express more concern for troop safety in combat operations than personnel of other [areas]. However [Quebec-based] personnel express more willingness to place troops in danger on non-combat ops compared to personnel of other areas."

These cultural differences have created new expectations, new demands, and new challenges for the leadership of the Canadian Forces. Dallaire puts it in graphic, explicit military terms. "You must be able to communicate in the language of the soldiers. No longer will soldiers die in the language of the officers."

But the realities of military life created its own problems in terms of language policy. To begin with, there is a geographic factor. The Army has an overrepresentation of francophones, while the Navy – based on both coasts – is only 16 per cent francophone, with one French-speaking ship, the *Ville de Québec.* "We can't force francophones to join the navy," one officer told me.

As National Defence's annual review of official languages for 2004–2005 put it, "Varied and repeated efforts to enforce compliance have been very strict and universally applied – in fact designed to result in over-compliance." The military set out to ensure that 70 per cent of the colonel-captains were bilingual, and found that doing so was a major drain on the organization: $19.2 million in training to get 84 officers and non-commissioned officers to the top level of language ability out of 1,178 who were tested.

The result was sometimes counterproductive, and the military has been working to develop "a functional approach," moving from universal bilingualism to bilingualism where required, with more flexibility in rotating bilingual members of the Forces in and out of positions where bilingualism is required. For the Canadian Forces, the military keeps trying to explain, does not function like the public service.

Other national organizations in Canadian life have not had to deal with the language implications of such a primal reality as the military faces. Nor have they been as successful. Jack Granatstein argues in his recent book *Canada's Army* that bilingualism has worked. "The resulting army was a better reflection of the country's duality than almost any federal institution – indeed, better than any Canadian institution of any kind."

ii: Voluntary Organizations

In contrast with the military, voluntary organizations are, by definition, voluntary; nobody is forced to follow orders or to function in a particular way, people can leave at any time, and the structures are less disciplined. Members are attracted out of a commitment to the subject, rather than to some abstract idea like civil society, social capital, inclusiveness, or linguistic equity. I discovered this through personal experience.

In 1978 and 1979, I was part of a group of journalists who decided that it would be worthwhile to set up an organization in which both English-speaking and French-speaking journalists could participate. While doing a book tour to promote his investigative work on Montreal real-estate manoeuvrings, *City For Sale*, Henry Aubin of the *Gazette* had met Jock Ferguson, then a CBC-TV reporter. That encounter, and their concerns about the state of investigative journalism, led to a wider continuing discussion; Nick Fillmore of CBC-Radio and Jean-Claude Leclerc of *Le Devoir* joined the group. A little later, I joined them, as did Gérald Leblanc of *La Presse*, Richard Cléroux of the *Globe and Mail*, and a number of others. Several Quebec journalists were skeptical; they already had La fédération professionelle des journalistes du Québec (FPJQ), and they did not want either to join a second parallel organization, or see one develop that would siphon off their members.

What was agreed upon was that the new group would focus on investigative journalism – investigative in its broadest sense – and as a result the Centre for Investigative Journalism (CIJ) was created. For several annual conferences, the enthusiasm was considerable; the contact between English-speaking and French-speaking journalists who were wrestling with many of the same issues seemed to generate energy. But the original idea did not survive longer than a few years; English-speaking journalists wanted a broader focus for the organization than simply investigation, no matter how that was defined. About 1986, there began to be pressure to change the name and the mandate and, after several debates at several conventions, the change was made. The CIJ became the CAJ – the Canadian Association of Journalists – and, with a sense of regret and lost opportunities on the part of some of the original organizers of the CIJ but no bitterness or hard feelings, the CAJ and the FPJQ ran from then on along parallel tracks, with amicable but distant relations.

"They run their show and we run ours," Robert Cribb, who was president of the CAJ from 2001–03, told me, adding, "There's

not a hint of ill-will between us." Alain Gravel, president of the
FPJQ, told me that there are almost no day-to-day relations
between the two organizations. "They are almost non-existent; we
have very, very few relations," he said. "I have no contact, there is
no follow-up. It's a shame, we have contacts with Reporters
Without Borders, and we are members of a bunch of international
organizations, we have connections almost everywhere, and with
the CAJ, very little. It's a pity; the same laws apply to us, but there
is no link, nobody calls. Mind you," he added thoughtfully, "I work
at Radio-Canada, and it's the same thing with the CBC."

But when it matters, the two organizations have worked closely
and effectively together. "There are occasional issue-based relations
that we have," Cribb said, and described how the two organizations
worked together when CanWest imposed a single editorial policy
on all the members of the newspaper chain. The two groups coordinated their efforts, put together a package of materials in both
languages, and sent it to all members of Parliament. Similarly,
Gravel said that when a reporter for the *Hamilton Spectator* was
fined for refusing to reveal a source, the FPJQ got involved, and sent
a member of the executive to the CAJ conference in Winnipeg.
"Large, overarching national issues bring us together to get a better
representation," Cribb said. "When you put us together we
effectively represent the whole country."

But the language that English Canadians use to describe
Canadian organizations usually does not acknowledge that those
groups that purport to be national in scope in fact are English-
speaking organizations. The CAJ is a good example; it has an
asymmetrically bilingual title on its website – a stylized lowercase
caj beside "Canadian Association of Journalists/L'association
canadienne des journalistes" – with the rest of the site in English
only. In its mission statement, the CAJ says, "The CAJ promotes
excellence in journalism, encouraging investigative journalism. We
serve as the national voice of Canadian journalists, and we uphold

the public's right to know." The bilingual title exists as a claim of national representativeness, but there is nothing in the statement, the goals, the caucuses, or the website of the organization that would suggest that journalism in Canada might occur in French.

The FPJQ has a larger membership than the CAJ – over 1,800 as compared to 1,500 – thanks to the fact that the employees of a number of media organizations are made members automatically, while every CAJ member is a volunteer. On its website – which is in French only – the FPJQ has a link to the CAJ, which it describes as "a kind of equivalent to the FPJQ, whose 1,500 members come, in the great majority, from English Canada."

It is, in effect, a form of sovereignty-association: two groups which have evolved with different cultural approaches, different structures, but which come together on occasion when their common interests are affected. Unwittingly, I had participated in one of the classic patterns of Canadian voluntary organizations. "That's such a common story," Susan Carter, a founding member of the Voluntary Sector Initiative, told me. "Language is a fault line in most large organizations in the voluntary sector, and there are very few organizations that do not have some parallel counterpart. Either they grew up that way, or they were one and spread apart in different ways."

The differences were not always so amicably resolved. In 1972, the Royal Commission on Bilingualism and Biculturalism published a study by John Meisel and Vincent Lemieux on ethnic relations in Canada's voluntary associations in which they described how organizations as various as the Boy Scouts and the Canadian Junior Chamber of Commerce had a history of differing values, mutual incomprehension, and even bitter conflict.

They found a situation where, in most organizations, unilingual anglophones predominated, and francophones had to function in English if they wanted to participate. The result, they observed, often involved "too great a cost in terms of effort, discomfort and possibly humiliation." The result was either withdrawal or embarrassing encounters (they describe a scout jamboree in Quebec where all the signs were in English, and the francophone scouts shouted insults that their anglophone fellow scouts, perhaps fortunately, could not understand), or a constant push for a recognition of difference. "The Anglophone leaders have consistently assumed their frame of reference to be one more or less homogeneous Canada, whereas their Francophone counterparts have thought of their organization as existing in a country with a dual character," Meisel wrote, describing the problem of the Jaycees. "A bilingual headquarters . . . would not make sense unless the whole organization were so changed as to promote values and produce programs of more or less equal appeal to both Francophones and Anglophones."

The problems of communication that Meisel and Lemieux observed continue in many areas as there has been a process of mutual disengagement. It is as if the academic, voluntary, and non-governmental sectors in Canada had quietly adopted a policy of sovereignty-association, with each sphere of activity quietly dividing along language lines. As York University's Daniel Drache and Blake Evans point out in a recent paper, academics attend different conferences; in all the social sciences, francophones and anglophones have separate academic journals. In addition, they point out, "Quebec and Canadian anti-globalization movements inherit very different organizational worlds," the Canadian Federation of Students has no French-language institutional members, and the Canadian labour movement has adopted a kind of sovereignty-association. "Almost every major civil society group has come to recognize the necessity of giving Quebec a special status in their organization," they write. "Amnesty International's Canadian Section, for example, maintains separate organizations, administrative councils and secretariats for

English- and French-speaking Canadians. Other groups, ranging from CUSO to the Red Cross to the Civil Liberties Union to the Boy Scouts to Development and Peace all have differential arrangements with their Quebec chapters."

The reason is both obvious and simple: they don't speak the same language. "Linguistic duality is a huge problem for grass-roots organizations," said Dr. Lisa Young of the University of Calgary. "The cost of simultaneous translation is staggering for groups trying to function on a shoe string. So most volunteer organizations are functionally unilingual."

She pointed out that it wasn't always this way. "The federal government was extremely involved in the 1970s and 1980s; the Secretary of State paid for translation to allow national organizations to be functionally bilingual, to create some bonds between the language groups, and to address fundamental linguistic issues in the country," she said. "As funding was reduced, and government greatly cut back its support, this stopped. Most of the organizations tend to be bi-national. It's one of the barriers to mobilization in the country."

One sector that has had particular difficulty with language has been amateur sport. As the Commissioner of Official Languages found in a report published in 2000, only two of ten national sports organizations provide simultaneous interpretation at their annual meetings. Athletes reported a series of language-related problems: documents sent to French-speaking athletes in English only, one national team with a majority of French-speaking members that trains in Montreal with a French-speaking coach and practises in English because one team member does not speak French.

"The inverse situation does not hold true," the report observed. "A unilingual French-speaking athlete training in an English environment is expected to learn English." A follow-up study found that efforts had been made by Sports Canada – but also found a lingering problem in many sports organizations and training centres; Montreal offered bilingual services to athletes, while by and large other cities did not.

This gap also exists in business, even in the cultural industries; the film industry is remarkable in its cultural divide. In 2003, one of the most successful English-Canadian producers, Paul Gross (who made *Men With Brooms*), and the most commercially successful Quebec director, Charles Binamé (who directed one of the most popular Quebec films ever made, *Séraphim*), were brought together to work on a TV series that Gross had written, a political thriller called *H2O*. The two men had not only never met or worked together before – neither one had ever heard of the other.

This gap caught public attention at the Genie Awards in 2005. Not only did French-language films, directors, and actors win the major awards – for films that had not been released in English Canada and would perhaps eventually make it, six months later, to the repertory art-house circuit – but the winners surprised the audience when they accepted their awards in French. The host (actor Andrea Martin) joked about the fact that English Canadians stay away from French-language films, quipping, "You didn't see *Mémoires affectives* but you spent $13.50 to see *Hitch*?" – but in fact, it simply wasn't possible; the film wasn't released in English Canada until months later, where it joined foreign-language films in art houses and repertory cinemas. "The Genies show was a depressing example of our two-solitudes divide between French and English Canada," wrote Peter Howell in the *Toronto Star* a few days later. "After decades of official bilingualism, we are still a land of mostly English-speaking provinces surrounding a separate nation of mostly French-speaking people."

For the winners, the ceremony was an equally odd experience; Roy Dupuis, who won for best actor, and Pascal Bussières, who won for best actress, had won in the same categories for the same roles a month earlier at the Jutra Awards in Montreal. They responded the way winners of the Best Foreign Language Film at the Academy Awards do: say a few words of thanks in English, and then speak their native language to their compatriots. Pascal Bussières said later it was like getting an award in Japan: addressing an uncomprehending audience in a foreign country. Howell was annoyed and disappointed, arguing that the French-speaking winners had missed an opportunity to reach out to a wider audience by saying more in English, adding, "It wouldn't have killed the English winners to make a bit of an effort toward addressing Quebec viewers either."

Award ceremonies in Ottawa, like the Governor General's Performing Arts Awards, are driven by concerns about carefully measured linguistic duality; in the private sector in Toronto, it is an afterthought, if it is a thought at all. At the Genies no one thought to organize simultaneous translation; no one thinks, as Howell suggests, to organize screenings of Quebec films in the rest of Canada. Quebec films are firmly in the category of "foreign films." The latest example of this cultural asymmetry was Denys Arcand's 2004 film *The Barbarian Invasions*, which won an Oscar for best foreign-language film, and earned $6.6 million at the box office in Quebec and $40 million in France – but barely $500,000 in English Canada. In contrast, it earned over $880,000 in Australia and $1.7 million in Spain – a grim commentary on English-Canadian interest in the first Oscar-winning Canadian feature film. (Denise Robert, the film's producer, politely refused to comment on this, pointing out that English-Canadian films are in the same category in English Canada, while Australia cherishes both its own films and foreign, non-Hollywood cinema. Indeed, Canadian films, regardless of their language, are often racked with foreign films in Canadian video stores.) In fact, the film industry is another example of the asymmetrical model for language relations in Canada: a

Canada-wide association which includes Quebec, but has little communication with or knowledge of it – and a Quebec organization that functions separately.

However, as was the case for English-speaking and French-speaking journalists, those in the cultural field showed they were able to come together when they faced a common threat. A similar pattern of divergence and co-operation occurred with the Coalition for Cultural Diversity – a group of artistic and cultural organizations, French- and English-speaking, that came together to lobby for the UNESCO Convention on the Protection and Promotion of the Diversity of Cultural Expressions.

"There were unilinguals in both groups, perhaps more on the English side," Pierre Curzi, co-chairman of the coalition told me, saying that everyone had come together for a common purpose, putting aside their broader political differences. "But very often, people would express themselves in their own language, no one would translate, but people would understand. Both sides were able to keep their linguistic space. We did that constantly; it was a success at that level."

There are other cultural factors at play. The Voluntary Sector Initiative, a project headed up by Ed Broadbent, was having great difficulty attracting Quebec social activists. Finally, Quebec community worker Pierre Ducasse said, "You have to understand that you won't get anyone as long as this is the language you use." He explained that the term "*bénévole*" was used for ladies who volunteered at church – a very narrow band of activity. Social activists used terms like "*adhérents*" or "*participants*." "The term 'voluntary sector' is not great, nobody likes it – but everybody dislikes it equally," Susan Carter, who worked on the initiative, told me. "In Quebec, it excludes the majority of what the sector is." So in French, the Voluntary Sector Initiative became "L'Initiative sur le secteur bénévole et communautaire."

In a forthcoming book, political scientists David Cameron and Richard Simeon set out to update the research that Meisel and Lemieux did in the 1960s and 1970s, and see how things have changed. They found that different organizations responded to the linguistic challenge in very different ways. Some transferred authority to their provincial organizations so that their Quebec wing could operate in French, while others adopted a bilingual public face, with the website, documents, and office staff all available in both languages.

Anglophones and francophones reacted very differently to the linguistic divide. Anglophones, Simeon found, were primarily concerned about the cost of operating in two languages, and the extra effort required to get agreement with francophone members. Organizations like the Heart and Stroke Foundation and the Huntington Society were better at developing a bilingual public face than in their internal operations. "These remain almost entirely unilingual English."

Francophones, on the other hand, had subtler and heavier burdens adapting to an English-speaking environment, since active participation required them to operate in their second language.

"It's easy to understand the extra effort that this requires," Simeon writes. "What we do not know is how many unilingual Francophones, or even those for whom English is a difficult stretch end up deciding not to participate at the national level, and instead decide to focus their involvement entirely within Quebec."

That observation could have been made forty years ago. However, there have been positive changes since Lemieux and Meisel did their research in the 1960s, when the tensions were palpable, the resentments considerable, and the mutual incomprehension much greater. Cameron and Simeon found that adjustments and organizational splits have occurred with much less bitterness. While voluntary associations do not bring individual French- and English-speakers together face-to-face very often, they found pragmatic co-operation on matters of shared interest – a pattern similar to the relationship between the Canadian Association of Journalists and the Fédération professionelle des journalistes.

Cameron and Simeon see some grounds for optimism, pointing out that francophones and anglophones have been able to work out relationships, structures, and practices that enable them to co-operate on shared goals while maintaining their autonomy and identity. Different groups do so in different ways, and language tensions persist in some of them, where the French-speaking members carry the burden of bilingualism. "Pragmatism tends to predominate over shared values; elitism and professionalism over mass involvement," they write. "Yet the co-operation we have described is no mean achievement."

One public organization that is trying to address the issue directly – at least in Ottawa, in its national bureau and head office – is the Canadian Broadcasting Corporation. In its structure and organization, the corporation has functioned as almost two separate public broadcasters: CBC and Radio-Canada. The programming is different, the market share is different (Radio-Canada has a much larger audience, both relatively and, for many popular programs, in absolute numbers), and in the past not much was done in common. Recently, partly for economic reasons, that has begun to change. It is so expensive to maintain foreign correspondents that the corporation has been increasingly looking for candidates who can report in both English and in French. As a result, Don Murray, Patrick Brown, Michel Cormier, and a number of other correspondents file to both networks, in English and in French.

As Quebec nationalism became a central part of the national political debate, relations between French and English journalists evolved from hostility to a kind of amiable camaraderie. In 1967, two reporters literally came to blows in the press room after General de Gaulle's "*Vive le Québec libre*" speech. Thirteen years later, as the bus full of reporters followed René Lévesque to Sherbrooke during the 1980 referendum campaign, Peter Cowan of Southam News (whose federalist credentials are unimpeachable, since he went on to work for Joe Clark when he was constitutional affairs minister and then the Council for Canadian Unity, but whose sense of humour remains mischievous) told the bus that reporters had a duty to vote Yes. "If the No wins, they will take away our American Express cards!" he said, in tones of mock seriousness. "They will make us write about education!"

But the emergence of even passively bilingual journalists in Ottawa is relatively recent. When Pierre Trudeau was prime minister, English-speaking reporters travelling with him in Quebec would sometimes have to huddle around his press aides for translation of his speeches. "The expectation in those years was that if you spoke French, that was fortunate, but it certainly wasn't obligatory," recalled former radio and TV reporter Jim Munson. (Although Trudeau's press attaché Patrick Gossage noted with awe in his journal that at a dinner of reporters on the road with Trudeau in Matane on June 23, 1977, there was a table of six English-speakers and six French-speakers. "All, but all, of the Anglos at the table spoke French.")

The language requirements for reporters covering the prime minister changed somewhat in 1984. Once Brian Mulroney decided that he would run hard in Quebec and would spend about a third of the campaign there, every major news organization realized that they should assign a reporter who was comfortable in French to his plane, at least when he was in the province – and if that proved difficult, TV networks ensured that a cameraman or a producer could speak French. To be senior enough to be assigned to a leader's plane and comfortable in French meant, almost inevitably, that the reporter had spent part of the 1970s working in Montreal. And any reporter who covered politics in Montreal in the 1970s, even occasionally, knew Brian Mulroney.

The result was that when Mulroney flew in to Baie Comeau, his home town, during the campaign, I looked around the plane and noticed that he was accompanied by a planeful of reporters who had been on a first-name basis with him, who had had lunches and drinks with him. In contrast, John Turner had a planeful of reporters who, with a few exceptions, knew him only as a former politician who had been out of politics for nine years. The difference in attitude was noticeable; one group quietly thought, "Hey, Brian's doing pretty well," while the other group thought, "Who does this guy Turner think he is?" (When Mulroney came to Ottawa, the situation was suddenly reversed: he faced a Press Gallery of largely unilingual journalists and commentators who wondered what qualified this smooth-talking Montreal lawyer who happened to be bilingual to be prime minister.) From that point on, the Ottawa bureaus of major English-language news organizations made it a point to have at least one reporter who was comfortable in French.

With few exceptions, the solitudes of the CBC and Radio-Canada did not connect, let alone, as the Rilke phrase that Hugh MacLennan used for the title of his novel put it, "protect and touch and greet each other." However, in the early days of television, one of the most popular programs was *Les Plouffe*, which was shot first in French and then in English – and was a hit in both languages. For several decades, that formula was not repeated, and when it was – with *Lance et Compte/He Shoots He Scores* – the result was very successful in Quebec and much less so in the rest of Canada.

One great exception to the solitudes rule was Mark Starowicz's massive project *Canada: A People's History*. At the cost of enormous effort, Starowicz piloted a joint, or collaborative, version of Canadian history, weaving together the narrative streams of aboriginal, French-speaking, English-speaking, and immigrant experience. In his candid, sometimes heartbreaking account of the production, *Making History: The Remarkable Story Behind* Canada: A People's History, Starowicz describes the constant problems he encountered in getting the two parts of the public broadcaster to work together, and the resentment the project inspired at Radio-Canada and in the French press. "For many Québécois, the word 'Canada' is a synonym for frustration, deception, combat and humiliation," Mario Cardinal, one of the editorial advisers for the series, explained to him when he asked about the journalistic hostility. "For the *indépendantistes* (that is to say, almost half the population and the majority of intellectuals, including journalists), the word 'Canada' is taboo. I have lost friends who no longer speak to me simply because I agreed to work on the series."

For all the frustration, Starowicz emerged optimistic from the experience. "The mystery of Canadian history is that we have every single ingredient for every Old World conflict, yet we are peaceful," he concluded. "Every toxin is here: two languages, two religions, different races, contested land, a devastated indigenous people. How we *haven't* become Kosovo, Northern Ireland, or the Middle East is a far more intriguing story, and more pertinent to the modern world."

More recently, the CBC decided to take one small step to reduce the gap between the solitudes that Starowicz encountered and described. For years, the corporation has had its resources scattered all over Ottawa: radio studios and offices shared by English and French radio on the seventh floor of the Fairmont

Château Laurier, the parliamentary bureaus of English radio and television on Wellington Street, the French radio and television bureaus on Sparks Street, local television on Lanark Road in the suburbs, and, until they were downsized and transferred to Lanark, a separate headquarters building. After he became president, Robert Rabinovitch decided that this made no sense; that there should be a single CBC building in Ottawa. He also decided that the building should operate in both languages.

"I guess I'm a product of Mr. Pelletier," he told me, referring to his first job in Ottawa as a political aide to Gérard Pelletier when the Official Languages Act was developed and introduced. He was also a product of his environment. He had spent his childhood in Lachine, gone to McGill, and been active in Quebec student politics before doing his doctorate in economics at the University of Pennsylvania. He then went to work for Pelletier, and worked in the federal government, first in the Privy Council Office and then as deputy minister of Communications until 1986 when he was fired by the Tories; he was too identified with the policies of the Trudeau regime. After fourteen years in the private sector, he was named president of the CBC in 1999, and renewed in 2004. "To me it wasn't even a question. The real strategy was news integration," he said, talking about bringing the services together. "And in order for news integration to occur, you had to get rid of the physical barriers."

News integration – bringing radio, television, news, and current affairs together – is a CBC strategy in a number of cities. However, Ottawa is the largest operation to attempt the exercise, complicated by the presence of the Ottawa bureaus in addition to local radio and television stations. Rabinovitch was, in effect, rolling six bureaus, which, he concluded, never talked to one another, into one operation; he was going to bring them together and force them to communicate. "Putting them all in one place, the intent was to get them to work together," he said. "That was the news integration model. The next thing was 'Fine. What language are we going to work in?' And I always say my francophone friends are too polite. And to get their point across, they often work in English. That's not acceptable. And I knew there was a slippery slope in this building which would lead to English." He had noted that a lot of the technicians were French-speaking, and had had to work largely in English.

"But I also, philosophically, said, 'How can somebody understand Gilles Duceppe without being able to ask him questions and listen to him in French?' It just didn't make sense to me. If you're going to be a national reporter, how can you do it without understanding French? If I had my way, I would have everybody do a *stage* in Montreal before they came here for the English network," he says, using the French word for internship. "But we don't have that type of money and that luxury. So from day one [of the planning of the single CBC building in Ottawa], as comfort for the francophones, but more importantly from my point of view because I believed it, this place had to be bilingual. This is Ottawa. It's the capital."

So in March 2005, the CBC's Senior Management Committee approved a bilingualism policy for Ottawa media and production employees. "Ottawa is unique in Canada for being the capital of an officially bilingual country and a bilingual city in itself," the policy read. "The Corporation views bilingualism for Ottawa media and production employees as not only a great asset to bring to the job, but also as an opportunity for employees to obtain training and gain opportunities in the workplace." It went on to say that English and French are the languages of work at CBC/Radio-Canada in Ottawa, that employees have the right to use either official language, but that not every employee needs to be bilingual. "At meetings or in conversation, employees have the option to speak in the language of their choice." Then, after establishing two levels – functionally bilingual and fluently bilingual – the policy goes on to state that "hiring processes for positions designated 'bilingual-ism essential' will consider only bilingual individuals, and that non-bilingual candidates will only be hired in exceptional cir-cumstances," and "then only on condition that the bilingualism requirement is met within a reasonable time frame (maximum two years)." The bilingualism requirement for national and parlia-mentary reporters is effective September 8, 2006.

Then, for the current national reporters, many of whom are unilingual, came the reassurance that the Corporation is commit-ted to ensuring that everyone, "without regard to their ethnic origin or first language learned," has equal opportunities for advancement. And then the chilling qualification followed. "However, it is possible that employees may have to look to other CBC/Radio-Canada locations for opportunities," the policy states. "Lack of ability to reach the level of bilingualism required will not be grounds for separation, but individuals may be reassigned." For a national reporter who has spent years working to get to Ottawa, this hardly qualified as reassurance.

Rabinovitch has been worried that there might be some slip-page or some resistance to the policy but, overtly at least, there hasn't been any. "I'm amazed there has been no push back on the floor," he said. "Because believe me, there was push back at the top." (There may not have been push back; there was and certainly still is skepticism and concern.) He argues that a good reporter will ask to spend some time in Quebec, saying that even if he or she speaks the language, a grasp of the culture is also important.

The CBC, however, is the only news organization to make lan-guage skill an explicit prerequisite for working in Ottawa and covering national politics. (Other news organizations occasionally pay a price for their unilingualism. In September 2005, CTV Newsnet erroneously reported that Lucien Bouchard had died after someone misunderstood a documentary on the 1995 referen-dum that was playing on Radio-Canada's news channel Le Réseau de l'Information, and included Bouchard's hospitalization and brush with death.) The result is the following paradox: ever since 1968, a significant number – usually a majority, now perhaps less than a majority – of the English-speaking members of the parliamentary Press Gallery have been unable to cover Pierre Trudeau, Brian Mulroney, Jean Chrétien, or Paul Martin when they were campaigning in Quebec or speaking to their constituencies, or debating during the French-language debate. It is ironic, for ever since Trudeau became prime minister, bilingualism has become a prerequisite for those who seek advancement and leadership in the military, the public service, or federal politics – but not for those who report on, evaluate, and criticize them.

chapter ten

Serving the Public, Passing the Test

> *It is important that you be physically and mentally fit to undergo a testing session on the scheduled day. If you are not, we invite you to set another date because the results of your aptitude tests will be valid for your whole career in the federal public service.*
>
> CANADA SCHOOL OF PUBLIC SERVICE WEBSITE

In the spring of 2004, Carolyn Adolph, a CBC-Radio reporter in Ottawa, began to notice the rising sense of panic among some of her neighbours. The government had decided, after years of lax application of the language requirements, to actually enforce the rules; people who had not passed the reading, writing, and oral interaction tests after three tries would not be able to keep their public-service jobs. One neighbour was fretting that they might not be able to keep their house if her husband failed the test a third time. Later, when he did pass the test, his young son wept with relief.

Convinced there was a story to be done, Adolph sent off a series of Access to Information requests before she went on holiday

with her family. When she got back, the Access requests were ready
– unusually quickly. She became convinced that, inside the system,
public servants wanted the story to get out. For, at the very top of
the very first file she opened, was a letter Chief Statistician Ivan
Fellegi had written to the recently appointed president of the
Public Service Commission, Maria Barrados, on December 23,
2003. Fellegi was the farthest thing from being a reactionary
opposed to bilingualism. In fact, he was one of the success stories
of official bilingualism; under his watch, Statistics Canada had won
an award for its provision of services in both languages. But in his
letter, he made it clear that the system wasn't working.

After apologizing for bothering Barrados so soon after her
appointment, Fellegi said that the problems that had been brought
to his attention seemed urgent, "in fact, the word 'crisis' might not
be inappropriate." Fellegi had just had a series of lunches with his
senior executives, and the issue that was overwhelmingly bothering
them was the language training and testing system. He listed off the
complaints: an "unbelievably high" failure rate; students who failed
being given little or no feedback; students being assigned self-study
when "given that the failure is, in most instances, due to problems
with oral interaction, self-study is clearly the least effective reme-
dial measure"; unspecified rules involving the use of certain grammatical forms; differing goals in terms of timing (students in a
hurry to get back to work, teachers unconcerned about this);
scheduling problems; unreliable diagnosis; and a feeling that the
standards to be met had been raised.

"I am told that depression and other health problems have
been reported to their managers by several of the recent course
participants," he wrote. "I can certainly underline the intensity of
feelings that I experienced among my senior managers – both
Francophone and Anglophone (all of them having reached their
[required] levels, most of them some time ago – i.e. they were not
complaining on their own behalf). Indeed, it is the real possibility

of a backlash against the entire language program that makes me take this issue very seriously."

Fellegi's letter set off a flurry of reaction inside the system, and Barrados's staff generated a series of answers to all of the points he made. But in the margin of the copies released under Access to Information, beside the statement that it was a myth that candidates had to use certain grammatical forms, sophisticated vocabulary, or impeccable pronunciation in order to pass the test, some anonymous public servant had written "B.S.!"

After reading the file, Adolph went in to the CBC-Radio story meeting for *CBO Morning*, the local Ottawa morning show, and announced, "Folks, our ship has come in." She spent five weeks researching the situation, and produced two and a half hours of radio that provoked more e-mails than anything else CBC-Radio in Ottawa had ever done.

None of the public servants she interviewed who described their experience in language training were prepared to be identified; their voices were distorted for the broadcast so that they would not be recognized. They told of being failed repeatedly, and having difficulty in finding out why, so that they could focus on the areas where they had made mistakes. As their failures mounted, they became increasingly tense, losing confidence and sleep; teachers recommended that they take beta blockers or other drugs to calm their nerves. One public servant told how he only passed when he smuggled wine into the examination room.

As I worked on this book, I began to hear a litany of similar stories. The anecdotes are endless, disturbing, and impossible to attach to names. A specialist from Alberta who was hired to work in the public service because of his expertise went cheerfully off to language training, and failed after the examiner led him into a conversation about his favourite pastime – hunting – and he found that he had no idea of the name of breeds of hunting dog in French. A contract communications employee, sufficiently comfortable in both languages that there was some discussion as to whether French or English should be designated as the second language for testing purposes, and who had been dealing fluently with French-language issues and the French-language media without problem or complaint for years, lost the job for not using the conditional enough in the examination – even though communications officials have drilled it into them not to use the conditional. A successful fifty-year-old executive with twenty-five years in government was told, on the basis of her earlier test, that she should expect to pass her C level (the highest level) in four months and, after six tests in eighteen months, is still trying. After years of success in government, including several where she worked closely with a Quebec minister, that woman's confidence has been so seriously undermined by her experience with language training that she has been referred to a psychologist to explain why she is unable to pass the test. A regional director in a Southern Ontario town almost devoid of francophones lost his job because his boss would not ask for an extension in the deadline for him to pass his French test. Executives in late middle-age are going for their tenth and eleventh tries to pass the test so they can be confirmed in their positions before they retire, thereby making them eligible for a better pension. A language teacher, baffled by his students' failure of the test, concluded that the problem was that the examiner simply didn't understand what the public servant was talking about when he described the complexities of his job.

The fears about losing jobs were not unfounded or unrealistic; Adolph reported that a total of six thousand people were disqualified from their jobs because they didn't pass the language test. Even those who passed the test the first time find the system flawed. "It's an examination-obsessed system," one senior public servant told me. "There's no incentive for keeping the language current, and there's no incentive to use the language on a daily basis. It's highly artificial. . . . I won't dare speak a word of French now because I haven't spoken it for two years. . . . The shelf life for the C level (the highest level) is about a month, maybe three weeks. You don't touch it for a month, I don't think you could pass the C test; you don't touch it for a year, I don't think you could pass B level."

There are three levels: A (basic), B (intermediate), and C (advanced) – and tests are given in reading, writing, and oral interaction. The C in oral interaction is the challenge for most English-speaking public servants, and what it requires is described by the Public Service Commission in the following terms:

- giving and understanding explanations and descriptions which may involve complicated details, hypothetical questions or complex and abstract ideas;
- giving and understanding detailed accounts of events, actions taken, or procedures to be followed;
- discussing or explaining policies, procedures, regulations, programs and services relating to an area of work;
- participating effectively in discussions which involve the rapid exchange of ideas;
- supporting opinions, defending a point of view, or justifying actions in meetings or discussions with employees, colleagues or superiors;
- counselling and giving advice to employees or clients on sensitive or complex issues;
- participating in selection boards;
- making presentations, giving training courses or defending appeals; and,
- dealing with situations which require quick and accurate use of both languages in rapid succession (such as those faced by a receptionist in a busy office).

At one level, the situation is extremely simple. Since the early 1960s, the federal government has recognized the need to establish a federal public service that can function in both official languages. The rationale is obvious, laudable, and as old as Maurice Lamontagne's 1962 memo. Since the Official Languages Act of 1969 that has been the objective. And in many ways, the objective was being achieved a few years after a difficult introduction in the 1970s. "By the early 1980s, one could find in Ottawa meetings of five or six anglophone officials with a francophone minister where the discussion was entirely in French," observed Arthur Kroeger, then deputy minister of Employment and Immigration, in 1989. "When I was in the Department of Energy, we conducted negotiations with officials from Alberta in English, and with officials from Quebec in French. Is the French that one hears at such meetings elegant? Not usually. One does not look to governments for elegance. One looks to them for competence, for the ability to do those things that have to be done." (One of the current complaints about language testing is that many students feel that competence is no longer enough, that elegance is now required, that the testing system has been taken over by obsessive grammarians, or, to put it more crudely, in water-cooler language, "grammar nazis.")

But after a decade of cutbacks in the 1990s, it began to be obvious that the system had eroded, language requirements were being quietly ignored, exceptions being made, and rules bent with a wink and a nudge. In 2001, in the Speech from the Throne, the government reiterated its commitment to linguistic duality. After years of postponed deadlines, extension orders, and exceptions (1978 became 1983, 1983 became 1987, and so on), in 2002 Treasury Board president Lucienne Robillard announced that enough was enough, and the rules would be enforced. As of March 2003, those in positions designated as bilingual would be required to be bilingual. This was headline news in Ottawa – rules to be enforced! Language requirements to be taken seriously! – and the reaction among public servants was a mixture of horror and skepticism. After so many postponements, why would this announcement be any different from all the others? "The question people asked me most often was 'When are you going to announce a new date?'" recalled Diana Monnet. "Well, no new date. Mme Robillard had decided to start, level by level, to make 'imperative' staffing obligatory." (It is an interesting reflection on bureaucratic language in Ottawa that it had not been obligatory to have a "bilingual imperative" position filled by a bilingual person.) Monnet is the vice president, Official Languages at the Public Service Human Resources Management Agency of Canada, which means that she is the senior official responsible for official languages.

The reasons for the policy are clear enough. Canadians should be able to address their government in the official language of their choice, and French-speaking citizens concerned about taxation or mining policy or the Kyoto Accord or Canada's policy on disarmament or Canada's negotiating position at the World Trade Organization have as much right to make their case in French to federal officials as English-speaking Canadians have the right to make their case in English. In 1978, one Quebec Liberal MP told me how furious he was that a delegation of concerned citizens from his riding came to Ottawa to meet departmental officials – and the department was unable to produce officials who could understand their concerns and respond in French.

Similarly, French-speaking cabinet ministers have the right to be served with documentations and briefings in French. Over the last two decades, several departments have had to do cartwheels to be able to cope when a cabinet shuffle produced a francophone minister, sometimes choosing the only bilingual assistant deputy minister to do all the briefings. "The word would come down that the minister would want everything in French – and there would be a loud groan," recalled one former public servant. "Because that meant that everything had to be done three days earlier than before to provide time for translation."

Finally, the right to work in one's preferred official language has been established for those working in areas that are designated bilingual: a belt that runs down the Ottawa River, includes the national Capital Region, goes along the St. Lawrence River, and covers part of New Brunswick.

That does not mean that everyone in the federal government has to be bilingual. In Western Canada, in 2000, fewer than 5 per cent of the over 30,000 federal government jobs in the West were designated bilingual. Over all, only 35 per cent of the 143,052 jobs in the public service were bilingual. (Since then, that has risen to 39 per cent.) "If you want to rise in the Public Service and, for whatever reason, you really don't want to learn French, you can do it up to the EX3 level – in Alberta and Saskatchewan," Monnet told me. "There are unilingual executive positions, and to a very senior level. But if you want to get ahead, if you want to be an assistant deputy minister, they're all bilingual, and the message has to be clear."

One thing certainly was clear – the government did not need Ivan Fellegi to tell it that there was a problem. For years, there have been surveys, studies, and reports by Treasury Board and the Public Service Commission, the ongoing work of the parliamentary committees on official languages, and the studies and annual reports of the Commissioner of Official Languages. All of them confirm that problems persist.

Language training is not a casual business. On the basis of three decades of experience, the government calculates that it takes 1,000 hours of instruction to reach level A, 1,300 hours to reach level B, and 1,860 hours to reach level C. The required level for executives is "CBC" – C in reading, B in writing, and C in oral interaction. On average, executives needed 883 hours to achieve their CBC level – which, at seven hours a day, works out to 126 days or eighteen weeks. Calculating the cost of an executive's salary and the cost of instruction – not to mention the executive's absence from his or her "real work" – the investment is considerable.

After the Public Service Commission asked for more money for language training in 2000, in the fall of 2001, the Treasury Board Secretariat and the Public Service Commission did a joint study of language training. They faced a problem: the government had announced that all executives would have to reach higher language standards by March 2003; almost five hundred executives had to be trained to reach that level, and yet the system could train only an additional fifty executives with the budget it had. In addition, there was what, in government jargon, is called "the EE community" – or those targeted by employment equity programs intended to increase the number of visible minorities, immigrants, and aboriginals – and what the report called "learners with physical and learning disabilities."

They also encountered a difference in how anglophones and francophones viewed the issue of official languages: anglophones saw it as a matter of getting an accreditation, without any real business need, while francophones saw it as a critical question of being able to work in their mother tongue. This was not a good mix.

There were a number of dilemmas: although the size of the public service was then shrinking, the demand for language training was increasing – and budgets were tight. One of the early drafts of the joint study in 2001 even raised some brave questions, wondering whether the government should be acknowledging that the language make-up of the country was changing, with new, growing linguistic minorities and a shrinking French minority. "As society becomes more diverse, there will be more need for the PS [Public Service] to become truly representative and respectful," the draft stated. "For example, if 20 per cent of a manager's clientele are Asian and two per cent are French, is that manager really better off to send staff on French training or Mandarin? What do we do if these growing minority groups become more militant and demand equal service (e.g. funding of primary schools)?" Those questions – almost subversive in the context of the government policy – disappeared in later versions.

The report made it very clear that there was a problem in meeting the March 2003 deadline that the government had set for government executives to reach the required levels; among other gloomy statistics on failure rates and the gap between the five hundred executives needing training while the system could only train fifty, it found that executives were twice as likely to fail the oral interaction test as non-executives. Pointing out that executives feel great pressure to pass the test, and that too much stress can inhibit performance on the tests, the report made a sensible suggestion: "The language program for senior executives should be reviewed and adapted to meet the needs and working conditions of executives rather than to expect the executives to adapt to the existing language training program."

Despite the continuing horror stories, there are some indications that this is happening. On an experimental basis, the government tried giving several executives their language tests by sending an examiner and a psychologist to their workplace and watching them function with colleagues and at meetings in French. Despite the potential for awkwardness, it proved successful.

Following that report, Treasury Board reached a number of conclusions about federal language policy. It found that, despite the progress that had been made, the reality fell short of the goal of linguistic duality; momentum had been lost during the cutbacks of the 1990s. Between 1994 and 2000, the availability of French on government toll-free lines dropped from 91 per cent to 75 per cent. The number of federal government offices and service points that were designated bilingual dropped from 31 per cent to 28 per cent between 1994 and 2000. And there was a major problem with respect to the use of French in the National Capital

Region. "It has become clear that social and cultural factors are at play which limit interaction in French," the analysis stated. "Anglophones take language training but many of them seldom use their new skills; as a consequence their capacities diminish. Francophones accommodate them by switching to English if they suspect there is a problem of understanding. The result is quasi-assimilation of French in the workplace. English becomes the lingua franca and the job gets done, but true bilingualism suffers."

In 2002, the Treasury Board Secretariat commissioned a study on attitudes toward use of French and English within the public service – and, after interviewing over five thousand public servants, found that opinions were all over the map, with varying degrees of support, concern, and resentment of the policy. But a clear majority – a total of 64 per cent of those surveyed – supported the language policy, and differed in degrees over how much more should be done. Skeptics, mainly in Ontario and British Columbia, thought the policy was a waste of money and it should be French in Quebec and English in the rest of the country, while a worried minority, mainly francophones from the West and the National Capital Region, felt the linguistic minority in their province was not being well served, and its future was threatened. But rumours of overwhelming opposition to the policy were unfounded. It was a study which showed how complicated the views on language policy are, even within the public service. Generalizations are unwise.

In March 2004, Official Languages Commissioner Dyane Adam published a study that reinforced these findings. *Walking the Talk: Language of Work in the Federal Public Service* was based on a survey of two thousand public servants in the National Capital Region, and found that francophones tend to adopt the language of their superior; that anglophones have a lack of confidence in work done in French – suggesting that francophones are right to suspect that their work will be taken more seriously if it is in English – and are rarely faced with the need to communicate with unilingual francophones. But the study also showed that anglophones would prefer to see French used more than it is now – during meetings, when dealing with senior management, or with superiors, and with francophone colleagues.

In April 2005, Adam's office published a report that further clarified some of the issues about language use in the public service. *Making It Real: Promoting Respectful Co-existence of the Two Official Languages at Work* found that the situation in Quebec was a mirror image of the situation in Ottawa; just as the default language in Ottawa is English, the default language in the federal public service in Quebec is French. Like francophones in Ottawa who hesitate to speak French, many anglophones in the federal public service in Quebec do not feel comfortable using English at work and prefer to work in French, feeling their work will be better understood and recognized in an environment where 97.5 per cent of the staff can communicate in French and 25 per cent of the francophones are unilingual.

Dealing with head office is different. E-mails in French get replies in English; when someone speaks French at a meeting in Ottawa, one Montreal manager observed in a focus group, "they stop taking notes or ask you to repeat yourself." As the report observed, "The organizational culture of the National Capital Region favours the use of English." Documents, training sessions, and work instruments are unavailable in French until later.

Other studies found that the federal government has never used the French-speaking environment of its Quebec offices as a way to provide English-speaking public servants with a career-shaping experience of working in a situation where French is the natural language of work, and that, despite the widely held view to the contrary, language requirements are no more of a barrier for visible minorities than for anyone else. It is hard to find an issue relating to language in the public service that has not been studied.

Without ever saying so, the studies suggest that language use is relationship-based. In other words, if two people establish a relationship in one language, it is very difficult to change the language. As a result, when managers or executives have established relationships with their colleagues in one language and then go off to language training, it is difficult to change the language of the relationship when they come back. An anglophone manager is unlikely to start speaking French to francophone colleagues when back at work, despite the hopes of the program.

Study after study has showed the same thing: public servants still don't understand the policy, and exaggerate its scope, believing that it applies in every part of the country; younger public servants are most likely to endorse the aims of the policy; and anglophones and francophones see the policy very differently. Anglophones see it as a barrier to their career aspirations, and as politically motivated; francophones see it as protecting their basic rights and protecting the survival of the French language. While the objections have become more muted, it is a pattern that has endured with anglophone public servants uttering some of the same complaints as their predecessors did, thirty years ago.

It seems incongruous that, four decades after Lester Pearson set out to make the public service functional in both languages, the government is still wrestling with the problem, and public servants who are much nearer retirement than entry into government are taking language training. The policy is thirty-five years old. It was introduced when people now reaching retirement were graduating from university. One would think that anyone who wanted to work in the federal public service should have recognized a long time ago that understanding both official languages was a prerequisite for advancement, and would have made a point of studying French in high school and beyond. But the problem, as one federal executive pointed out to me, is that high-school students do not generally aspire to be federal bureaucrats.

More to the point, the federal government does not seek out bureaucrats – or even political science graduates – when it hires. It seeks secretaries, administrators, economists, lawyers, scientists, agronomists, doctors, trade experts, health-policy analysts, labour mediators, engineers, public-relations specialists, foreign-policy wonks, and all the other experts that a modern state requires. At the moment they are hired, and in the jobs where they are needed, language is not a requirement. It is only when they want to be promoted that it becomes an issue.

The further problem is that government departments have developed, over the years, a linguistic culture; some, like Finance, National Defence, Agriculture, Natural Resources, Fisheries and Oceans, and Indian and Northern Affairs are overwhelmingly anglophone in their culture. Others, like Foreign Affairs, CIDA, and Canadian Heritage have a significant French-language presence – but even at Foreign Affairs, in the lecture hall, the large sign at the front announcing translation facilities is in English only, reflecting the unconscious assumption that, even though many diplomats from French-speaking countries come to lectures there, the only purpose of translation is to convert French into English.

On the face of it, the system is not rational. It is easier – and much cheaper – to teach students a second language than it is to teach adults. And it is triply expensive to take a forty-seven-year-old manager out of his or her job to teach him or her French: the government is paying for the training itself, paying the manager's full salary – an expense that does not exist for students – and also has to pay the replacement cost of having someone else fill in for the absent employee. "You could train all the kids in Canada," one federal official observed, "for the cost of training the public service." There are huge effects on efficiency (executives and managers detached from their jobs for weeks to go "on French") and,

unexpectedly, on internal mobility and advancement. One executive told me that she had several people on her staff determined
never to leave their current job because they never wanted to take
another language test again.

The fact that universities have not assumed this language
responsibility has created an additional barrier for hiring new
blood into the senior levels of the public service. This is one of
those ideas everyone endorses. Bring in top people from the
private sector, enrich the public sector, increase understanding
between government and business. Terrific. But language requirements have become a hidden barrier to turning the theory into
practice. Toronto consultant and former headhunter Robin Sears
embarked on a number of head-hunting projects for the federal
government, seeking out experienced executives on Bay Street.
The executive would be interested, the negotiations would be
underway, and at one point he would be told, "Your job will start
with five months in French-language training." "There would be a
laugh – and he would hang up," Sears said. What he found more
frustrating was that his client – the federal government – refused
to acknowledge that this was a problem. "I felt like [Mississippi
Senator] Trent Lott complaining about affirmative action," he
said. "I told them, 'Look, I understand the objectives – I was in
Ottawa then. I'm trying to tell you it isn't working.'"

The unforeseen problem was that those members of the
public service elite who had passed their language tests and
advanced – the great majority – had acquired a skill that the business elite had simply not bothered with. The unintended effect,
Sears said, was something similar to what he had observed in Asia:
the emergence of post-colonial leadership castes: the Tamils in Sri
Lanka, and the Sikhs in India.

The Asians, he pointed out, had developed an informal solution. Companies that needed contact with the English-speaking
world developed an informal system of support: if the boss was

English-speaking, the number two would be Asian, and vice versa. Sears found it frustrating that no one in Ottawa was prepared to consider that kind of approach where, if the deputy were an anglophone, the assistant deputy would automatically be a francophone, with the reverse being the case as well.

There have, however, been improvements to the system. For years, an aptitude test was given to see whether people had the ability to learn French, using a language that they were unlikely to have heard in order to check their ability to learn languages. So, for several days, people were immersed – in Kurdish! Those days are gone now, and the government is wrestling with various recommendations on how to make the language-testing system more flexible, and more focused on the requirements of work. One approach that is being considered is developing a different method of teaching French to those whose mother tongue is tonal, like Chinese or Japanese.

In March 2003, the federal government announced the Action Plan to address the tenacious problems surrounding the issue of official languages. Introduced by Stéphane Dion, who had been given overall responsibility for language within the Chrétien cabinet, the plan involved the injection of $751.3 million over five years. It had two explicit goals: doubling the number of bilingual high-school graduates from 25 per cent to 50 per cent, and increasing the number of francophones outside Quebec who send their children to French school from 68 per cent to 80 per cent. Unusually for any government report, the plan acknowledged that "the official languages program has been losing steam for the last decade or so, while the country and the public service focussed on taming the deficit." The Action Plan vowed to "make official languages a priority again and change the organizational culture of the public service."

The Chrétien government changed, however. Dion was dropped from cabinet before returning as Minister of the Environment, and Deputy House Leader Mauril Bélanger, the minister responsible

for Official Languages, had his hands full as the Martin government wrestled with the day-to-day crises of managing a minority
government.

At the end of October 2005, Bélanger tabled a mid-term
report on the Action Plan, which showed progress – but in scattered fashion. There were some bright spots – the target of
increasing French-speaking immigrants to communities outside
Quebec from 3.1 per cent to 4.4 per cent in 2008 had been sur-
passed, with 4.9 per cent of French-speaking immigrants settling
outside Quebec in 2004. But the report was vague about the hard
targets, saying, "Objectives are being phased in over a ten-year
period, and while investments to date have been made in the targeted areas, it is too soon to predict their effect." Only $123.4
million of the $751.3 million had been spent, two and a half years
after the Action Plan had been launched.

There were a host of small initiatives – an Innovation
Program which, among other things, granted $1,450,000 to Sport
Canada to improve its services to the public and to Canadian athletes; in addition, $2.5 million over five years to develop strategies
to recruit bilingual candidates for the public service and fund a
study on language training, and $400,000 to promote the hiring of
bilingual people. But the Mid-Term Report was shrouded in
jargon, claiming proudly that "one of the major achievements of
the Action Plan is undoubtedly the new horizontality practices
introduced within communities and a number of departments."
Come again? Horizontality?

The Mid-Term Report also included, indirectly, a series of
admissions: the government is still "exploring options to raise
awareness of parts . . . of the Official Languages Act and explain
clearly to public servants the values that underpin government
policy and the inherent rights and obligations." In other words,
public servants still don't understand the policy. Demand for
training increased more rapidly than expected. In addition, the

Mid-Term Report conceded, a survey of community activists revealed that the actions from the action plan had been almost invisible: "Over 75 per cent of respondents saw no impact of the Action Plan on members." That figure provoked Conservative MP Guy Lauzon, a member of the committee, to issue a statement criticizing the government for inaction, saying, "The Action Plan is a failure all along the line."

On October 27, 2005, the day that Bélanger tabled the Mid-Term Report, Official Languages Commissioner Dyane Adam told a parliamentary committee that in some regions, service is provided in both languages less than 50 per cent of the time. "We discuss the implementation of the Action Plan and we highlight the same problems that you have discovered: slow delivery and inertia have real consequences for communities and create impatience," she said. She heard some of the same stories from MPs that have been told for decades: Air Canada flight attendants unable to understand a request for a glass of water, officials at the Meteorological Service in Halifax unable to give warnings about Hurricane Wilma to the Acadian community in New Brunswick on the radio in French, Air Canada employees in Moncton unable to serve customers in French. And she told the MPs about the court cases that Air Canada is appealing, challenging its obligations to provide services in both languages.

It was only the latest indication that the public service is caught on the horns of a dilemma. On the one hand, it is the only Canadian institution that has enshrined the right to work in one's mother tongue and that has the obligation to be ready to serve ministers and the public in the language of their choice – which it still finds difficult. On the other hand, it is expected to be as diverse as the country has become. And, despite the injection of money from the Action Plan, the funds to make the public service a genuine bridge between English-speaking and French-speaking Canada are simply not there. So that job is left to our politicians.

The Political
Imperative

> To become a truly national leader in Canada and
> to function effectively in the Parliament of Canada,
> it is necessary to understand and speak French
> with some degree of proficiency.
>
> *PRESTON MANNING*

At the end of May 1983, in the lobby of the Holiday Inn in Longueuil, John Crosbie demonstrated that the political world in Canada had changed. He was campaigning for the leadership of the Progressive Conservative Party, and he was questioned by reporters about his lack of French. "I was tired, frustrated and angry about this constant harping on my French," Crosbie recalled in his memoirs. "I said 'I am not some kind of criminal, I am just an ordinary Canadian who has been in politics for a long time and has a lot to offer. Just because I'm not fluent in the French language doesn't mean a disaster is going to occur. . . . There are 20 million of us who are unilingual French or English . . . I don't think the 3.7 million who are bilingual should suddenly think of themselves as some kind of aristocracy and only leaders can come from their small group.'"

It was the fullest expression of unilingual frustration at the new rules of the leadership game made by a leadership candidate for a major party. Lester Pearson once said that he would be the last unilingual PM – and he was correct. Crosbie was in the middle of proving him right.

That spring, Crosbie was emerging as the dark-horse candidate in the Progressive Conservative leadership race. Highly intelligent, candid, and quick-witted, he had been a cabinet minister in Joey Smallwood's Newfoundland government before storming out to become a Conservative, and had been the finance minister in Joe Clark's short-lived government. Starting at 3 per cent support with Conservative delegates, he was gaining support fast, and his impressive campaign became a *Maclean's* cover story. Then came the scrum in Longueuil.

Crosbie went on to say that he understood many of the problems of Quebec and could talk to the people of Quebec. Then a reporter asked him the obvious question: how could he do this if he spoke only English. Crosbie's reply, he realized later, killed his leadership hopes. "I can't talk to the Chinese people in their own language either . . . I can't talk to the German people in their own language," he snapped. "Does that mean there should be no relationships between China and Canada or Canada and Germany or whatever? . . . There are many different languages." It's true, there are. But while Crosbie may have expressed solidarity with unilingual French-speaking Canadians, there was little indication that he would be any more successful in communicating with them or winning their votes than he would have been in winning hearts and votes in China or Germany. And, as he bitterly concluded in his memoirs, reporters had succeeded in getting what they wanted: a provocative quote. "They knew my goose was cooked," he wrote.

"So did I when I saw the newspaper headline: 'For Crosbie, French is not more important than Chinese or German.'"

Over two decades, the bar for linguistic competence had been raised. Leadership meant crossing swords in the House of Commons – and in a French-language debate – with Pierre Trudeau. Trudeau had changed the nature of the game; Quebeckers had made it clear that, henceforth, they would vote only for parties led by individuals who could communicate with them in French. Previously, English-speaking leaders from John A. Macdonald to Lester Pearson had got by with Quebec lieutenants. Suddenly, particularly with the prospect of a televised debate in French with Pierre Trudeau, this was not enough. Substitutes were no longer acceptable.

But it was more than just Trudeau. It was also the impact of television, which required a greater intimacy, a personal connection between political leaders and voters. "The revolution has already happened at home," Marshall McLuhan wrote in his eccentric classic look at communications, *Understanding Media*. "TV has changed our sense-lives and our mental processes. It has created a taste for all experience in depth that affects language learning as well as car styles. Since TV, nobody is happy with a mere book knowledge of French or the bard. The unanimous cry is 'Let's talk French' and 'Let the bard be heard.'"

So Joe Clark built his successful but surprising leadership win in 1976 on the plausible claim that he was bilingual – as was the number-two candidate, Claude Wagner, and the relatively unknown Montreal lawyer who finished third, Brian Mulroney.

The election of the Parti Québécois in 1976, with its promise of a referendum on sovereignty-association, heightened the uncertainties and unease over language. Patrick Gossage sardonically noted some of them in his journal in May 1977, after returning to the Prime Minister's Office from a trip to Quebec. "Back at Langevin [the building where the PMO is located], I enjoy the paradox of the top political strategists, [Jim] Coutts, [Keith] Davey, and [Tom] Axworthy, discussing election plans that will assure Quebec's future in Confederation in the only language and outlook they know – English!" he wrote. "A weird scene."

Clark's mastery of French won him respect in Quebec, but few votes – and did nothing to temper the sense of resentment of bilingualism in his home province of Alberta. He faced down his critics, however. At one all-candidates meeting, when people were complaining about language regulations, Clark said suddenly, "I want everyone in this room who has had to learn French to do their job to raise their hand." No one in the room put up their hand except Clark himself.

When Clark decided that the 67 per cent leadership vote was insufficient and called for a leadership race in 1983, Mulroney built his campaign around the idea that there were one hundred seats in Canada where francophones determined the outcome – and that the Conservatives had, in the past, simply conceded those seats to the Liberals. Mulroney won.

In the 1984 election, the French-language debate proved to be a turning-point – not because John Turner's French was inadequate (some columnists argued that it was more precise and grammatical than Mulroney's), but because Mulroney successfully hammered home that he was a Quebecker. A few days later, when Mulroney's campaign was mobbed in Quebec City, a local organizer told me, "Brian uttered the two most beautiful words in the French language during that debate – *chez nous*." At home. Where we live. Mulroney went on to win the largest majority in Canadian history, establishing a working coalition between small-town, largely unilingual Quebec, and small-town largely unilingual Western Canada.

Several of his Quebec ministers, in particular Benoît Bouchard, arrived in Ottawa unable to speak a word of English, just as his ministers from Western Canada spoke no French. The differing response was revealing; none of the Western ministers learned French. Bouchard – who had voted Yes in the 1980 referendum – became determined to learn English, hiring staff who would speak to him in English and listening to CBC-Radio in the morning as he shaved. He embraced the country, a country he had never known, and became a fervent federalist. Others, like Marcel Masse and Monique Vézina, became passionate sovereigntists after the failure of the Meech Lake Accord and campaigned for the Yes in the 1990 referendum.

As was the case in 1958 and 1963, the arrival of a significant number of unilingual francophone MPs who were not part of the culture of the Liberal Party created a certain momentum to change language policy and practice. Mulroney brought back simultaneous translation to the cabinet room, and, despite strong objections from Western MPs, introduced significant advances in language policy in 1988 with the amendments to the Official Languages Act, to bring the act into conformity with the Charter.

Language also became a part of the political cut-and-thrust of Question Period. The House of Commons had been televised since 1978, and the television news broadcasts in both languages would use the most dramatic exchanges. But TV producers hate broadcasting exchanges in a second language; the simultaneous translation gets in the way. So Mulroney would be adept at responding in the language that would be less likely to go on the air if he wanted to keep his response from helping to illustrate a story that might embarrass his government in Quebec or, if he spoke in English, in the rest of Canada. In February 1988, for example, Mulroney broke his habit of replying to Commons questions in the language in which they were asked when New Democrat MP Michael Cassidy asked, in French, about the loan problems of former Supply and Services Minister Michel Côté. Mulroney replied in English, taking a poke at an earlier statement by Cassidy that part of a frigate contract should have gone to Quebec instead of all of it going to New Brunswick. It was a triple-play partisan gibe: Mulroney avoided saying anything more in French about Côté, keeping the exchange off the French news; New Brunswickers were reminded in English that Saint John got the whole frigate contract; and Mulroney also avoided saying anything in French about the fact that Quebec failed to get part of the frigate contract.

Similarly, when Lucien Bouchard was sworn in as Secretary of State on March 31, 1988, Mulroney said – in French only – that part of Bouchard's mandate was to examine the question of party ethics and fundraising, and make recommendations to cabinet. Bouchard also spoke about this only in French. As a result, reporters who spoke no French came away from Rideau Hall unaware of this part of Bouchard's responsibilities.

The 1993 election resulted in a political fracture, largely along language lines. The Meech Lake Accord, and its failure, blew apart the fragile coalition that Mulroney had constructed between small-town Western Canada and small-town Quebec. The Progressive Conservatives were reduced to two seats, Lucien Bouchard became Leader of the Opposition leading fifty-four Bloc Québécois MPs, and Preston Manning came to Ottawa leading a caucus of fifty-two Reform MPs.

As prime minister, Jean Chrétien told his ministers that they should respond in the language of the question, if they were able to do so. In some areas, this became a political necessity; Bouchard, a former ambassador to France, wanted to show that he represented a people who could become a country – it was essential that his questions should be answered in French, by a Minister of Foreign Affairs who could be just as articulate and politically astute in the House as Bouchard: his former law-school classmate André Ouellet.

The fact that the Bloc formed the Official Opposition was a shock for English-speaking Canadians, and represented a critical rupture in Canadian politics. For the first time Quebeckers had not only voted for a party that was not about to form a government – rare in itself, since Quebec voters had been remarkably pragmatic in the way they invested their votes in the winning bandwagon in the past – but a party that could never form a government, whose goal was only to represent Quebec's interests, and that, after starting out as a nationalist anti-Chrétien coalition, was in the process of evolving into an *indépendantiste* party at the federal level.

Preston Manning observed later that Question Period became a family feud between Quebeckers, which shaped the body language of the House. "While the Quebec Liberals and Bloc members would be leaning forward – half rising from their seats, yelling at each other, and even shaking their fists – the majority of other MPs would be literally leaning back in their seats, as if to distance themselves from the fracas," he wrote in his memoir *Think Big*. "On such occasions even the most talkative non-Quebec MPs were strangely silent and bewildered: 'What the heck is this?'" It was a graphic illustration of some of the continuities of Canadian politics, and of the inability of the vast majority of English-Canadian politicians to understand or participate in one of the central debates over the future of the country: the place of Quebec. To address that issue, Manning did a number of things. He bravely set out to try to learn French himself.

In the fall of 2002, after he had left politics, I asked Manning about what that attempt represented, both as a personal and as a symbolic challenge. "Well, it's one of those things you know you should have done earlier," he said. "But to start trying to do it when you're a member of Parliament, particularly with a new party and being leader, it was very hard to do. Plus, my personality – I'm a perfectionist, which language teachers will tell you is the worst possible trait, because you won't try and settle for imperfection, so you don't do it at all." He recounted, laughing, that when he and his wife, Sandra – a warm, outgoing person – both showed up at the language school in Jonquière, it took the instructors about fifteen minutes to figure out that she had potential. "I could see these profs looking at each other, as if to say 'Who gets her and who gets him?'" he said, chuckling. Then, more seriously, he said, "I never thought the key to getting Quebec and French-speaking people was me learning French. I mean, I knew I had to get to a certain level for courtesy's sake and for the symbolic thing, but I really felt that what I needed was a Quebec general. I used to say a lieutenant, but I meant a higher rank than that."

In his speeches in Quebec, he would evoke the memory of Baldwin and Lafontaine, the two nineteenth-century reformers, and would always ask, "Où est Lafontaine?" Where is Lafontaine? No one ever emerged. "I think that probably kind of subconsciously inhibited my . . ." he paused. "I didn't think me learning French was the answer to anything. I mean it was necessary, yes, but that was not how this was going to be sold in Quebec. It was going to be sold by one of their own, having a different view of federalism."

I asked him what his response was to the idea that learning French, or having a mastery of French, was part of the distinction between having a national political culture and a regional political culture. Regional politicians, I suggested, whether they are in Quebec or in Alberta, don't have to learn the other language. In fact, at that point, a significant number of the members of Bernard Landry's Quebec cabinet were unilingual francophones, meaning that there were some portfolios requiring contact with other provinces that Landry had trouble filling. Manning responded, saying, "In the West, that's not as much a symbol of . . . I mean, if you're a national politician and you speak two languages but you know absolutely nothing about the economics or politics of Western Canada, to our people that is as

big a disqualifier for you presenting yourself as a national statesman as the bilingualism thing."

He then said something which illustrated, in my view, one of
his great misunderstandings about the nature of language and language politics in Canada. "I mean, ideally, yes, you should have the
language thing – but in the future, it's going to get even more
complicated than that," he said. "You're not going to be seen as a
national statesman in that Lower Mainland area [of British
Columbia] unless you've got some grasp of Mandarin. There are
huge chunks of Toronto there where if you say, 'This is a meeting
of the founding races, cultures and peoples' . . . [they'll say]
'Toronto is a meeting of the Italians and the rest.'"

But politics in Canada happens in one of two languages; only
376,000 Canadians speak neither official language – and over 40
per cent of these are age sixty-five and over. When I pointed out
that there were no Ontario or British Columbia politicians who
spoke no English – and that there were a sufficient number of
Bernard Landry's cabinet who spoke no English that it made
cabinet shuffles difficult – he acknowledged that it was true, and
that French remained important.

But it was a reluctant admission. Like many of the critics of
bilingualism, Manning instinctively turned John Crosbie's argument on its head, suggesting that Chinese would soon be just as
important as French in Canada. Well, no. There are all kinds of
good reasons for learning Chinese. It is the language of one of the
great world civilizations and cultures, and the language of a
surging Asian economy. Learning Chinese opens a door to an
ancient culture and an economy of the future. There are economic, business, diplomatic, cultural, even military reasons to
learn Chinese.

But becoming a national politician in Canada is not one of
them. There are 1 million speakers of Chinese in Canada – 3.5 per
cent of the population (872,400 who speak it as their mother

tongue, and 156,000 who have learned it as a second language). A small proportion of them are unilingual, and virtually none will remain unilingual in the next generation; their children either learn English or French or both. In his book *The Practice of Language Rights in Canada*, Michael MacMillan cites what he calls "the third generation rule of thumb" as a test for the validity of language rights: if a language minority sustains its language use for three generations, it is entitled to seek some guarantees of rights. Pointing to the Minority Report in the Royal Commission, which argued for official recognition of Ukrainian, MacMillan traces the steady decline of Ukrainian as a home language: from over 350,000 in 1951 to 46,150 in 1986. "The case for some recognition of Ukrainian, whatever legitimacy it might have had, is clearly past," he wrote. In contrast, there are almost 4 million unilingual francophones in Canada – more than half of the French-speaking population of Quebec, and more than there were when the Royal Commission on Bilingualism and Biculturalism was established. And yet, reflexively, those skeptical of the importance of learning French in Canada suggest that, somehow, it would be wiser to learn another world language. In fact, those Canadians who have learned other world languages are much more likely to have started with the other official language. As James Moore, a Conservative MP from British Columbia who went through school in immersion, pointed out, this only makes sense. Whatever instrument they ended up playing, most musicians started out with piano lessons. Learning one language makes learning other languages easier; it reduces the inhibition, sharpens the part of the brain that uses language, and generates the unconscious understanding that another language is just another code.

While Mulroney was comfortable in both languages, he did not have the same kind of impact on the political culture of the Progressive Conservative Party that Trudeau did on the Liberals. Of the young Tories attracted to Ottawa to work in ministers' offices, few took advantage of the language classes available – Stephen Harper being a major exception. But Trudeau influenced a generation of young university graduates who were drawn to Ottawa in the late 1960s and early 1970s, many of whom went on to have significant careers in the public service or in politics. Inspired by his bilingualism, they learned the other official language.

Even before Trudeau, by the 1960s, it was clear that bilingualism was not only going to be a criterion for advancement in the public service, it was also going to be a badge of honour for ambitious Liberals. So Trudeau's cabinet was full of English-speaking ministers who could answer questions in the House of Commons and from journalists in French: John Turner, Mitchell Sharp, Donald Macdonald, Bryce Mackasey, and several others. It set an example for future ambitious Liberals; in Jean Chrétien's cabinet twenty years later, Sheila Copps, John Manley, Allan Rock, David Collenette, and Bill Graham were all comfortable in French. They were all Ontario MPs who, as young people, had decided that learning French was important, and would be important in their lives.

As, of course, did Paul Martin. From the age of eight until he left high school, Martin was educated partly in French, and partly in English. It was an experience comparable to immersion: French immersion didn't exist when he was going to school, but true French-language education in Ontario didn't exist either. The result was that his French was good enough to embrace the idea of moving to Montreal not long after he graduated from law school and, after two decades of living in Montreal and conducting business there, he spoke colloquial French easily and comfortably. (When he is tired, however, his syntax sags – resulting in the incongruous suggestion in *Le Devoir*, on the eve of the French-language debate in the 2004 election, that his French was not as good as that of Stephen Harper.)

When Paul Martin Sr. joined the cabinet in 1946 and moved his family from Windsor to Ottawa, his cabinet colleagues were likely to live in Rockcliffe Park and send their children to Rockcliffe Park Public School. But French had been Paul Martin Sr.'s home language – although James Martin was of Irish descent, his wife was a Chouinard – and he was of the generation that had lived through Ontario's decision to abolish French-language teaching in the province, Regulation 17. His mother had been a schoolteacher. "So my father felt very strongly, as a Franco-Ontarian, about the language issue and the role of French-Canadians in government," Martin told me. "I didn't know it at the time, but it would have been a betrayal if he had not sent me to French school." Doing so coincided with his sense of roots, family identity, and his nationalist idealism about the country and its future.

The family lived in a duplex in Sandy Hill – then a partly French-speaking neighbourhood not far from the University of Ottawa – and young Paul was sent to a French school, the École Garneau. Percy Philip, the Ottawa correspondent for the *New York Times*, who spoke French, lived downstairs. Paul's mother Nell, who didn't speak a word of French, would send Paul downstairs for help with his homework when his father was busy.

Martin learned the hard way about Canada's language tensions. "They put me into this French school and I didn't speak a word of French," Martin recalled. "So naturally, the first couple of years of grade school, I learned how to fight. Then I would walk home, and I would have to walk past St. Joseph's School (the Irish Catholic school), where I would have to fight all over again, because this was when the fights between the French Catholic kids and the Irish Catholic kids would take place. I found I had to fight at the school I was going to, and then fight with the Irish Catholic kids who decided I was French – and then three blocks later I had to go by a school called Osgoode, which of course was the public school, and the same battle would start all over again."

Martin learned French, and went from the École Garneau to Ottawa University High School – the only French-language high school that then existed in Ontario, which drew students from Northern Ontario. (At that time it was a bilingual education rather than a French education; Martin always studied maths and sciences in English.) It gave him first-hand contact with the other language and culture, and he realized very young that perspective on an issue was shaped very strongly by the language one thought and spoke in. He became aware of the frustration of French Canadians in Ottawa, who, in the years before official bilingualism existed in the public service, were severely limited in how high they could rise. "My closest friend was a kid named Dickie Robillard, who later became a trade commissioner and died in Africa," Martin said. "He lived not far from the school. They were French, and I remember conversations with them, and the feeling in that family that his father could not rise in the civil service because he was French. I remember those discussions as a kid growing up." Later, he told me, "I went to school with the sons, and later the sons and daughters, of French Canadians – and it was easier for them to become Prime Minister of Canada than to rise in the public service."

Martin had a kind of double life: growing up both in Windsor, where he spent his early childhood and every summer at the family cottage in Colchester, among Irish Catholic relatives in Essex County, and in Ottawa, where he went to school, often visiting his grandmother and aunts in Pembroke. After he graduated from the University of Toronto law school, he moved to Montreal with his wife and young family, and took a job at Power Corporation as personal assistant to the president, Maurice Strong. It was a turning-point for Martin. Montreal was an exciting place in 1966; the city was buzzing with preparations for the World Fair, Expo 67, and politics was bubbling with action. "I also came to Montreal because I had a tremendous interest in the Quiet Revolution," Martin said. "This gave me a chance to learn about it."

But while Martin spent two decades in Montreal before running for office in 1988, and insisted on running in a Montreal riding, when his primary political team came together in 1990 for his first race for the Liberal leadership it consisted largely of unilingual anglophones. Mulroney and Chrétien had both carried on much of their working day with their senior political and bureaucratic advisers in French, and their English-language confidants were bilingual. This was not the case for Martin, whose most intimate and constant advisers were unable to follow if the issue at hand was being discussed in French. Martin insists that this is not a problem; that he has a wide network of friends and contacts in Quebec, that he returns to Montreal and his farm in the Eastern Townships constantly, and that he is not constrained in any way by the unilingualism of his closest circle of political advisers in the Prime Minister's Office. Yet it is odd and revealing that the small, deeply loyal team of advisers and friends who have been part of Martin's entourage since his first leadership campaign in 1990 would have remained unilingual, cut off from the political energies and ideas that had drawn Martin to Montreal and led him to decide – against the advice of many Liberals – to make his political base in Montreal rather than in Windsor.

Similarly, events conspired to create a situation in which fewer of Martin's English-speaking cabinet members were able to respond in French to questions in the House of Commons than has been the case since Mulroney's cabinet. Martin insists that this is not a problem in caucus or in cabinet, but acknowledges that there are times when to be sure that they are understood, French-speaking MPs or cabinet ministers make their case in English. Martin himself asks his cabinet members to speak in French if they so choose, and always responds in the language of the person addressing him.

"It is a problem [in Question Period] when questions are posed in French to individual ministers and individual ministers are unable to answer in French," he acknowledged to me. "One would wish it to be otherwise, but that's just the way it is." For the senior members of Martin's English-speaking cabinet – where one would expect the leadership successors to come from – are largely unilingual: Ralph Goodale, Anne McLellan, Ken Dryden, Ujjal Dosanjh, Reg Alcock, Tony Valeri, and Belinda Stronach are all unable to answer questions in the House in French. The Martin government speaks with authority on finance, national security, national child care, health, treasury, parliamentary matters, and employment strategies in English only. National Defence Minister Bill Graham and National Revenue Minister John McCallum are the only senior ministers from outside Quebec who can respond effectively in French; the others – Joe Volpe, John Godfrey, Scott Brison, Claudette Bradshaw, Jim Peterson, Albina Guarnieri, and Aileen Carroll – are either less comfortable in French or more junior. Those watching the news in French generally hear about federal policies from Quebec ministers only; most senior ministers from the rest of the country cannot speak to Quebec in French.

Stephen Harper learned French very differently. In the summer of 1968, when he was nine years old and his father was working for Imperial Oil in Toronto, and the family lived in Leaside, his mother read an advertisement for a particular kind of summer school. Ontario was teaching French teachers, and looking for students. So that summer, young Stephen would take public transit to Deer Park School to be taught French by student teachers. Harper then took French in Grade 5 and through high school – not immersion, which did not exist in Toronto when he was in school, but core French. He was a good student and, he observed, "at the end of Grade 13, I could read and write French as fluently as I can today. In fact better, because I seldom write French any more. I haven't in a long, long time. But I could not understand or speak a word. It was learned strictly scholastically. And most of the French teachers, I would say in that era . . . were conversationally limited. Their own knowledge was scholastic." He took full credits in French and full credits in Latin, and observed wryly that he had about the same level of comprehension in both. But where he really learned French was in a summer immersion program in Victoria in the summer of 1978. He observed that while the program was half francophone students learning English and half anglophone students learning French, there was almost no mixing. "The Quebec students, who were almost all sovereignists, stayed to themselves and the English students – who were by and large less serious about this as a language course, anyway – had a lot of fun."

It was almost a decade later, in Ottawa – first as a staffer for Progressive Conservative MP Jim Hawkes in 1985–86 and then in 1989, when he became the chief policy officer of the Reform Party and worked for Deborah Grey – that he started working on his French and using it in earnest. "I mean, I actually started doing interviews [in French] and it was really through necessity." In addition to the classes that were available for Parliament Hill staff, which he enrolled in but attended sparsely, Harper chose an unusual method of improving his French. Whenever he attended the House of Commons or parliamentary committees as a staffer, he would tune to the translation channel for whoever was speaking, and listen to those speaking English in French translation, and to those speaking French in English translation.

In the late 1980s, he embarked on a personal study of language policy internationally. It had a significant impact on his thinking – and coincided with his dim view of government intervention of any kind.

"The first thing I learned about language policies is that they have been extraordinarily unsuccessful at changing social realities. Trying through language policies to get populations to speak different languages is almost impossible," he told me, sitting in his office on Parliament Hill. He concluded that governments had been able to establish a standard version of language over a long period of time through national education systems, but had only changed actual language use through displacing populations, through genocide, or through what is now called ethnic cleansing: mass movement of populations.

"Government policies do not change people's language, even, fascinatingly, in totalitarian states," he said. "The decades-long attempts by the Soviet government to make Russian the effective reality in large parts of the Soviet Union, only happened where Russians were actually moved to those areas, [through] Russification." Harper argues that Russification was a complete failure as a language policy, and may have increased ethnic identities and contributed to the dissolution of the Soviet Union.

"And in France, which is probably, among non-totalitarian systems, the most extensive use of governments trying to change linguistic reality through the use of policy, it took literally hundreds of years to assimilate the regional dialects and, in the end, the disappearance of the non-French languages has been only marginally due to language policy itself," he said, adding that the near disappearance of Breton has been the result of three hundred years of policy and enormous state resources. "So language policies don't change the way people speak and the languages they use," he said. "In the case of Quebec, and in the case of Canada, as we know, the Trudeau bilingualism policies continued by future governments – including my own – won't change the actual usage of the French or English language in parts of the country as a social or economic reality. Only at the margins. They'll be determined by other things."

In fact, it is easy to show that Harper's claim that governments cannot affect language use is simply not true. Scandinavian governments have made the learning of English a significant priority, and have encouraged this by refusing to allow English films or television programs to be dubbed, insisting on subtitles. Partly as a result, 94 per cent of Swedes, 87 per cent of Finns, and 84 per cent of Danes between fifteen and thirty-nine say they know English.

And, as Harper himself acknowledges, Quebec's language legislation has had a significant impact on language use in Quebec; when Martin moved to Montreal in the mid-sixties, it was rarely used in business, and now it is a language of work. Harper's summary is an intriguing one that hinted both at his fundamental skepticism about the utility of language legislation – any language legislation – and his recognition that, politically, he would be unable to change the main elements of Canada's language policy.

At the same time that Harper was doing his private study of language policies in other countries, a fellow Reform Party staffer was doing a study of language policy in Canada. Now an Ottawa-area MP and then a Reform party researcher, Scott Reid wrote *Lament for a Notion* in 1989, laying out the case against the current form of official bilingualism, and arguing for the Finnish model. It is a highly researched polemic, with a number of problems: a false premise (that the purpose of the policy was to make everybody in Canada bilingual) and a disconcerting assumption that everyone has a right to work for the federal government, and God forbid that they be required to learn another language. Reid argued that the policy discriminates against unilingual francophones and overly favours francophones from outside Quebec. He called for the creation of French-language units – the idea proposed by Laurendeau–Dunton that there should be units inside the federal government that worked only in French, but that was never implemented – and the introduction of an education voucher system as a low-cost alternative to minority-language education. Highly critical of the costs of the government-language policy, he concluded by arguing, "Official bilingualism has come as close as any policy in the history of Canada to accomplishing the opposite of its intended objectives. Founded with the intention of uniting the country, it has at best failed to limit the allure of Québécois nationalism, and at worst it has driven Canadians further apart. Designed to correct historic wrongs, it has created new injustices. Intended to help create a new national identity in which all Canadians could share, it has instead become a symbol of section-alism, elitism and division."

Some influences of Reid's work can be seen in a memorable column that Harper wrote in the *Calgary Sun* in May 2001 entitled "The God That Failed." He argued that the policy did not reflect the country, and was unfair because of Quebec's language law.

"Real bilingualism in Canada is quite geographically isolated," he wrote. "Most Francophones actually live in French unilingual regions of Canada – mainly in Quebec – and most Anglophones live in English unilingual regions outside the province. Areas with significant numbers of both linguistic groups are almost all nar-rowly concentrated near the New Brunswick–Quebec and Quebec–Ontario borders, where most genuinely bilingual Canadians reside."

He argued that the federal government applied a double stan-dard: one set of rules for Quebec, and another for the rest of Canada. "While there have been ongoing and unsuccessful attempts to promote French outside of Quebec, the federal gov-ernment has increasingly surrendered to Quebec's activist policies of official unilingualism. And now the double standard has reached new heights with the appointment of Stéphane Dion as Minister of Official Languages. Dion is an unabashed supporter of the French-only Bill 101 inside Quebec and official bilingualism elsewhere. As minister, he immediately declared his view of national bilingualism as being 'to promote French.'"

Harper's last paragraph included a phrase – used as the title of a memorable 1950 anti-communist classic – that gave the column its headline. "As a religion, bilingualism is the god that failed. It has led to no fairness, produced no unity, and cost Canadian taxpayers untold millions."

When I asked him about the column four years later, Harper laid out his diagnosis without hesitation, with the calm deliberation of someone who has carefully thought out his position. He started by talking about the objectives of the policy. "For some people, it's merely a way for Quebeckers to feel more comfortable with the federal government," he said. "For others, it really is a massive social engineering exercise, in which Canada is supposed to become a genuinely bilingual country. And most people, at least upwardly mobile people, genuinely bilingual." His piece in the *Sun*, he said, focused on the idea – false, in my view – that Canada was supposed to become a genuinely bilingual country. "On that criteria, bilingualism is a dismal failure." He argued that it was quite shocking how few people had become bilingual, given the resources devoted to French. "Relative to the resources that have been piled into it – I am actually shocked at how many were bilingual before we got into it in the first place," Harper said. "Quebec is more French, the rest of the country is more English today, than at any time in our history. Those are the realities."

Then, in more measured tones than Reid fifteen years earlier, Harper addresses whether this means the policy is a failure. "Well I guess, once again, it depends on what you think the policy was designed to achieve. If it was designed to change the country, then by that measure it is a failure. If it was designed to end the sovereignty movement and make the country think of itself as one country as opposed to two solitudes or two peoples, I think it is also a failure by that measure. If, in fact, the scope of bilingualism was much more limited, and its only real objectives were to make it easier for francophones to join and participate in the civil service and make the federal government less, not necessarily less English but less British than when my father worked on the Glassco Commission in 1961, then on that score it's actually been a success." But Harper does not think that was the original intent of the policy. "If we want to accept today that we'll say that that was its original intent, and therefore it's a success, I'll go along with that interpretation; I'm not convinced that's true."

Harper argued that there has been a persistent historical misconception about the origins of the country. "There's a statement that goes around that Canada is a bilingual country, and Canada was conceived as a bilingual country, a country of two nations, whatever the various phrases are," he said. "In my judgment, both statements are false. There's no doubt – and you've read Scott Reid's book – there's no doubt Canada was not conceived in 1867 as a bilingual country. Canada was conceived as an English-speaking country where the presence of French, particularly in Quebec, would be recognized. And more than recognized, given some status and allowed to develop its own existence. But really, primarily in Quebec." Bilingualism in the 1867 Constitution, he said, was included to protect English in Quebec rather than to make Canada a bilingual country.

But Harper acknowledged that the conception of the country did change with Pierre Trudeau, becoming a country with two national languages. "What has changed is that Canada now has no truly national language of any kind. But it has two major languages that are dominant in their sections of the country. And large areas of the country where . . . [the other] official language is [not] very significant. Once you leave Montreal, with a few exceptions in Quebec, English is not an important language any longer. That's not because of Trudeau, that's because of Bill 22 and Bill 101 and things that happened from the Bertrand government on. And in the rest of the country, it hasn't changed because notwithstanding whatever Pierre Trudeau may have wanted to do or spent resources on doing, that hasn't been achieved."

Interestingly, Harper acknowledges that Quebec language law did change Quebec, despite his claim that governments are unable to influence language use. But while his diagnosis of the policy is as severe as ever, Harper has come to terms with the political realities; any suggestion that the Conservatives are going to change the language law raises red flags. When I asked him what elements of the policy he would change, he was very modest in his ambitions. "I think some of the regulatory aspects are too costly and elaborate that really have nothing to do with the efficacy of the policy, or its value as a symbol," he said. "And this is where I would probably disagree with most of the advocates of bilingualism, but I think the evidence is that if you wanted to strengthen French as an actual language of use in the federal public service, it would be better to go to the original B&B model of language work groups."

But he acknowledges these are details in a broad-ranging process; that creating French-language work groups could simultaneously preserve French as a working language and reduce the discontent among English-speaking public servants. (The problem is that someone has to communicate with these groups – and the language requirements for senior managers would remain intact.)

"But as I say, it's a continuum," Harper said. "The civil service could never conceivably be completely balkanized into two separate linguistic services, nor will it ever be one undifferentiated bilingual whole across the country. I would argue that moving a little bit in the other direction would be a practical one. But I think that's probably the extent."

Harper has become resigned to the political realities that surround discussion of language in Canada. Asked if he thinks it is possible to have a public debate on bilingualism now, Harper replied, "Not today, but some day" – and explained that the Liberal Party has succeeded in making language policy a symbol, and in conveying the view that Reform Party and Conservative language policies were and are more radical than is actually the case. "And as you know, Scott Reid's own prescription – while his evaluation of the system, like mine in the *Sun* article, is radical, in the end the conclusions from it are not that radical. . . . You toy around with the system at the margins," he said, adding that nobody is advocating rolling back the clock to pre-1968. Instead, he says, he agrees with Scott Reid: the Royal Commission's recommendation of bilingual districts should have been adopted.

"But the Liberal Party has made it a symbol: they're the party of the Canadian State and other parties have . . . strategies to undermine the state. And the fact that they may talk differently on this means that they actually want to dismantle the state," he said. "So until we're back to a point in the country that we perceive that we have two national parties that are fighting about governing the country and not about its radical restructuring, I think it's off the map."

He actually doesn't think there is much interest in a debate about the policy. Change will be on the margins. In other words, while the emperor of language policy may be wearing no clothes, Harper is not going to say so any more, because that has become a metaphor for dismantling the state.

It seems to me that there is a grudging, resentful quality to this analysis: a sense that the original, English nature of the country has been lost and cannot be recovered, and a very reluctant acknowledgement of the need to recognize that the country has changed, that there is a new Constitution with a Charter of Rights and Freedoms and that the clock cannot be turned back.

Reid's views, however, remain a sufficiently hot-button topic that when he uttered a fairly mild version of them during the 2004 election campaign, telling a New Brunswick newspaper that a Conservative government would ease the language requirements for public servants, the Liberals jumped on his remarks. Harper immediately dropped him as Official Languages critic. (Reid's views did not change; a few months later, he indicated his support for a lawsuit against the City of Ottawa over its language policy, saying it was unfair to unilingual anglophones.)

However, the Conservative caucus listened when veteran Tories like Hugh Segal reminded them of how the party had bitterly divided over language in the past. Harper made it "a three-line whip" – an obligatory caucus position – and the Conservatives swallowed whatever misgivings they might have had and voted to strengthen the Official Languages Act in November 2005. It went virtually unnoticed in the press – while an internal squabble would have made headlines.

Clearly, even in Harper's Conservative Party, challenging the assumptions of official bilingualism is politically unacceptable – which, in itself, speaks to widespread public support for the policy. Leadership aspirants in every party have grasped this.

Jack Layton grew up in Hudson, Quebec, an affluent conservative suburb west of the Island of Montreal. His father, Robert Layton, was an active Liberal, and in 1962 worked as the campaign manager for Paul Gérin-Lajoie, who went on to be Jean Lesage's Minister of Education. Layton has a vivid memory of helping his father put up election signs.

"At first, [I learned French] badly, because the English education system in Quebec at the time was not focused on communicating in the language," he said. "It was focused on memorization of rules. There wasn't any such thing as French immersion, and there was no effort to teach you how to listen or communicate in conversation. We were very definitely living in the two solitudes. . . . Hudson was not a place very friendly to the French-speakers. It was a divided community." (He still bristles with indignation at the dressing down he received when he threw a young people's party at the Hudson Yacht Club and opened it to the French-speaking teenagers in the town.)

Later, when he was a university student, he worked during the summer on construction sites for his father's engineering firm. "That's where I learned my French, because then suddenly I had to communicate," he said. "It was rough; I can't use some of the vocabulary I perfected there." In his fourth year, after marching in the massive McGill Français demonstration of 1969, he took a conversational French class every morning – a class that involved simply reading that morning's *Le Devoir* and talking about it.

Layton then moved to Toronto for graduate school at York University, and stayed on to teach at Ryerson and run municipally, where, after thirty years in Toronto, his French became rusty. When he ran for the NDP leadership in 2004, it became clear that the party had quietly made competence in both official languages one of its leadership requirements. Bill Blaikie and Lorne Nystrom, both from Western Canada, had learned French as MPs, and spoke it well. Joe Comartin had grown up in a small French-speaking village near Windsor, and surprised delegates with the quality of his French. Pierre Ducasse, the ebullient community worker from Quebec, was eloquent in both languages. Only Bev Meslo, the token candidate of the far left from Vancouver, was unable to participate in the French-language debate.

As a leadership candidate and as leader, Layton went to work on his French, taking French lessons for an hour twice a week, using his press secretary, Karl Bélanger, as an additional resource to help him improve his French, and periodically taking immersion weeks in Jonquière and Saint-Jean. "I'm determined to crack the subjunctive," he quipped. "You need to constantly work to improve your French; there are just too many elements of it to ever really stop trying to improve. It's getting a little better; I'm finding, bit by bit, my comprehension is improving and I'm more comfortable. I used to be very nervous about French interviews, particularly on the radio where I couldn't see people. Especially in the regions, or phone-in shows; people are speaking very fast, they're speaking idiomatically, using lots of expressions you just wouldn't know. But I'm gradually learning those."

There is a great disparity between the NDP's support for official language policy and language equity (significant) and its electoral support in Quebec (minimal). The lone francophone New Democrat MP is Yvon Godin from New Brunswick, and Layton acknowledges that when he first became leader, most caucus meetings featured Godin's complaints about a lack of complete commitment to the reality. "I can tell you we have had virtually none of that grousing for about a year, because we went to work on the issue," Layton said. "It's a long-term investment on our part, but, more important, it is a recognition of what we are and who we are."

Caucus meetings have simultaneous translation, and several MPs speak very good French, and others are learning. So far, that investment has gone unrequited in Quebec. "But at some point, the fissure line in Quebec politics may open up," Layton said. "Was Michaëlle Jean being prophetic [when she said in her installation speech that 'the time of the two solitudes that has for too long described the character of this country is past']? I like to think so. We want ourselves to be in place . . . so that when and if that happens . . ." He leaves the wistful thought uncompleted.

In the two decades since John Crosbie's humiliating experience and angry outburst in Longueuil, it had become clear that effectiveness in both official languages was a prerequisite for national party leadership. Manning lost the leadership of the Canadian Alliance in part because he had been unable to learn French. (As the experience of Stockwell Day showed, however, speaking both languages was a necessary condition, but not a sufficient condition, for effective leadership.)

For any politically ambitious young person, the rules are clear. If you want to be a doctor, you have to go to medical school; if you want to be a lawyer, you have to go to law school – and if you have national ambitions as a politician, you have to learn French. Already, a younger generation has learned that lesson.

James Moore was elected in 2000 at the age of twenty-four, making him still one of the younger Conservative MPs. Born and raised in Coquitlam, he was in French immersion from kindergarten to Grade 11, dropping out of immersion for his last year of high school because he found it difficult to do math in French. His parents, he quipped, thought that Pierre Trudeau was right about only two things: that the state had no place in the bedrooms of the nation, and that learning a second language was important for intellectual development. His mother was a French teacher, and he and his two sisters both went into immersion. Despite dropping out a year early, Moore emerged comfortable and articulate in the language. After a year in broadcasting in 1996, he went to Ottawa to work for the Reform Party, returning to British Columbia to get a degree in political science at the University of Northern British Columbia.

In an interview, he told me that he found his French to be "invaluable" as a member of Parliament. "It means I can stand in the House toe to toe with a member of the Bloc, telling them they are wrong in their own language," he said. "I have also been able to talk to public servants whose first language is French." He also found it important as a political science student to be able to read René Lévesque, Jacques Parizeau, and Claude Ryan in the original; he felt he understood them better.

So at the top and the lower levels of the parties in Ottawa, French is being recognized as important, and is improving. What is not yet clear is whether French-speaking Quebeckers are paying any attention. The last time that a significant number of Quebec voters chose a party led by a non-Quebecker was in 1965, when Lester Pearson's Liberals won 56 of 75 seats. Since then, whenever Quebec voters have had a choice between a party led by a Quebecker and one led by a non-Quebecker, they have voted for the Quebecker every time, shifting their support from Trudeau to Mulroney to Lucien Bouchard and then to Gilles Duceppe, despite a grudging acceptance of and perhaps even some admiration for Jean Chrétien, whose Liberals won 36 seats in the 2000 election. But the revelations of the sponsorship inquiry drove Paul Martin's Liberals down to 21 seats in Quebec in 2004, while the Bloc matched its previous 1993 record of 54 seats.

The Conservative convention in Montreal in March 2005 was an attempt to reach out to Quebec – but it was a flawed attempt. "They are the kind of minor irritants that grate mightily on fragile Québécois sensibilities, and despite the best intentions, this weekend's Conservative convention was rife with them," observed Sean Gordon in the *Toronto Star* of March 21. "Improperly translated policy resolutions, mangled French syntax from keynote speakers, and, especially the sight of some francophones addressing the crowd in English because most delegates didn't bother wearing headphones for simultaneous translation."

There is little evidence, in fact, that this kind of courtship of Quebec brings positive electoral results. The more reasonable assumption is that Ontario voters might lose their suspicion of Harper's Conservatives if he gains any popularity in Quebec. The ability to manage an effective relationship with Quebec is seen in Ontario as a critical criterion of leadership – and Preston Manning's "no more leaders from Quebec" ad in 1997, while it may have played well in the West, was particularly damaging to his chances in Ontario.

On the other hand, those who think that Quebeckers will only support those who are descendants of the original settlers should consider that two of the people who had the most impact in Quebec in 2004 and 2005 were clearly anglophone federalists, and, as it turns out, both from Huntington, an English farming town southwest of Montreal: Auditor-General Sheila Fraser and Commissioner of Inquiry John Gomery.

Conclusion

> *. . . even if the legends were like oil and alcohol in the*
> *same bottle, the bottle had not been broken yet.*
>
> HUGH MACLENNAN

In the fall of 1995, thousands of English-speaking Canadians crowded into the Place du Canada in Montreal to make an emotional plea to Quebec voters to vote No in the referendum. The federal government, along with hundreds of private companies, gave employees the day off to attend the rally, and between 15,000 and 20,000 people came to the Montreal event from outside Quebec, taking advantage of special low fares offered by Canadian Airlines, Air Canada, and the bus companies. Thousands squeezed together and listened to Quebec politicians – Jean Chrétien, Daniel Johnson, Jean Charest, Liza Frulla – give speeches, large parts of which they could not understand, but which they applauded furiously anyway.

I was there that day, and found it hard to see how the rally would have a positive impact on how Quebeckers voted. Later that night, as crowds of people wandered the streets, I was reminded of a crowd after a university homecoming or a championship game: people seemed satisfied and self-absorbed. The result, as Edward

Greenspon and Anthony Wilson-Smith concluded in their book *Double Vision: The Inside Story of the Liberals in Power*, was that while most people on the No side went home feeling better about themselves, the actual impact was negative rather than positive. The media response was certainly negative, with the *Journal de Montréal* describing it as an invasion by English Canada. The tracking polls conducted by the No campaign showed that support actually dropped after the rally from a 3.7 per cent lead to a 2.5 per cent lead. The final result was 2,362,648 No votes to 2,308,360 Yes votes: a margin of 54,288 or 1 per cent of the vote. The rally at Place du Canada serves as a kind of metaphor: English Canada has been largely listening to Quebeckers talk for and against Quebec remaining in Canada (without necessarily understanding the exchanges), or has been talking to itself rather than connecting with Quebec.

In a paper he wrote for a group of Ukrainian officials who were baffled by Canada's language policies, University of Toronto political scientist David Cameron traced the contradictions – sometimes direct and unavoidable, sometimes intended and designed – between federal language policy and Quebec language policy. "For years, then, Canada has known two distinct language regimes, conceived for different purposes, framed in different ways and sometimes conflicting directly with one another," he wrote. "Both are responses to the transformation of Quebec."

For as recently as fifty years ago, Quebec – as represented by the Tremblay Commission, Quebec's Royal Commission of Inquiry on Constitutional Problems – defined the identity of the society in terms of religion. "French-Canadian culture is, in fact, a particular form of the universal Christian concept of Man and of order," the commissioners wrote in 1956, describing this culture as spiritual and anti-materialist. ". . . The principal characteristics of the French-Canadian culture [are] Christian in its inspiration and of French genius; spiritual, personalist, communal, qualitative, centred on Man, ordered for his perfectioning and for the full realization of his natural and supernatural vocation." In that era, the Canadian economist Harold Innis once noted that the secret of political success in Canada was "keeping Scottish Presbyterians and French Canadians in the same party."

Now, no one seems to have figured out what the secret is. As the power and influence of the Church collapsed in the 1960s, that sense of defining identity and community was replaced by language, and reinforced by the role of the state. As religion receded as the communal bond, the French language became the critical connecting tissue for Quebec society as a whole. As Quebec has grown and matured over the last four decades, it has moved from being a defensive, self-contained, religious society to an open, secular, integrating one. The challenge for the rest of Canada is to recognize how that society has changed and continues to change, and to develop ways to connect to its energy and dynamism. And to recognize, above all, that this is a society that defines itself by language – as a French-speaking unit in an English-speaking continent.

Some of the critics of the official languages policy argue that it would, in fact, be better for English-speaking Canada if Quebec did separate and become a French-speaking country. This was the argument by J.V. Andrew in *Bilingual Today, French Tomorrow* ("My reason for recommending a division of Canada into two separate countries is to get French- and English-speaking Canadians off each other's backs once and for all . . .") and, in more sophisticated rhetoric, a decade later by Peter Brimelow in *The Patriot Game*. Brimelow – who now runs an anti-immigration website in the United States – argued that Canada's contradictions cannot be resolved within Confederation, that Quebec is emerging as a nation, and that "English Canada will – sooner or later – recover from its post-Imperial hangover and will increasingly assert its North American identity." Others, like Reed Scowen and Jane Jacobs, have suggested that the natural and preferable course for the country would be an amicable disengagement between the rest of Canada and Quebec. But these are distinctly minority views; most English-speaking Canadians prefer the idea of living in a country in which there is an effective working relationship with French-speaking Canada. Stephen Harper has learned that, and has had to swallow his harsher criticisms of federal language policy. The Conservative Party has strongly endorsed official bilingualism and strengthened minority language rights. But Canadians must wake up to the fact that there are consequences of this understandable preference.

It is possible to see the recent history of the interaction between Canada's linguistic majorities as a series of near-misses by satellites on a different orbit. With each near-miss, there is a recalculation, a recalibration, and an attempt to avoid a collision in the future. The political unrest in Quebec led to the creation of the Royal Commission; the intensification of that unrest led to widespread acceptance of the Commission's recommendations. The election of the Parti Québécois silenced many of the objections to federal language policy, and the 1980 referendum made the patriation of the Constitution possible. The death of the Meech Lake Accord in 1990 increased the sense of bitterness in Quebec; the near-death experience in 1995 increased the sense of anxiety in the rest of Canada. Consistently, English-speaking Canada has tended to be a decade out of date in its perception of Quebec, still seeing it as a priest-ridden province in the midst of the transformation that was the Quiet Revolution, and reacting to the Parti Québécois government as if it had hijacked an aircraft. English Canadians have found it difficult to recognize the ambiguities in the views in Quebec toward the rest of Canada, preferring to see a harsh division between "separatists" and "federalists." But instead of that black and white world, there is a range of shifting, often contradictory views, and an overwhelming belief in the importance of Quebec's survival as a flourishing French-speaking society. Any attempt to overlook that reality, and to lump French-speaking Canadians into a multicoloured Canadian mosaic raises hackles – just as would any suggestion by an outsider that English Canadians are just Americans who say "eh" instead of "huh."

In the months and years that followed the razor-thin 1995 referendum victory, Jean Chrétien's Liberal government embarked on a two-pronged strategy. The first was a series of concessions or transfers of authority to Quebec, and a concentrated plan of visibility for federal symbols in Quebec: a.k.a the sponsorship program. The second prong, Plan B, involved a much tougher response to Quebec's assertion that international law supported its claim that a positive referendum result – 50 per cent plus one – would be sufficient to result in Quebec achieving independence. This led to the Supreme Court reference and the Clarity Act, laying out the terms under which Quebec could accede to independence. But whatever positive impact that may have had was blown away by the revelations of the corruption, sleaze, and favouritism that characterized the sponsorship program.

What is interesting is what was not done during that period. No effort was made to increase the contact between the rest of Canada and Quebec. There were no Quebec Studies programs established in the rest of Canada with a strategy of simultaneously teaching English-Canadian undergraduates about contemporary Quebec and attracting young Quebec academics to study and work in English-speaking universities. By contrast, the late Barry Farrell, who ran the Canadian Studies Program at Northwestern University for many years, managed to create both a pool of American graduates who knew Canada, thanks to a series of summer jobs and internships he organized, and to the involvement of a group of sophisticated American-trained Ph.D.s from Quebec – a group that includes well-known Quebec academics like Guy Lachapelle of

Concordia, Pierre Martin of l'Université de Montreal, Antonia Maioni of McGill, and Luc Bernier of L'École nationale d'administration publique.

There was no systematic effort to introduce the equivalent of a junior year abroad and to make it much easier for students in French-speaking and English-speaking universities to spend a year in an institution of the other official language. There was no movement by English-speaking municipalities outside Quebec to twin with Quebec municipalities and organize exchanges. There was no attempt to increase the linkages and connections between English-language and French-language non-governmental organizations. There was no systematic attempt to make unilingual Quebeckers aware that they could be served in French in national parks across Canada – and no renewed effort to ensure that this was, in fact, the case. There was a short-lived tourism ad campaign urging Quebeckers to visit the rest of Canada, but no systematic strategy to woo French-speaking Quebec tourists away from the beaches of Maine and Florida (where their loyalty has resulted in services being offered in French) to neighbouring provinces, which have been churning out immersion graduates for years. In the same way, there has been no effective system of directing those immersion students to summer jobs where they could serve French-speaking visitors in their own language. (There are some small, individual exceptions to this; a tourist lodge in Ontario's Rideau Lakes, for example, has been quietly hiring Quebec teenagers and offering them a chance to learn English during a summer job. Similarly, many Quebec young people quietly make their way to the mountain resorts in the Rockies.) Exchanges do exist – there are school exchanges, and a bilingual monitors program, and the Action Plan lays out an ambitious program for increasing them – but they were never coordinated as part of a national strategy to build links, connections, and networks between English-speaking and French-speaking Canada.

The Mid-Term Report on the Action Plan indicates how limited the programs are: despite $6 million invested in bursaries and monitor programs, the number of bursaries for French enrichment for minority francophones rose from 153 to 156, while the number of second-language bursaries rose from 6,614 to 7,341 and the number of monitors of French as a first language rose from 199 to 225, while the number of second-language monitors actually dropped from 733 to 602. The phrase "a drop in the bucket" comes to mind.

English-Canadian authors are now read as avidly in Quebec as in other parts of the world, but few tour the province to promote their books. Few English-Canadians ever address the Chambre de Commerce de Trois-Rivières. (In fact, when he was the chief Liberal political organizer for Quebec, Alfonso Gagliano, of Gomery Commission fame, refused to book ministers from outside Quebec to speak in the province.) The *Gazette* and *La Presse* exchanged reporters, who wrote about the experience of working in a newsroom in another language – but the two newsrooms were only a few blocks apart; no other newspapers, radio stations, or television networks followed the example. In other words, there was no strategic attempt to introduce Quebeckers to the country that they had almost abandoned, and no effort on the part of those who had organized the rally in Montreal to attempt a deeper exploration of the society that had almost left.

From the outset, the federal government's language policy has been characterized by defensiveness. Rather than promoting the importance of learning Canada's two official languages, Pierre Trudeau spent his time explaining how people would not have to learn French, and should turn the cornflakes box around if the sight of French offended them. (In fact, W.K. Kellogg first put French on his cornflakes boxes in 1907, so that French-speaking customers would buy them – not because of federal labelling requirements.) That defensiveness never worked; it was seen as hypocritical, fibbing, and, in Richard Gwyn's phrase, "white lies." It was also an example of failure of nerve.

The federal government continues the cycle of sending middle-aged executives to learn French. Over the years, the government has bent over backward to avoid offending unilingual anglophones – and has continued to build in on-the-job training, at public expense. "It is the only requirement in the public service where you bring people in and then train them in the capacity," Diana Monnet pointed out to me. "You want an engineer, you go and get an engineer." Canada does not name judges and then send them to law school – yet for over three decades, it has been appointing public servants who need to be able to understand the country to do their jobs, and then sending them to learn French.

Conversely, public administration is the only area where universities produce professionals who are unable to meet the requirements of their expected employer. If architecture schools produced graduates unable to do architectural draughting, or engineering school graduates unable to use computers, the industry would immediately make it clear that this was unacceptable. Yet journalism schools produce graduates who are unable to understand the prime minister when he speaks to his constituents, or the governor general when she speaks French. Most law schools, political science faculties, and public administration programs in English-Canadian universities cheerfully off-load language training to the federal government – to be done at an age and stage where it is most expensive, and least likely to be effective. As a result, there are fewer bilingual people in Canada than there are in Britain – which has fewer second-language skills than any other European country.

As part of the war on the deficit, funds for second-language teaching were capped or cut; the Collège Militaire Saint-Jean was shut down; and various government services were privatized, reducing the requirement that both languages be used. As the federal government cut programs and funding, "withdrew," "downsized," "off-loaded," and "out-sourced," the presence of both official languages in different parts of the country shrank. Non-governmental organizations lost funding for translation – and often travel grants that made face-to-face national meetings possible in the first place – so the gradual process of disengagement between Canada's English-speaking and French-speaking societies continued.

Sadly, there has been little effort to dispel the persistent, tenacious myths and errors that still cling to the public perception of language policy. It is still a commonplace observation that Trudeau's dream was to have a country that spoke both languages coast to coast, and it is still true, as Victor Goldbloom plaintively observed in 1992, that "people cannot be expected to support what they do not understand."

That defensiveness has been reinforced by the fact that, from its introduction in 1969 by Gérard Pelletier, the lead minister responsible for official languages has almost always been a francophone. This has only reinforced the quiet, unspoken, politically incorrect assumption in English Canada that language policy is only of importance or of benefit to francophones. If the federal government believes in the importance of language policy as a critical link between English-speaking and French-speaking Canada, a bilingual English Canadian should be given the job in cabinet of promoting language policy, which is too often seen as reserved for francophones. Keeping that responsibility in the hands of francophones reinforces the perception that French is a minority language, not a Canadian language that is an asset to all Canadians.

In his journal, Frank Scott enumerated a series of Quebec francophone myths about English Canada (quoted here in Chapter

Three); there is a similar, equally tenacious list of English-Canadian myths about French-speaking Quebec.

English Canadians tend to believe that all French-speaking Quebeckers speak English. This is understandable, since only the bilingual appear on English television – unless there is a bus accident or natural disaster. In fact, there are almost 4 million unilingual French-speaking Quebeckers. Those Quebeckers who live outside Montreal hear very little English and have little reason to speak it. They live in a culturally self-sufficient world, and have little contact with English-speaking Canada. They live, in Michel Côté's phrase, in a bubble. It has been the persistence, from one generation to the next, of a community for which English plays little or no role, that has ensured that Canada has needed to maintain its commitment to having national institutions that can respond in both official languages.

At the same time, there is a deeply ingrained assumption that English Canadians don't speak French. In fact, the 2001 census showed that there are 1.3 million bilingual Canadians of English mother tongue outside Quebec, while 67 per cent of anglophones in Quebec are now bilingual – compared to 37 per cent for francophones in Quebec. A much higher proportion of young Quebec anglophones are now bilingual than are young Quebec francophones.

There is a tendency in English Canada to think of language as yesterday's issue. In fact, it remains the central political and social fact of Canadian life, and the most critical fault line. If Canada cannot produce leaders who can speak to the whole country, it is difficult to see how the country can function effectively. "Bilingualism is one of the defining characteristics of the country," University of Toronto political scientist Richard Simeon observed to me. "If we lose it, we may lose the country."

A lingering complaint from the critics of the government's language policy is that if Quebec is going to be unilingual French, the rest of the country should be unilingual English. In fact, it is because the two societies are largely unilingual that the national leadership and the national institutions of the country should be able to function in both languages. As William Mackey pointed out years ago, at the time of the Royal Commission, there are fewer bilingual people in bilingual countries than there are in so-called unilingual countries, since the countries became officially bilingual to guarantee the maintenance and use of both languages.

One of André Laurendeau's deepest concerns – that Quebec could not only survive but thrive as the home of a distinct French-speaking society – has been satisfied. The income gap that the Royal Commission identified between francophones and anglophones has vanished. The underrepresentation of fran-cophones in the Armed Forces and the federal public service has been eliminated; it is no longer seen as a strange eccentricity for a foreign-service officer to write dispatches in French, as it was four decades ago, when such dispatches would simply not be read by anyone important.

In 1965, when he toured Western Canada, Quebec premier Jean Lesage told Western audiences the story of two engineers, one English Canadian in Vancouver, and one a French Canadian in Montreal. Both worked for a national company. Each was offered a promotion to the other city. "For the English Canadian pro-moted to Montreal, it's just an ordinary move. He can accept without hesitation. His children will go to school as usual, their lives will not be changed," he said. "But for the French Canadian promoted to Vancouver it's a terrible choice. If he accepts, his chil-dren must give up their language."

In 2005, the balance had shifted. The Vancouver engineer's wife (or husband) would now have trouble getting a job in Montreal without French, and the children would only be able to go to English school if one parent had been educated in English in Canada. The Montreal engineer would be able to keep his child

in French school (there are several French-language schools in the
Vancouver area, in Vancouver, North Vancouver, and Surrey – in
addition to schools in Victoria, Kelowna, Chilliwack, Mission, Port
Coquitlam, Powell River, Prince George, and Delta) and they could
continue to watch TV and listen to the radio in French. In fact, the
growth of French-language education outside Quebec has become
an attraction for international talent: at least one high-profile
physicist was wooed back from the United States to Waterloo
because he wanted to have his children educated in French. Since
Laurendeau's death in 1968, French-language universities,
scientific research, financial services, radio, television, publishing,
recording, film, and public service in Quebec are all immeasurably
stronger than they were four decades ago. As Pierre Bourgault put
it so memorably, "We have won!"

A number of other dramatic changes have occurred since the
Preliminary Report was published and Lesage travelled West in
1965. Immersion French has become a permanent part of
Canadian education, producing thousands of graduates who,
while not necessarily enjoying the mastery of native speakers, are
comfortable in French in a way that no previous generation of
high-school graduates have been. This has been one of the building blocks of a new internationalism on the part of Canadian
young people.

One of the most significant changes has been the explosion
of English as a lingua franca in Asia and in Europe. At the same
time, the expansion of the European Union has meant the
official recognition of twenty-five languages. Belgian scholar
Philippe Van Parijs has made a complex and compelling argument in favour of establishing English as a common language of
exchange in Europe, and, at the same time, guaranteeing the survival and predominance of national languages. If this were done,
he argues, the message the European Union would be sending

to its citizens would be "Free movement within the European Union is one of our great achievements. But if you move for more than a short time to any part of the EU's territory whose official language happens to be different from your mother tongue, you must have the courage and the humility to learn that language if you do not know it already." He is proposing, in effect, the Belgian solution – since in Belgium, average competence in English among young adults is considerably higher than average competence in the other national language, whether French or Flemish.

But he was talking about a Europe of twenty-five languages, not two; Canada has always rejected the Belgian solution, seeking something that was more generous and more flexible. The problem for English Canada now is not how to end the discrimination against a subordinate, neglected society, as French-speaking Quebec once was, but how to connect with and benefit from the energy and creativity of a dynamic one. For proficiency in French is our doorway to a vibrant society that is within our boundaries, whose culture we already help support. Canadians, through their taxes, contribute significantly to the flourishing of French-language culture in Canada: through Telefilm, Radio-Canada, the Canada Council, the National Theatre School, and a variety of public subsidies for publishing, recording, and performing. Rather than begrudge this contribution, Canadians should insist on having access to the fruits it has helped produce: the Quebec films, novels, and recordings that are virtually inaccessible outside Quebec and parts of New Brunswick.

Instead of learning French, Preston Manning implied in his conversation with me, children should be learning Chinese. In fact, French is a bridge to other languages, not a barrier. Anecdotally, those young English Canadians who are learning Spanish, German, Chinese, Japanese, Vietnamese, and Hindi, working around the world, are frequently immersion graduates, who, like musicians, have moved on from the piano to other instruments.

Some fear that Canada can no longer be bilingual if it is going to be multicultural. But respect for multicultural communities flows from an innate understanding that there is not a single Canadian culture or language. And there are many indications that Canada's multicultural communities have embraced bilingualism. Montreal has seen the emergence of the phenomenon of "trilingual Montrealers," and the Chinese communities in both Vancouver and Toronto have been strongly supportive of French-language education. In Vancouver, the Chinese community asked the French Embassy to have the Alliance Française located in a Chinese community centre, and in Toronto, the Chinese community has provided strong financial support for the expansion of the Toronto French School. Often it is recalcitrant Anglos who use concern for immigrants and visible minorities as grounds to oppose the federal government's language policy; the grounds are false. In fact, it is Canada's acceptance, however inarticulate, of the reality of another culture and language within its national fabric, and its attempt to accommodate that reality – rather than the desire to undermine Quebec that Quebec nationalists feared – that has made multiculturalism possible.

One of the current definitions for insanity (also applied to stupidity) is continuing to do the same thing and expecting a different outcome. If you think of language policy as an ecological system, Canada's approach has some crazy dysfunctionalities. It is silly that English Canadians reach their peak in French-language facility at nineteen, and then start to lose it when they enter university. It is crazy that it is easier for English-speaking Canadian teachers to have exchanges with Australia than with Quebec, and for

French-speaking Quebec teachers to have many more exchanges with France than with other provinces. It is bizarre that, instead of giving teenagers an incentive for continuing to study French, making it an asset for them in getting into university, the education system builds in an incentive to drop French by neglecting to take it into account, let alone making it a prerequisite for university admission. It is insane that Canadian universities continue to treat French as a foreign language, to be taught in literature departments, rather than as a language of instruction in history, political science, and public administration classes. It is absurd that there are so few links and connections between English-speaking and French-speaking non-governmental organizations and voluntary associations. It makes no sense that it is virtually impossible to see popular Quebec films in the rest of Canada until months, if not years, after they have been shown in Quebec. It is madness that the federal government is still spending millions on teaching middle-aged bureaucrats how to pass language tests rather than sending young, enthusiastic recruits to the public service to work in another language and culture. A comparable exercise would involve sending middle-aged athletes to hockey camp to improve Canada's chances at the Olympics.

But there are hopeful signs. Immersion has had its impact: French-speaking television viewers have been pleasantly surprised at the number of young Canadian athletes in international competitions who give interviews in both languages. In 2005, the junior hockey phenomenon Sidney Crosby showed French-speaking television viewers that he had learned French during his time in Rimouski – a stark contrast with Eric Lindros, who caused an uproar in 1991 when he refused to sign with the Quebec Nordiques. The cynical can argue that both decisions were driven by marketing, but at nineteen, Crosby apparently had a much more generous view of the country, the world, and the market than Lindros did.

The Supreme Court decisions, over the years, have tacitly recognized Quebec's distinctness while striking down foolishly discriminatory regulations, such as the policy that prevented immersion students from outside Québec (because they had been educated in French) from attending immersion school in Quebec (because it was part of the English, and not the French school system, and only the children of those educated in English are admitted to English schools). At the same time, the court has forced provinces to make the right to French-language education, guaranteed in the 1982 Constitution Act, more of a reality. The successful fight to keep the Hôpital Montfort alive in Ottawa has led to funding to enable the hospital to grow and expand its role as a French-language teaching hospital while continuing to provide medical care in both languages.

Another book could be written on New Brunswick's adoption of official bilingualism, and how it has made its ability to offer services in both languages a commercial asset, most notably through call centres. In contrast, Ontario has adopted a kind of stealth policy: shrinking from any formal declaration of official bilingualism while, at the same time, gradually increasing the services that are available in both languages, and making many official documents – like the Ontario driver's licence and health cards – rigorously bilingual. The panels explaining the exhibits at the Royal Ontario Museum are in English and in French. The Trillium Prize ceremonies, giving out Ontario book awards, are entirely bilingual, provoking occasional surprise when those present think, "Wait a minute, this isn't federal."

The late Quebec premier Daniel Johnson used to say he wanted Quebec to be as French as Ontario is English. Bernard Landry never used to say that – since Ontario is making slow progress on the language issue; he would say he wanted Quebec to be as French as Argentina is Spanish. It is a tribute to the flexibility

of Canadian federalism that this is the case. Quebec's transformation has been possible within Canada, in the context of a language
policy that is more flexible and generous-spirited than that of
Belgium or Switzerland.

What needs to be done to make Canada's language challenge
a success? Have we simply strayed from the faith and need to go
back – or do we need a new policy for new times? Certainly, the
determination, optimism, and realism of Lester Pearson needs
to be understood and revived; Canadians need the opportunity to
learn French, and the right to speak it. Pearson recognized that
Quebec was a nation; the richness and opportunity of having a
vital, dynamic French-speaking society within Canada needs to be
appreciated. Canada's role in the world has been earned in part for
its (often unjustified) reputation for bilingualism; one of the
incentives for the military to improve its approach to language
occurred in the early 1960s when the senior authorities realized
that language ability was one of the reasons Canada was being
asked to contribute to United Nations peacekeeping missions.

At the same time, there has to be a higher priority placed on
welcoming that French-speaking society into the broader
Canadian framework. Francophones should be targeted as a
market – particularly since tourism from the United States has
dropped dramatically since the terrorist attacks of 2001 and SARS.
But we need to use the new technologies; just as bank machines
across Canada serve cardholders in their language of choice, information for unilingual travellers should be instantly available in
every airport, station, post office, and hotel lobby in the country;
French-language and English-language schools should be twinned
through e-mail.

The universities need to recognize their responsibilities, and
look for support for an equivalent to the European Union's
Erasmus Mundus program. The EU has committed serious

resources to encouraging university students to study in other parts of Europe. Since 1987, 1.2 million students have participated in the program – and in 2004, the EU spent 187.5 million euros on the program, with over 2,100 students from thirty-one countries participating annually. The budget for the 2004–2008 period is 230 million and involves the encouragement of joint degrees by universities in different European countries, attracting non-Europeans to study in European universities, and sending European students to study in other parts of the world. Canada has never embarked on a program of that magnitude, or even taken steps to make it dramatically easier for students to spend a year at a university of the other official language.

Nevertheless, most of the ingredients are there: for all its problems, the public service has gone through significant changes in adapting to the requirement that it be able to serve French-speaking Canadians. And year in, year out, there are three hundred thousand English-speaking children in French immersion. But the public servants – and immersion students – need to connect to a French-speaking society; immersion curriculums should reach beyond provincial borders. Minority French-language communities should be more visible.

In the past, the argument has been made that English Canadians should learn French for the sake of Quebec and national unity. No, dammit, we should do it for ourselves. Learning another language is the first step to understanding the rest of the world, not just the country we live in. By failing to make French a significant part of Canadian life, we are limiting our ability to connect with the whole country, and with the rest of the world. The idea that we should be learning Chinese instead is a fallacy; one can lead to the other. Instead of failing French, we can embrace it and make it fully part of the country's identity and stop wasting the resources that we have invested over the last forty years. It is telling that English Canadians are most bilingual between the ages of fifteen and nineteen – and spend most of the rest of their lives losing what they have learned.

In the decade that followed the 1995 referendum, several of the efforts intended to connect Quebeckers to the rest of the country, in particular the sponsorship program, have proven counterproductive. The controversy surrounding the nomination of Michaëlle Jean as governor general in the summer of 2005 illustrated once again the gulf between English-speaking and French-speaking Canada, as the nominee and her background were first unknown and then baffling to much of Canada outside Quebec, who found the ambiguities in her background hard to understand. Then, when she said in her installation speech that the time of two solitudes is past, ordinarily skeptical columnists in English Canada cheered and it was the turn of Quebec journalists and intellectuals to raise a quizzical eyebrow and of *indepéndantistes* to attack her.

Ten years have passed since the last referendum, and many of the fundamental realities that led to that bitter and divisive outcome remain unchanged. Polls suggest that support for sovereignty remains high: 55 per cent of Quebeckers – which means well over 60 per cent of French-speaking Quebeckers – say they would vote Yes in another referendum, indicating they would prefer Quebec to be independent. The Charest government remains unpopular and the Parti Québécois is determined to hold a referendum on independence as soon as possible should it win the next election. But there are ambiguities in that support for sovereignty – many Quebeckers want to retain a connection with the rest of Canada – and those ambiguities are misunderstood or resented by Canadians in the rest of the country.

There is little public indication that the federal government has developed a referendum strategy, or a longer-term strategy for connecting Quebec francophones and their sense of the future to

the country as a whole. As the prospect of another Quebec referendum looms, the fundamental question that André Laurendeau
and Davidson Dunton asked so often will be relevant again: "Can
English-speaking and French-speaking Canadians live together,
and do they want to do so?"

The question remains pertinent, four decades later. The answer
will determine whether, and how, Canada survives.

Sources

While much of this book was based on what I have observed and reported over four decades, a great deal of it is based on the scholarship of many who have spent their careers studying each aspect of things that I have only touched on. Without pretending to be an academic, I have tried to give credit and indicate my sources so that others can follow some of the paths I have pointed out.

chapter one: Two Hundred Years of Language Relations

I consulted *The Confederation Debates*, and found the Perrault–Rémillard exchange in *Canada's Founding Debates*, edited by Janet Ajzenstat, Paul Romney, Ian Gentles, and William D. Gairdner; Sir Edward Thurlow is quoted by William Moore in *The Clash: A Study in Nationalities*; I reread *Lord Durham's Report*, edited by Gerald M. Craig, and Mason Wade's classic *The French Canadians, 1760–1945* for the pre-Confederation history; John Ralston Saul's comment is from *Reflections of a Siamese Twin: Canada at the End of the Twentieth Century*. Marc Levine quotes Robert Linteau and Ralph Heintzman and summarizes "the rules of the game" in *The Reconquest of Montreal: Language Policy and Social Change in a Bilingual City*; Donald Creighton quotes Sir John's letter to Brown Chamberlin in *John A. Macdonald: The Young Politician* and Ramsay Cook quotes George Brown in *Canada and the French-Canadian Question*. Alastair Sweeny's remark is in *George-Étienne Cartier: A Biography*; Everett Hughes's observation about a culturally alien employer is in *French Canada in Transition*; his remark about assumptions about assimilation are in Jean C. Falardeau's collection *Essais sur le Québec contemporain*. I found Michael Oliver's comments in the 1956 introduction he wrote to his thesis, published as *The Passionate Debate: The Social and Political Ideas of Quebec Nationalism 1920–1945*, and Arthur Lower's comment is in *Canadians in the Making: A Social History of Canada*.

chapter two: The Pressures Converge

This chapter is based largely on Maurice Lamontagne's papers, and André Laurendeau's diary. Monica Heller's observation about legitimacy is in *Éléments d'une sociolinguistique critique*. For Laurendeau's diary, I consulted the French edition, and the version published in English. In addition, I read Philip Stratford's collection and the anthology *Ces choses qui nous arrivent: Chroniques des années 1961–66*. I also consulted *André Laurendeau* by Denis Monière, *André Laurendeau: un intellectuel d'ici*, *sous la direction de Robert Comeau et Lucille Beaudry*, *André Laurendeau: French Canadian Nationalist, 1912–1968* by Donald J. Horton. I read Lester Pearson's posthumous memoir *Mike: The Memoirs of Rt. Hon. Lester B. Pearson, Vol. III*, Jean-Louis Gagnon's memoirs, Gérard Bergeron's *Ne Bougez Plus! Portraits de 40 de nos politiciens*, *The Great Scot: A Biography of Donald Gordon*, by Joseph Schull, *Réal Caouette: l'homme et le phénomène* by Marcel Huguet, Gilles Grégoire's self-published *Aventure à Ottawa*, and Keith Davey's memoir, *The Rainmaker: A Passion for Politics*. For surveys of the period, I found the following to be useful: *Canada, 1957–1967: The Years of Uncertainty and Innovation* by J.L. Granatstein, *Lester Pearson and the Dream of Unity* by Peter Stursberg, *Mandate '68* by Martin Sullivan, and *The Search for Identity, Canada, Postwar to Present*, by Blair Fraser.

chapter three: Two Éminences Grises

Most of this chapter was based on the journals that André Laurendeau and Frank Scott kept. I also consulted Sandra Djwa's biography of Scott, *The Politics of the Imagination: A Life of F.R. Scott*, Jean-Louis Gagnon's memoir, Gérard Pelletier's three volumes of memoirs, the biographies of Laurendeau, Guy Laforest's essay "The Meech Lake Accord: The Search for a Compromise between André Laurendeau and F.R. Scott" in *Trudeau and the End of a Canadian Dream*, and Pierre Elliott Trudeau, "Quebec and the Constitutional Problem," written in March and April 1965, published in *Federalism and the French Canadians*. Michael Oliver described Scott and told the story of Laurendeau meeting the elderly Albertan in his introduction to the *McGill Law Journal*'s special issue on F.R. Scott, Vol 80. No. 1; Scott's anecdote about translating the Coûtume de Paris is from his introduction to *Poems of French Canada*; Scott's poem "Bonne Entente" was first published in *Events and Signals*. The press reaction to the Preliminary Report is taken from a press summary by James Ferrabee in the *Gazette*, February 26, 1963; "Bizarre Algèbre" appears in the December 1965 edition of *Cité libre*; the reaction to the Report of the Royal Commission was compiled by the Commission, and a copy is filed in the Archives du Centre de Recherche Lionel-Groulx. The reactions to the death of André Laurendeau were published in *Le Devoir*, June 3, 1968.

chapter four: Two Friends, Two Views

The anecdote about Trudeau and Laurin can be found in my piece "L'insondable Dr Laurin et ses 6 millions de patients," *L'actualité*, septembre 1978. Trudeau and Laurin were interviewed together on November 11, 1992, and the transcript can be found in the Trudeau Papers, MG 26 03 f 13; my thanks to John English for generously sharing this and other insights with me. In addition to reviewing the chapter I wrote on Laurin in my book *PQ: René Lévesque and the Parti Québécois in Power*, I also consulted Jean-Claude Picard's book *Camille Laurin, L'homme debout*. I reread Laurin's own writings, *Ma traversée du Québec*. The story about Trudeau presenting Scott to the Queen can be found in the *Toronto Star*, October 1, 2000. Ron Graham recounted to me Scott's rueful retelling of the story in an interview, June 23, 2005. The observation by Sandra Djwa is from the *Toronto Star*, April 13, 2002; Scott Reid's view of Trudeau's Messianic vision is in Scott Reid, *Lament for a Notion:*

The Life and Death of Canada's Bilingual Dream; Trudeau's presentation
before the Royal Commission was on November 7, 1963, and begins on
p. 200 of the transcript, which is in box C4884 of the microfilms at the
National Archives; Scott observes that Trudeau has lost touch with
Quebec in his journal on p. 33 in the entry that begins on November 6,
1963; Trudeau's address to the Canadian Bar Association is in *Federalism
and the French Canadians*; his comment that what French Canadians
want is language rights was in *Le Devoir*, le 7 février 1968, quoted by
Joseph Magnet in *Official Languages of Canada*; Gordon Robertson made
his comment to me in an interview, January 27, 2005; Michael
MacMillan's comment on rights is in *The Practice of Language Rights in
Canada*, p. 74; Trudeau's comment that bilingualism unites people and
dualism divides them was in Senate Debates, 2nd session, 33d Parliament,
vol. 132, March 30, 1988, p. 2993; quoted by Kenneth McRoberts,
Misconceiving Canada: The Struggle for National Unity, p. 107, and in
Serge Joyal's preface to Michael Behiels's book *Canada's Francophone
Minorities: Constitutional Renewal and the Winning of School Governance*.
Reid quotes Trudeau on the difficulty of testing cabinet ministers in
Lament for a Notion, p. 29; see Trudeau, "Quebec and the Constitutional
Problem," in *Federalism and the French Canadians*; the observation that
Trudeau kept translators out of cabinet meetings is from Michel Vastel,
Trudeau le Québécois, p. 180; Kenneth McRoberts's comment about the
irony of the Charter is from his lecture at the Robarts Centre for
Canadian Studies Lecture Series, York University, March 5, 1991.

chapter five: Ottawa Tries to Learn French
Pearson's comment about the Preliminary Report is in his memoirs;
Robertson writes about Pearson's announcement in his *Memoirs of a
Very Civil Servant*, and we discussed the policy in an interview on
January 27, 2005; Granatstein quotes his letter to Pearson in *Canada
1957–1967: The Years of Uncertainty and Innovation*; Peter Stursberg
quoted Maurice Lamontagne and Judy Lamarsh in *Lester Pearson and the
Dream of Unity*; Gérard Pelletier's remark is in the third volume of his

memoirs; Dennis Braithwaite's column was in the *Toronto Telegram*, June 11, 1969; Trudeau's comment about recalcitrant public servants being put in charge of elevators was quoted in the *Ottawa Journal*, October 17, 1968 – and repeatedly by Tory MPs opposing the Official Languages Act; Fortier's experience with a unilingual elevator operator is recounted in the *Ottawa Citizen*, March 29, 1985; Trudeau's conversation with Anthony Westell was in the *Toronto Star*, February 7, 1969, and quoted in his book *Paradox: Trudeau as Prime Minister*; Dalton Camp's comments are in his book *Points of Departure*; Pelletier's hiring of Spicer is told in Keith Spicer, *Life Sentences: Memoirs of an Incorrigible Canadian*; the Zolf news item was posted on the CBC website in the series *The Road to Bilingualism*; Erna Paris's comment is from her article "Guilt, Anxiety and Bilingualism in the Civil Service," *Saturday Night*, March 1972; Gwyn quotes Camp, and devotes a chapter to the language issue in *The Northern Magus: Pierre Trudeau and Canadians*; Pelletier's angry reaction is from "1968: Language Policy and the Mood in Quebec," in *Towards a Just Society: The Trudeau Years*; Gwyn's response is from a letter to Pelletier written on April 18, 1990, a copy of which he sent to me after I quoted Pelletier's comments in a review; Spicer describes himself as a guy of thoughtful recklessness in *Life Sentences*; he talks about the need for French to be established as the key working and social language in Quebec in his *Third Annual Report, 1972–73*, p. 26; his remark that there is room for the Canadian who wants to learn only one official language is in his *Second Annual Report, 1971–72*, as is the one about etiquette; his "Sorry, I don't speak French" story is from his *Sixth Annual Report, 1976*; John Carson's remark is from "La Grande Peur des Anglophones," par Gilles Racine, *Le Magazine Maclean*, août 1972; Sandra Gwyn's observations are from "Twilight of the Ottawa Man," *Saturday Night*, January 1971; Spicer's comment about dreary tensions and hang-ups is from his *Fifth Annual Report, 1975*; Conn Smythe's comment is from Scott Young, "Language Policy Is a Bloody Bore," *Globe and Mail*, September 23, 1976; the summary of the air traffic controllers' dispute is from research I did for *Maclean's* for a story published in October 1976, from John Saywell's *Canadian Annual Report on Politics and Public Affairs, 1976* and Sandford Borins's *Language of the Skies: The Bilingual Air Traffic Control Conflict in Canada*; Bergeron's comments on Marchand are from his profile in *Ne Bougez Plus*, p. 70; Spicer's conversation with Trudeau about quitting is from *Life Sentences*; Gossage's bleak observation is in *Close to the Charisma: My Years Between the Press and Pierre Elliott Trudeau*; Spicer's list of the government's vices and his communications advice is from his *Sixth Annual Report, 1976*. Dunton's comment was in an article he wrote for Canadian Press published in the *Gazette*, August 16, 1978; the comments from Yalden, Fortier, Goldbloom, and Adam are from their annual reports.

chapter six: Montreal and the Changing Etiquette of Language Use

I have drawn much of my inspiration for this chapter from the work of Monica Heller. My piece on the twenty-fifth anniversary of the Quebec language law appeared in the *Toronto Star* on January 4, 2003, where I quoted Michael Goldbloom, Marcel Côté, and Sarah Saber-Friedman. Josh Freed describes the use of *allô* in the *Toronto Star*, October 1, 2005. The statistics on emigration from Quebec and language use are from *New Canadian Perspectives: Language on Canada 2001 Census*, by Louise Marmen and Jean-Pierre Corbeil; Uli Locher's study "Les Anglophones de Montréal: emigration et évolution des attitudes 1978–1983," Québec, Conseil de la langue française, 1988, is quoted by Martha Radice in *Feeling Comfortable? The Urban Experience of Anglo-Montrealers*; Jacques Henripin's comment is from Jacques Henripin, "Quebec and the Demographic Dilemma of French Canadian Society," in Dale Thomson, ed., *Quebec Society and Politics, Views from the Inside*; Julius Grey's argument about the need to demystify the language law was published in *La Presse*, August 18, 2005; Jacques Godbout's article appeared in the *New York Times* on September 16, 2001; Mordecai Richler's *New Yorker* pieces were compiled and expanded on in *Oh Canada! Oh Quebec! Requiem for a Divided Country*; Scowen's comment is from *The Time to Say Goodbye:*

The Case for Getting Quebec Out of Canada. Soma Day's comments are from "Please Don't Switch," the *Montreal Star*, January 26, 1978; Monica Heller's comment that something strange is going on in Montreal is from "Bonjour, Hello?: Negotiations of Language Choice in Montreal"; Nicole Dominingue's comment is from "L'usage bilingue dans le centre de Montréal," in *Aspects of Bilingualism*, ed. Michel Paradis. Heller's teasing out of the meaning of the language switch is from "Bonjour, Hello?: Negotiations of Language Choice in Montreal," paper presented to the Berkeley Linguistics Society, 1978. François Grosjean's observations are in *Life with Two Languages: An Introduction to Bilingualism*; Heller's observations of the Montreal brewery are from "Ethnic Relations and Language Use in Montreal," in *Language of Inequality*, eds., N. Wolfson and J. Manes; Michaud's testimony before the Larose Commission is included in *Les raisons de la colère*; the Supreme Court reference that discusses immersion is Solski (Tutor of) v. Quebec (Attorney General), [2005] 1 S.C.R. 201, 2005 SCC 14; Statscan figures on immigrant language transfers in Quebec are from "Language Trends in Quebec," a paper prepared by Michael O'Keefe for the Official Languages Branch of the Privy Council Office; the Supreme Court reference dismissing the challenge is Gosselin (Tutor of) v. Quebec (Attorney General), [2005] 1 S.C.R. 238, 2005 SCC 15; Christine Fréchette's comment is in Alexandre Stefanescu's collection *Le Français au Québec: Les nouveaux defis*; Radice's description of comfortable Montrealers is in *Feeling Comfortable*; and Patricia Lamarre's bilingual shopping experience is in *Le Français au Québec.*

chapter seven: The Federal Capital – and David Levine's Ottawa Castonguay's comments about behaving like a minority are from *L'aut'journal*, no. 221, juillet 2003; Daniel Poliquin's description of Quebec intellectuals in Ottawa is on p. 17 of his novel *L'Écureuil noir*; the anecdote about Trudeau and Marcel Rioux is in Jules Duchastel's *Marcel Rioux: Entre l'Utopie et la raison*, p. 33; the quotation from the Royal Commission is from Book v: *The Federal Capital*, Ottawa, 1970, pp. 5-6; Christina Spencer's observations are from "How French Falters in

Canada's Capital," *Ottawa City*, vol. 6., no. 3, August–September 2003; Earl McRae's column was in the *Ottawa Sun*, June 16, 1998; his comment to me was in an e-mail, March 16, 2005; Ron Corbett's column was "Gauthier's Brave, New Bilingual World," *Ottawa Citizen*, June 23, 2003; the comments about the David Levine controversy are taken from Randal Marlin's *The David Levine Affair: Separatist Betrayal or McCarthyism North?*; I interviewed David Levine on August 31, 2005; Raffarin's remarks were reported in the *Toronto Star*, May 22, 2003; Charles Castonguay's observations are taken from "Nation Building and Anglicization in Canada's Capital Region," *Inroads* 11, and *L'aut'journal* no. 221, juillet 2003.

chapter eight: Talking to Ourselves

I read a number of studies on immersion, but most of the sources I cite are from the collection *French Immersion: Process, Product and Perspectives*, compiled by Sandy Rehorick and Viviane Edwards. I also consulted Fred Genesee's *Learning Through Two Languages: Studies of Immersion and Bilingual Education* and *Raising Children Bilingually: The Pre-school Years*, Michael Behiels's *Canada's Francophone Minority Communities: Constitutional Renewal and the Winning of School Governance*, Matthew Hayday's *Bilingual Today, United Tomorrow*, and J.L. Granatstein's *The Ottawa Men*. Richard Gwyn makes his observation about the impact of dropping French as a prerequisite on p. 230 of *The Northern Magus*.

chapter nine: Bumping Together, Drifting Apart

Roméo Dallaire talks about his experience as a French-Canadian in the Canadian Forces in his book *Shake Hands With the Devil*, and I interviewed Dallaire on September 4, 2004. The history of language policy in the Canadian Forces is told in detail in the two-volume history of bilingualism in the Armed Forces by Jean Pariseau and Serge Bernier, which is available on the Department of National Defence website. I also consulted *The Memoirs of General Jean V. Allard*, J.L. Granatstein's *Canada 1957–1967: The Years of Uncertainty and Innovation* and *Canada's Army: Waging War and Keeping the Peace*, and Jocelyn Coulon's *En première ligne: grandeurs et misères du système militaire canadien.* Drapeau's comment is from his article "Ottawa, l'armée et les francophones," *Journal de Montréal,* le 4 octobre 2005. Desmond Morton's is from his *A Military History of Canada.* My conversation with Robert Cribb was on August 17, 2005, and my conversation with Alain Gravel on August 24, 2005. The box-office figures for *The Barbarian Invasions* are reported in the *Globe and Mail,* October 10, 2005, and from figures compiled from *Variety* by Simon Beaudry of Cineac. I talked to Pierre Curzi on October 3, 2005. Daniel Drache presented the paper he worked on with Blake Evans at a conference at Glendon College in February 2005 and kindly sent me a more developed version; Lisa Young made her remarks at a news conference in Ottawa on March 11, 2005; the research by David Cameron and Richard Simeon is being published in a forthcoming book entitled *Patterns of Association;* Patrick Gossage's observation is in *Close to the Charisma: My Years Between the Press and Pierre Elliott Trudeau;* Mark Starowicz quotes Mario Cardinal in *Making History: The Remarkable Story Behind* Canada: A People's History. My interview with Robert Rabinovitch was on June 7, 2005.

chapter ten: Serving the Public, Passing the Test

The starting point for this chapter was the series that Carolyn Adolph did for CBC-Radio, broadcast in the fall of 2004. The documents that she and others had acquired under Access to Information were helpfully provided by Access officials at the Public Service Commission and the Privy Council Office. Reports by the Office of the Commissioner of Official Languages are on the website. Arthur Kroeger's comment is from his speech to the Public Policy Forum Testimonial Dinner, Toronto, April 17, 1989. The language levels are described on the Public Service Commission website at http://www.psc-cfp.gc.ca/ppc/sle_pg_06_e.htm; questions about whether staff should study French or Mandarin: Improving the Language Training System: A Joint Report of Treasury Board Secretariat and the Public Service Commission. October 2001 draft. p. 17; visible minority problems: "Official Languages and Visible

Minorities in the Public Service of Canada: A Quantitative Investigation of Barriers to Career Advancement," p. 6.

chapter eleven: The Political Imperative

John Crosbie describes the experience in his memoirs; his advance in the polls is described in *Leaders and Lesser Mortals*, by John Laschinger and Geoffrey Stevens. I interviewed Stephen Harper on June 17, 2005; I interviewed Paul Martin in August 2002 for a profile published on November 15, 2003, and interviewed him for this book on July 21, 2005; the comment by Marshall McLuhan is from *Understanding Media: The Extensions of Man*; the political use of French in Question Period is described in the *Globe and Mail*, April 7, 1988; Preston Manning described the cut and thrust in the House in his memoir *Think Big*; I interviewed Manning on October 15, 2002; figures on Canadians who speak neither official language and on Chinese-speakers are from *New Canadian Perspectives: Languages in Canada 2001 Census*, Louise Marmen and Jean-Pierre Corbeil. Michael MacMillan refers to "the third generation rule of thumb" in *The Practice of Language Rights in Canada*; the figures on European knowledge of English are quoted by Philippe Van Parijs in "Europe's Three Language Problems"; Scott Reid's conclusion is on p. 251 of *Lament for a Notion: The Life and Death of Canada's Bilingual Dream*; I interviewed Stephen Harper on June 17, 2005; Jack Layton on September 16, 2002, and September 29, 2005; and James Moore on June 14, 2005.

Conclusion

Greenspon and Wilson-Smith's description of the polling after the pro-Canada rally is in Chapter 20 of *Double Vision: The Inside Story of the Liberals in Power*. David Cameron provided me with a copy of his paper for Ukrainian officials. The quotations from the Tremblay Commission are from Vol. II of *Report of the Royal Commission of Inquiry on Constitutional Problems*; Jean Lesage's speech in Western Canada is quoted in "How Lesage Unsettled the West," by Blair Fraser, *Maclean's*,

November 15, 1965; Philippe Van Parijs's argument is in "Europe's Three Language Problems." The CROP poll which showed that 55 per cent of Quebeckers would vote yes was reported by Canadian Press on July 2, 2005. Laurendeau quotes the question he asked in his journal (1990): "Ces deux peuples, l'anglophone et le francophone, veulent-ils et peuvent-ils vivre ensemble?" – which is cited in the French version of the Preliminary Report in Chapter One. Interestingly, the word *peuples* was left untranslated in the English version.

Bibliography

Papers

The Maurice Lamontagne Papers, National Archives of Canada
Collection André Laurendeau, La Fondation Lionel Groulx
The F.R. Scott Papers, National Archives of Canada

Reports and Government Documents

Canada, Provincial Parliament of. *Parliamentary Debates on the subject of the Confederation of the British North American Provinces*, 3d. Session, 8th Provincial Parliament of Canada, Hunter, Rose & Co., Parliamentary Printers, Quebec, 1865.

Preliminary Report, The Royal Commission on Bilingualism and Biculturalism, 1965.

Reports of the Royal Commission on Bilingualism and Biculturalism, Books I-V.

Annual Reports of Commissioner for Official Languages, 1970–2005.

Department of the Secretary of State. *Official Languages Act: A Guide for Canadians.* 1993.

Government of Canada. *The Next Act: New Momentum for Canada's Linguistic Duality: The Action Plan for Official Languages*, 2003.

National Defence, Official Languages: National Defence Annual Review, 2004–2005.

Government of Canada. *Update on the Implementation of the Action Plan for Official Languages: Midterm Report*, 2005.

Office of the Commissioner of Official Languages. *Cooperation between the government and the communities: New models for service delivery*, 2000.

———. *Official Languages in the Canadian Sports System*, 2000.

———. *Official Languages and Immigration: Obstacles and Opportunities for Immigrants and Communities*, 2002.

———. *Official Languages in the Canadian Sports System: Follow-Up*, 2003.

———. *A Look at Bilingualism*, 2003.

———. *Walking the Talk: Language of Work in the Federal Public Service*, n.d.

Ottawa, City of. *Business Assistance Project Pilot Phase Evaluation Report and Phase 3 Action Plan*, French Language Services Division, June 2004.

Quebec. *Report of the Royal Commission of Inquiry on Constitutional Problems, Vol I & II*, Province of Quebec, 1956.

Books and Articles

Ajzenstat, Janet, Paul Romney, Ian Gentles, and William D. Gairdner, eds. *Canada's Founding Debates*. Toronto: Stoddart, 1999.

Allard, Jean V. *The Memoirs of General Jean V. Allard*. Written in Cooperation with Serge Bernier. Vancouver: University of British Columbia Press, 1988.

Andrew, J.V. *Bilingual Today, French Tomorrow: Trudeau's Master Plan and How It Can Be Stopped*. Richmond Hill, Ont.: BMG Publishing Ltd., 1977.

Arnberg, Lenore. *Raising Children Bilingually: The Pre-school years*. Clevedon: Avon Multilingual Matters Ltd, 1987.

Axworthy, Thomas, and Pierre Trudeau, eds. *Towards a Just Society*. Markham, Ont.: Viking, 1990.

Behiels, Michael. *Canada's Francophone Minorities: Constitutional Renewal and the Winning of School Governance*. Montreal: McGill-Queen's University Press, 2005.

Bergeron, Gérard. *Ne Bougez Plus! Portraits de 40 de nos politiciens.*
Ottawa: Éditions du Jour, 1968.

Borins, Sandford. *Language of the Skies: The Bilingual Air Traffic
Control Conflict in Canada.* Montreal: McGill-Queen's University
Press, 1983.

Brimelow, Peter. *The Patriot Game: Canada and the Canadian Question
Revisited.* Toronto: Key Porter, 1986.

Cameron, David, and Richard Simeon, eds. *Patterns of Association,*
forthcoming.

Camp, Dalton. *Points of Departure.* Ottawa: Deneau and Greenberg
Publishers, 1979.

Canadian Parents for French. *The State of French Second Language
Education in Canada, 2001–2005.*

Castonguay, Charles. "Nation building and anglicization in Canada's
capital region." *Inroads* 11.

Comeau, Robert. *André Laurendeau: un intellectuel d'ici.* Sous la direction
de Lucille Beaudry. Sillery: Presses de l'Université du Québec, 1990.

Coulon, Jocelyn. *En première ligne: grandeurs et misères du système militaire canadien.* Montréal: Le Jour éditeur, 1991.

Craig, Gerald M., ed. *Lord Durham's Report.* Toronto: McClelland &
Stewart, 1963.

Creighton, Donald. *John A. Macdonald: The Young Politician.* Toronto:
Macmillan of Canada, 1952.

Crosbie, John C., with Geoffrey Stevens. *No Holds Barred: My Life in
Politics.* Toronto: McClelland & Stewart, 1997.

Dallaire, Roméo. *Shake Hands With the Devil.* Toronto: Random House
of Canada, 2003.

Davey, Keith. *The Rainmaker: A Passion for Politics.* Toronto:
Stoddart, 1986.

De la Tour Fondue, Geneviève. *Interviews Canadiennes.* Montréal: Les
editions chantecler Ltée, 1952.

Djwa, Sandra. *The Politics of the Imagination: A Life of F.R. Scott.*
Toronto: McClelland & Stewart, 1987.

Dominingue, Nicole. "L'usage bilingue dans le centre de Montréal." *Aspects of Bilingualism*, ed. Michel Paradis. Columbia, S.C.: Hornbeam Press Inc., 1978.

Duchastel, Jules. *Marcel Rioux: Entre l'Utopie et la raison*. Montréal: Nouvelle Optique, 1981.

Falardeau, Jean-C., sous la direction de. *Essais sur le Québec contemporain*. Québec: Les Presses Universitaires Laval, 1953.

Fraser, Blair. *The Search for Identity, Canada, Postwar to Present*. Toronto: Doubleday & Co., 1967.

———. "How Lesage Unsettled the West," *Maclean's*, November 15, 1965.

Fraser, Graham. *P.Q.: René Lévesque and the Parti Québécois in Power*. Toronto: Macmillan, 1984.

———. "L'insondable Dr Laurin et ses 6 millions de patients." *L'actualité*, septembre 1978.

Friedenberg, Edgar Z. "Splitting Up," *The New York Review of Books*, vol. 21, no. 18, Nov. 20, 1980.

Gagnon, Jean-Louis. *Les Apostasies, Tome III, Les palais de glace*. Montréal: Les Éditions la Presse, 1990.

Genesee, Fred. *Learning Through Two Languages: Studies of Immersion and Bilingual Education*. Cambridge, Mass.: Newbury House Publishers, 1987.

Gossage, Patrick. *Close to the Charisma: My Years Between the Press and Pierre Elliott Trudeau*. Toronto: McClelland & Stewart, 1986.

Granatstein, J.L. *The Ottawa Men: The Civil Service Mandarins 1935–1957*. Toronto: Oxford University Press, 1982.

———. *Canada, 1957–1967: The Years of Uncertainty and Innovation*. Toronto: McClelland & Stewart, 1985.

———. *Canada's Army: Waging War and Keeping the Peace*. Toronto: University of Toronto Press, 2002.

Gratton, Michel. *Montfort: La lutte d'un peuple*. Ottawa: Centre franco-ontarien de resources pédagogiques, 2003.

Grégoire, Gilles. *Aventure à Ottawa*, 1969.

Greenspon, Edward, and Anthony Wilson-Smith. *Double Vision: The Inside Story of the Liberals in Power*. Toronto: Doubleday Canada, 1996.

Grosjean, François. *Life with Two Languages: An Introduction to Bilingualism*. Cambridge, Mass.: Harvard University Press, 1982.

Gwyn, Richard. *The Northern Magus: Pierre Trudeau and Canadians*. Toronto: McClelland & Stewart, 1980.

Gwyn, Sandra. "Twilight of the Ottawa Man." *Saturday Night*, January 1971.

Gzowski, Peter. "B. and B.'s desperate catalogue of the obvious." *Saturday Night*, April 1965.

Hayday, Matthew. *Bilingual Today, United Tomorrow*. Montreal: McGill-Queen's University Press, 2005.

Heintzman, Ralph. "The Political Culture of Quebec, 1840–1960." *Canadian Journal of Political Science* 16:1 (March 1983).

Heller, Monica. "Bonjour, Hello?: Negotiations of Language Choice in Montreal." Paper presented to the Berkeley Linguistics Society conference, February 18–20, 1978; proceedings, Berkeley, California, 1978; pp. 588-596.

———. "Language, Ethnicity and Politics in Quebec." Ph.D. thesis, Department of Linguistics, University of California, Berkeley. 1982.

———. "Negotiations of language choice in Montreal," in *Language and Society*, J. Gumperz, ed. Cambridge: Cambridge University Press, 1982.

———. "Ethnic Relations and Language Use in Montreal," in *Language of Inequality*, N. Wolfson and J. Manes, eds. Berlin: Mouton, 1985.

———. *Linguistic Minorities and Modernity: A Sociolinguistic Ethnography*. London and New York: Longman, 1999.

———. *Éléments d'une sociolinguistique critique*. Paris: Éditions Didier, 2002.

Henripin, Jacques. "Quebec and the Demographic Dilemma of French Canadian Society," in Dale Thomson, ed. *Quebec Society and Politics: Views from the Inside*. Toronto: McClelland & Stewart, 1973.

Hoffman, Eva. *Lost in Translation: A Life in a New Language*. New York: Penguin Books, 1989.

Horton, Donald J. *André Laurendeau: French Canadian Nationalist 1912–1968*. Toronto: Oxford University Press, 1992.

Hughes, Everett C. *French Canada in Transition*. Chicago: University of Chicago Press, 1943.

Huguet, Marcel. *Réal Caouette: l'homme et le phénomène*. Montréal: Les Éditions de l'homme, 1981.

Ignatieff, Michael. *Blood and Belonging: Journeys into the New Nationalism*. Toronto: Viking, 1993.

Jacobs, Jane. *The Question of Separatism: Quebec and the Struggle over Sovereignty*. New York: Random House, 1980.

Johnson, William. *Stephen Harper and the Future of Canada*. Toronto: Douglas Gibson Books, McClelland & Stewart, 2005.

Kaplan, Alice. *French Lessons: A Memoir*. Chicago: University of Chicago Press, 1993.

Laforest, Guy. "The Meech Lake Accord: The Search for a Compromise between André Laurendeau and F.R. Scott," in *Trudeau and the End of a Canadian Dream*. Montreal: McGill-Queen's University Press, 1995.

Laschinger, John, and Geoffrey Stevens. *Leaders and Lesser Mortals: Backroom Politics in Canada*. Toronto: Key Porter Books, 1992.

Laurendeau, André. *Journal tenu pendant la Commission royale d'enquête sur le bilinguisme et le biculturalisme*. Outremont: vlb/le septentrion, 1990.

———. *Ces choses qui nous arrivent: Chronique des années 1961–66*, préface de Fernand Dumont. Montréal: Éditions HMH Ltée., 1970.

———. *The Diary of André Laurendeau*, selected and with an introduction by Patricia Smart, translated by Patricia Smart and Dorothy Howard. Toronto: James Lorimer & Co., 1991.

Laurin, Camille. *Ma traversée du Québec*. Montréal: Éditions du Jour, 1970.

Levine, Marc. *The Reconquest of Montreal: Language Policy and Social Change in a Bilingual City*. Philadelphia: Temple University Press, 1990.

Locher, Uli. *Les Anglophones de Montréal: emigration et évolution des attitudes 1978–1983*. Québec: Conseil de la langue française, 1988.

Lower, Arthur. *Canadians in the Making: A Social History of Canada*. Toronto: Longmans, Green and Co., 1958.

MacLennan, Hugh. *Two Solitudes*. Toronto: Collins, 1945/New Canadian Library, McClelland & Stewart, 2003.

MacMillan, Michael. *The Practice of Language Rights in Canada*. Toronto: University of Toronto Press, 1998.

Magnet, Joseph. *Official Languages of Canada*. Sainte-Marie, Que.: Les Éditions Yvon Blais, 1995.

Manning, Preston. *Think Big: My Adventures in Life and Democracy*. Toronto: McClelland & Stewart, 2002.

Marlin, Randal. *The David Levine Affair: Separatist Betrayal or McCarthyism North?* Halifax: Fernwood Publishing, 1998.

Marmen, Louise, and Jean-Pierre Corbeil. *New Canadian Perspectives: Languages in Canada 2001 Census*. Statistics Canada, 2004.

McLuhan, Marshall. *Understanding Media: The Extensions of Man*. New York: McGraw-Hill, 1965.

McRoberts, Kenneth. *Misconceiving Canada: The Struggle for National Unity*. Toronto: Oxford University Press, 1997.

———. "English Canada and Quebec: Avoiding the Issue," Robarts Centre for Canadian Studies Lecture Series, York University, March 5, 1991.

Meisel, John, and Vincent Lemieux. "Ethnic Relations in Canadian Voluntary Associations." Documents of the Royal Commission on Bilingualism and Biculturalism no. 13, Information Canada, 1972.

Michaud, Yves. *Les raisons de la colère*. Montréal: Fides, 2005.

Monière, Denis. *André Laurendeau*. Montréal: Québec Amérique, 1983.

Moore, William. *The Clash: A Study in Nationalities.* Toronto:
    J.M. Dent and Sons, 1918.
Morton, Desmond. *A Military History of Canada.* Toronto: McClelland
    & Stewart, 1992.
Newman, Peter C. *The Distemper of Our Times.* Toronto: McClelland &
    Stewart, 1968.
O'Keefe, Michael. "Language Trends in Quebec." A paper prepared for
    the Official Languages Branch of the Privy Council Office, n.d.
Oliver, Michael. *The Passionate Debate: The Social and Political Ideas of
    Quebec Nationalism 1920–1945.* Montreal: Véhicule Press, 1991.
Paris, Erna. "Guilt, anxiety and bilingualism in the civil service,"
    Saturday Night, March 1972.
Pariseau, Jean, and Serge Bernier. *French Canadians and Bilingualism in
    the Canadian Forces,* vol. I 1763–1969: The Fear of a Parallel Army,
    on the Department of National Defence website:
    http://www.forces.gc.ca/hr/dhh/publications/engraph/
    Online_e.asp?cat=6
———. Vol. II, *Official Languages: National Defence's Response to the
    Federal Policy,* on the Department of National Defence website:
    http://www.forces.gc.ca/hr/dhh/publications/engraph/
    Online_e.asp?cat=6
Pearson, Lester. *Mike: The Memoirs of Rt. Hon. Lester B. Pearson, Vol. III.*
    Toronto: University of Toronto Press, 1975.
Pelletier, Gérard. *Les années d'impatience, 1950–1960.* Montreal:
    Stanké, 1983.
———. *Le temps des choix, 1960–1968.* Montreal: Stanké, 1986.
———. *L'aventure du pouvoir, 1968–1975.* Montreal: Stanké, 1992.
———. "1968: Language Policy and the Mood in Quebec," in *Towards a
    Just Society: The Trudeau Years,* edited by Thomas S. Axworthy and
    Pierre Elliott Trudeau. Markham, Ont.: Viking, 1990.
Picard, Jean-Claude. *Camille Laurin, L'homme debout.* Montreal:
    Boréal, 2003.
Poliquin, Daniel. *L'Écureuil noir.* Montréal: Boréal, 1994.

Racine, Gilles. "La Grande Peur des Anglophones," *Le Magazine Maclean*, août 1972.

Radice, Martha. *Feeling Comfortable? The Urban Experience of Anglo-Montrealers*. Saint-Nicolas, Que.: Les Presses de l'Université Laval, 2000.

Rehorick, Sandy, and Viviane Edwards, ed. *French Immersion: Process, Product & Perspectives*. Welland, Ont.: The Canadian Modern Language Review, 1992.

Reid, Scott. *Lament for a Notion: The Life and Death of Canada's Bilingual Dream*. Vancouver: Arsenal Pulp Press, 1993.

Richler, Mordecai. *Oh Canada! Oh Quebec! Requiem for a Divided Country*. Toronto: Penguin, 1992.

Robertson, Gordon. *Memoirs of a Very Civil Servant*. Toronto: University of Toronto Press, 2000.

Saywell, John. *Canadian Annual Report on Politics and Public Affairs, 1976*. Toronto: University of Toronto Press, 1977.

Scott, F.R. *Events and Signals*. Toronto: Ryerson Press, 1954.

————. *Poems of French Canada*. Blackfish Press, 1977.

Spencer, Christina. "How French falters in Canada's capital," *Ottawa City*, vol 6, no. 3, August-Sept. 2003.

Spicer, Keith. *Life Sentences: Memoirs of an Incorrigible Canadian*. Toronto: McClelland & Stewart, 2004.

Starowicz, Mark. *Making History: The Remarkable Story Behind Canada: A People's History*. Toronto: McClelland & Stewart, 2003.

Stein, Michael B. *The Dynamics of Right-Wing Protest: A Political Analysis of Social Credit in Quebec*. Toronto: University of Toronto Press, 1973.

Stefanescu, Alexandre, et Pierre Georgeault, sous la direction de. *Le Français au Québec: Les nouveaux defis*, Conseil supérieure de la langue française, Montréal, Fides, Montréal, 2005.

Sullivan, Martin. *Mandate '68*. Toronto: Doubleday Canada Ltd., 1968.

Supreme Court of Canada. Solski (Tutor of) v. Quebec (Attorney General), [2005] 1 S.C.R. 201, 2005 SCC 14.

————. Gosselin (Tutor of) v. Quebec (Attorney General), [2005] 1
    S.C.R. 238, 2005 SCC 15.

Van Parijs, Philippe. "Europe's Three Language Problems," prepared for
    Multilingualism in Law and Politics, R. Bellamy, D. Castiglione & C.
    Longmans, eds., Oxford: Hart, 2004.

Vastel, Michel. *Trudeau le Québécois*. Montréal: Éditions de l'homme,
    1989.

Saul, John Ralston. *Reflections of a Siamese Twin: Canada at the End of
    the Twentieth Century*. Toronto: Viking, 1997.

Schull, Joseph. *The Great Scot: A Biography of Donald Gordon*.
    Montreal: McGill-Queen's University Press, 1979.

Scowen, Reed. *The Time to Say Goodbye: The Case for Getting Quebec
    Out of Canada*. Toronto: McClelland & Stewart, 1999.

Stratford, Philip, Editor and Translator. *André Laurendeau: Witness for
    Quebec*, Introduction by Claude Ryan. Toronto: Macmillan, 1973.

Stursberg, Peter. *Lester Pearson and the Dream of Unity*. Toronto:
    Doubleday, 1978.

Sweeny, Alastair. *George-Étienne Cartier: A Biography*. Toronto:
    McClelland & Stewart, 1976.

Thorne, Stephen. "Quebec soldiers find war-fighting roles lower prior-
    ity than relief, rescue," Canadian Press, March 9, 2005.

Trudeau, Pierre. *Federalism and the French Canadians*. Toronto:
    Macmillan of Canada, 1967.

Wade, Mason. *The French Canadians, 1760–1945*. Toronto:
    Macmillan of Canada, 1955.

Westell, Anthony. *Paradox: Trudeau as Prime Minister*. Scarborough:
    Prentice Hall, 1972.

Acknowledgements

This book has its origin in a chapter that was never included in my 1984 book on René Lévesque and the Parti Québécois, and, in different form, in a book that I considered writing in 1991, in the bitter fallout from the death of the Meech Lake Accord. The idea, like the country, evolved in the fifteen years that followed. Doug Gibson has been my publisher and my friend for three decades and three books now, and I am grateful for his enthusiasm, his patience, and his confidence. Jenny Bradshaw was a scrupulous and supportive copyeditor.

In various ways, over the years, other friends have encouraged me in this project, including George Anderson, Stephen Bornstein, Wendy Bryans, Peter Calamai, Susan Carter, Andrew Cohen, Sheila Fischman, Bill Fox, Carol Goar, Charlotte Gray, Chantal Hébert, Michael Ignatieff, L. Ian MacDonald, Marie-Louise Perron, Alan Pickersgill, Bob Rae, Jeffrey Simpson, Jim Travers, Paul Wells, Don Winkler, and Hugh Winsor. *Toronto Star* editor-in-chief Giles Gherson, former National Editor Alan Christie, and my bureau chief, friend, and colleague Susan Delacourt made it possible for me to take time off to work on the book; my colleagues in the Ottawa bureau, Bruce Campion-Smith, Sean Gordon, Tonda MacCharles, Andrew Mills, and Les Whittington, cheerfully shouldered the extra work my absence forced upon them.

In the course of my research, a number of people have been particularly helpful, sharing their insights and their knowledge, and sometimes giving me an opportunity to organize my thinking on the subject.

Monica Heller first made me aware of the fascinations of sociolinguistics when she was a graduate student in the late 1970s, and her work has continued to give me rich insights. Others have included Simon Beaudry, Mauril Bélanger, Alvin Cader, David Cameron, Linda Cardinal, Michel Côté, Tim Creery, Sandra Djwa, Lt. Col. Brigid Dooley-Tremblay, Chris Dornan, Daniel Drache, John English, Graham Fox, Jean-François Garneau, Jack Granatstein, Denis Gratton, Chris Hall, Matthew Hayday, Norman Hillmer, Arthur Kroeger, Simon Langlois, David Mitchell, Jim Mitchell, Ken McRoberts, Anne Moreau, Gisèle Quenneville, Rob Renaud, Gordon Robertson, John Ralston Saul, Richard Simeon, Pat Smart, Donald Smith, Keith Spicer, Stephen Thorne, Jodi White, Konrad Yakabuski, Max Yalden, and the staff of the Commissioner of Official Languages, the Ottawa Public Library, and Library and Archives Canada. A number of federal public servants have been extremely helpful but asked that I not mention their names. The mistakes are mine alone.

My sons, Malcolm and Nick, have been inspirations in more ways than they know; in addition, Malcolm pitched in on some research for me.

I could not have done this without the constant, unflagging support, encouragement, wisdom, patience, and love of Barbara Uteck.

Graham Fraser
Ottawa
November 7, 2005

Index